From These Roots

FROM THESE ROOTS

My Fight with Harvard to Reclaim My Legacy

Tamara Lanier

with Liz Welch

CROWN
NEW YORK

CROWN
An imprint of the Crown Publishing Group
A division of Penguin Random House LLC
crownpublishing.com

Photo from *Free Renty: Lanier v. Harvard*, Courtesy David Grubin Productions, Inc.

Photo from Sasha Huber, Rentyhorn, Switzerland, 2008. Photo: Siro Micheroli.
Courtesy of the artist.

Library of Congress Cataloging-in-Publication Data
Names: Lanier, Tamara, 1962- author.
Title: From these roots : my fight with Harvard to reclaim my legacy / Tamara Lanier.
Identifiers: LCCN 2024013459 (print) | LCCN 2024013460 (ebook)
ISBN 9780593727720 (hardcover) | ISBN 9780593727737 (ebook)
Subjects: LCSH: Lanier, Tamara, 1962- —Trials, litigation, etc. | Harvard University—
Trials, litigation, etc. | Reparations for historical injustices—United States.
African Americans—Genealogy. | Enslaved persons—United States—Genealogy.
Slavery—Law and legislation—United States—History.
Classification: LCC KF229.L36 L36 2025 (print) | LCC KF229.L36 (ebook)
DDC 342.74408/7—dc23/eng/20241022
LC record available at https://lccn.loc.gov/2024013459
LC ebook record available at https://lccn.loc.gov/2024013460

Hardcover ISBN 978-0-593-72772-0
Ebook ISBN 978-0-593-72773-7

Editor: Madhulika Sikka
Assistant Editor: Fariza Hawke
Production editor: Serena Wang
Text designer: Andrea Lau
Production managers: Dustin Amick and Jessica Heim
Copy editor: Tom Pitoniak
Proofreaders: Barbara Jatkola, Hope Clarke, Alison Miller
Publicist: Felix Cruz, Stacey Stein
Marketer: Chantelle Walker

Manufactured in the United States of America

9 8 7 6 5 4 3 2 1

First Edition

A special tribute to Mattye Pearl Thompson Lanier

"The Keeper of Our Family Story"

My Grandma's name was Mattie Pearl,
She was a special Woman of style and grace.
In January of 2010, God saw fit to call her home,
And now she is resting in a heavenly place.

My Grandma loved her grandchildren,
More than anyone could know.
She held us and she rocked us,
And she was there to watch us grow.

My Grandma was the Boss,
And what she said had to be.
For things I wanted, but couldn't have,
My Grandma would say, "Meg come to me."

My Grandma was my greatest teacher,
She never left our education to the schools.
She would write me little notes of encouragement,
Hard work and perseverance were her golden rules.

My Grandma had a special chair,
Where she would sit and recount our history.
We would gather at her knee and listen,
As she told of things that used to be.

My Grandma is gone now,
And surprisingly I am not a wreck.
It's the fond memories that get me through,
"I love you a bushel and a peck and a hug around the neck."

by Megan Lanier Gomez, April 2010

Contents

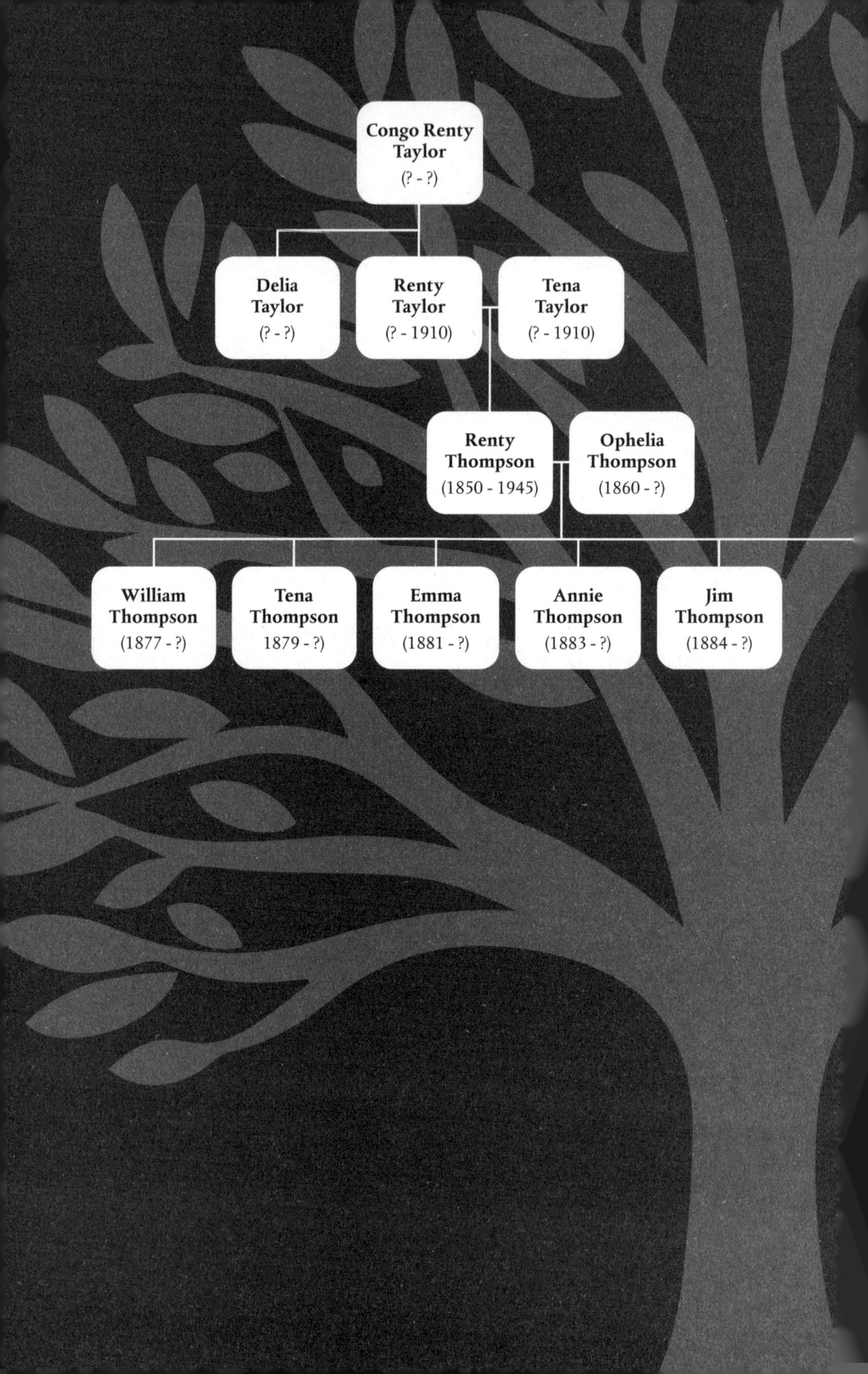
Congo Renty Taylor (? - ?)
Delia Taylor (? - ?)
Renty Taylor (? - 1910)
Tena Taylor (? - 1910)
Renty Thompson (1850 - 1945)
Ophelia Thompson (1860 - ?)
William Thompson (1877 - ?)
Tena Thompson 1879 - ?)
Emma Thompson (1881 - ?)
Annie Thompson (1883 - ?)
Jim Thompson (1884 - ?)

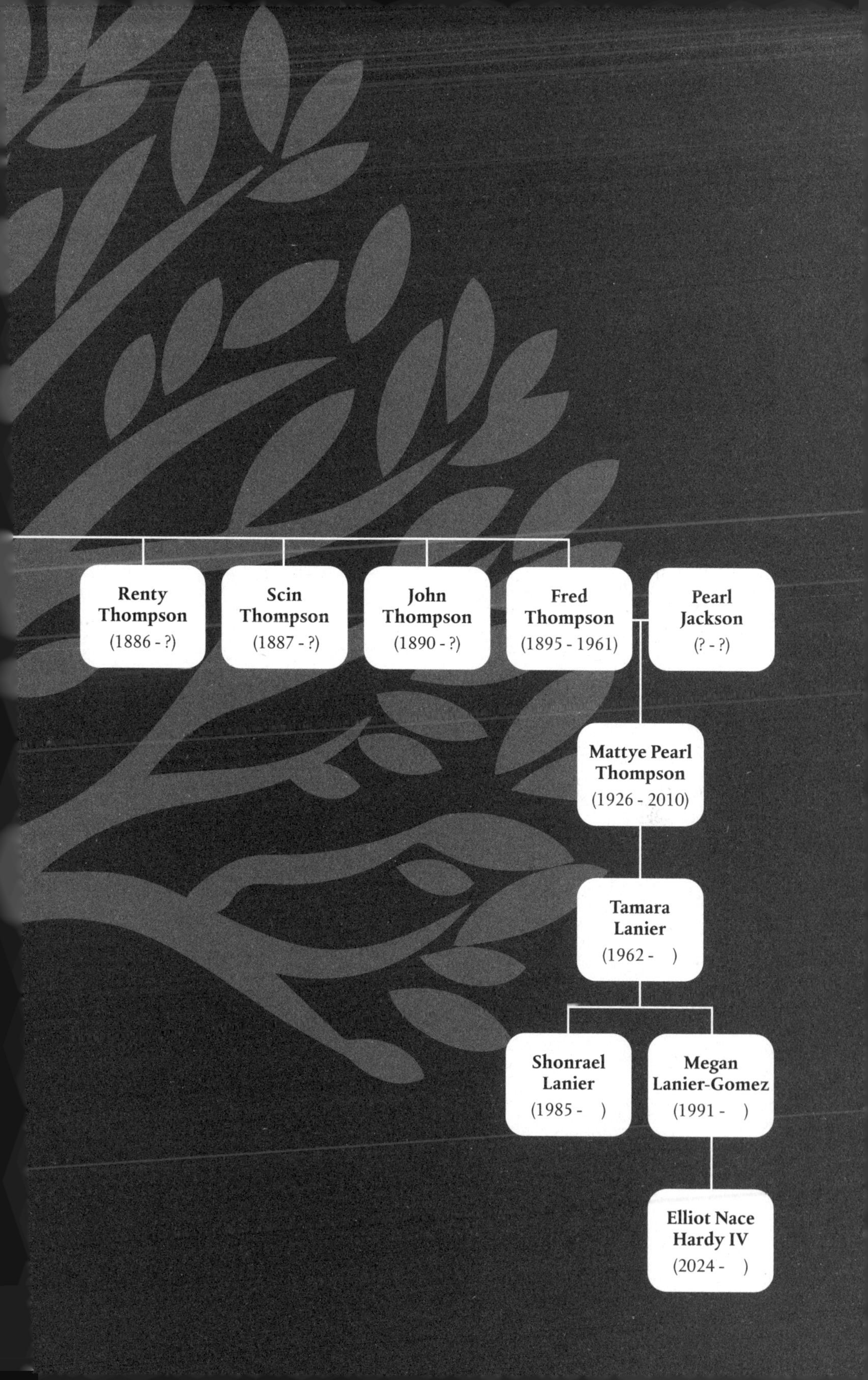

Renty Thompson (1886 - ?)
Scin Thompson (1887 - ?)
John Thompson (1890 - ?)
Fred Thompson (1895 - 1961)
Pearl Jackson (? - ?)
Mattye Pearl Thompson (1926 - 2010)
Tamara Lanier (1962 -)
Shonrael Lanier (1985 -)
Megan Lanier-Gomez (1991 -)
Elliot Nace Hardy IV (2024 -)

From These Roots

1

Sankofa

"It is not taboo to fetch what is at risk of being left behind."

Trending on college campuses and used in the names of many social justice organizations is the African term *sankofa*. But what does it mean? In the simplest of terms, it means "to go back and get it." The majestic bird that presses forward while looking back, safeguarding and nurturing the promises of life, is both a visual and symbolic reminder. It represents the foretelling and prophetic message of the past that cries out to the present: "Never forget where you come from."

On January 8, 2010, I lost my mother, Mattye Pearl Thompson-Lanier. Her death predated the popularity of Ancestry.com, 23andMe, or any of the other social media sites designed to assist families with their genealogy. But my mother was the keeper of our family story, and from as far back as I can remember, she talked of our ancestry. She talked of an African-born enslaved man named Renty, whom she fondly referred to as Papa Renty. My mother told these stories as they were told to her. Papa Renty was called the

Black African; his pride and reputation were revered by all. To his children, Papa Renty was larger-than-life; he was self-taught and stubbornly insisted on two things: education and faith in God. He was a determined man who worked the fields by day and taught himself to read at night. He understood the value of education; Papa Renty learned and taught others to read using a book called the Blue Back Speller, originally published in 1783 by Hartford, Connecticut's textbook pioneer and father of education, Noah Webster Jr., who went on to create the first dictionary in 1828. My mother called it the Blue Back Webster, as did the enslaved people who used it back then.

This is a story of generational love and perseverance. It is also a story of promises made and promises kept.

"Papa Renty was fondly known as 'the Black African.'"

She repeated these stories to me throughout my life, her voice growing more urgent as she neared the end of hers.

"Always remember," she'd often say. "Never forget." And "Write it down."

My mother, Mattye Pearl Thompson-Lanier, was born on June 8, 1926, in Mount Meigs, a small township in Montgomery County, Alabama. She was the fourth of six children born to Pearl Jackson and Frederick Douglass Thompson, whom everyone called "Fed." They were sharecroppers who grew up in what she called "the cradle" of the Jim Crow South, and while she knew of the racist violence that permeated the region, she was protected from it by her family. She also talked about working from "kin" to "can't," or from sunrise when you can first see, to sunset when you can no longer because it is too dark. Of going into the fields to cut grass that she tied on a stick to sweep out the house. She talked about the corn husk doll that one of her relatives handcrafted for her during harvest time in the African and Native American traditions. She also talked about going to church on Sundays, and how the elders might give you a stern look or a pinch if you misbehaved.

Sitting for hours tossing multicolored "jacks" across the kitchen floor was one of my favorite pastimes as a child.

I'd play for hours; I was good at it!

One afternoon the repetitive beat of the bouncing rubber ball and the scratching of the jacks along the tiled kitchen floor caught my mom's attention.

"You think that's easy?" she asked. "Try playing jacks with rocks."

Puzzled, I asked, "How do you play jacks with rocks?"

She sent me out into the yard to gather eleven rocks.

"Now, this rock is your ball, and the rest of the rocks are your jacks—starting with 'onesies,' let's see how far you can get."

I quickly mastered from "onesies to tensies" but there was one uniquely African tradition that I simply failed to grasp: the art of playing "hambone" with spoons. In many parts of the South, playing the drum was forbidden. To make music, enslaved men and women would use metal spoons, clapping and slapping their bodies in rhythmic patterns. Hambone was often accompanied by a scripted or improvised song that spoke of Black culture and the lived experiences of the formerly enslaved. Whenever my uncles and mother would play, I would look on in amazement. My girls would often joke, "We inherited Grandma's stories, not her rhythm."

The recounting of our oral history always began with Papa Renty. Over time, we would come to learn that there are five generations of men named Renty in my family, four directly descending from the African-born Papa Renty. My grandfather Fred was the youngest of Renty Taylor Thompson's ten children, all of whom lived in Mount Meigs. The story my mother told was that Renty, her grandfather, was the grandson of Papa Renty, the "Black African" and our first ancestor to set foot on American soil. My mom's oldest brother was also named Renty, but everyone called him Bubba.

"The old folk gave their children unusual names because families were so often violently separated during slavery," my mother explained. "This was how kinfolk could keep track and later found their loved ones."

She'd also say, "Always remember, we are Taylors, not Thompsons." This was our oral history, and she knew it because her grandfather, Renty Taylor Thompson, told her these stories when she was a child. Specifically, that he was born into slavery on the Taylor Plantation, but then he and his mother, Tena, were separated from their family and sold "south."

My mother was our family historian and chief storyteller. One of her favorite stories was that Papa Renty taught himself to read using the Blue Back Speller during a period where it was still illegal to teach slaves how to read in parts of the South. "A literate slave is dangerous" was the common thinking among slave owners, which explains why this book was so highly in demand among enslaved people. My mother often said, "Back then, finishing the Blue Back Webster was the equivalent of graduating with a PhD today."

She was especially proud that Papa Renty had mastered the entire book. "If you had a desire to read, Papa Renty would teach you," she'd say proudly.

Judging from her conviction, I concluded that Papa Renty's children had no choice but to embrace learning. "Education has always been a priority in our family," she'd say. She also loved to tell childhood stories of how she walked "country miles" to school, which was a one-room, dirt-floor shack with hand-me-down books that already had the answers written in them and pages torn out. She graduated from high school with honors and in 1942 entered Alabama's Teachers College, where she helped her schoolmate, the civil rights icon Ralph Abernathy, with his class work. During the summers she participated in a popular work exchange program where students from the South would migrate to the Northeast to work in hotels and restaurants, or on farms. In 1944 my mom got a job in a hotel in Connecticut, the same summer that Martin Luther King Jr., through the same program, worked as a farm hand on the Cullman Brothers tobacco farm in Simsbury, Connecticut.

After graduating, my mother took a teaching position and then became principal of the Free Mount School of Barbour County in Eufaula, Alabama. She continued to spend the summer months in Connecticut to earn extra money. That was how she met my father, Ennis M. Lanier, who was stationed in Groton, on the US naval base. They met in the fall of 1949 and married on August 27, 1950. My brother, Ennis, was the firstborn, followed by my sister, Cynthia, and finally me.

While my mother stopped teaching full-time to be a stay-at-home mom, she continued to be active in both education and civil rights. She was the PTA president at my school and instrumental in starting the local NAACP chapter in Norwich, Connecticut, going as far as paying the three-dollar application fee out of my father's military allotment to make sure people were able to join who could otherwise not afford it.

I was in seventh grade when my mother's cousin Charles Williams sent her a genealogy book that he had compiled of his and my mother's maternal ancestors. It chronicles the life, journey, and children of Big Mammy, my great-great-great-grandmother, who, according to the oral history, was born in Africa, brought to Virginia, and then sold south to Mount Meigs, Alabama. She loomed as large in our life as did Papa Renty.

My mother always wanted to create a family tree of Papa Renty's roots, like her cousin did for Big Mammy.

Big Mammy's children were part Cherokee and practiced both Native and African American culture and traditions. Charles

Williams documented all of this in a hand-bound book titled *From These Roots*. There was a tree trunk drawn on the bright yellow cardboard cover above three distinct branches of roots, each pointing to different family names: Williams, Murdock, and Lightfoot.

"Big Mammy may have been a descendant of an African king and queen. Her forefathers were among the thousands who were sold into slavery in the 1600s. Her name was MARY. To her family, she was known as Big Mammy," was how the book begins. "Like most slaves, she married at a very early age and began her family. Her first husband, Jake, and her children were left in Virginia when she was sold away from them to a plantation owner in Montgomery County, Alabama."

I had heard versions of these stories throughout my life, and after it arrived in our house, my mom started saying, "I want to put a similar book together tracing our paternal family history from Papa Renty. We need to write these stories down."

Around that same time, she was in the process of becoming a foster parent in Connecticut and needed her birth certificate for the application. My mother was born at home and, like many people born to sharecroppers, there was no documentation of her birth, so she had to send a sworn affidavit to the state of Alabama to request a birth certificate—and when she learned how long the process would take, she contacted her siblings to suggest that they do it all together, at the same time. When the package arrived in the mail, she was shocked to see that her legal date of birth was listed as December 23, 1923, three years earlier than she was born. My aunt Sarah's birthday was also incorrect. Uncle John was misgendered. Everyone's information was wrong. Since each child had been delivered at home in Mount Meigs by a midwife named Kizzy Ivery, it was decided that Kizzy just didn't keep good records. My mom knew that proving her real birth date would be a labyrinthine and laborious process, so she decided to leave it be.

"I figured, it put me that much closer to receiving Social Security," she said with a shrug. "Why change it now?"

I grew up hearing these stories of our ancestors, as did my daughters, Shonrael and Megan. My father had a very serious stroke in 1989 and spent the last years of his life at a veterans' rehabilitation center in New Haven, Connecticut, where he died in 1990, five years after Shonrael was born. I gave birth to Megan in 1991, so she missed him by one year. My mother made up for the loss, with her love and her stories. She'd sit in her favorite armchair, in the sunny corner of the living room in her ranch house in Norwich, where I grew up.

"Papa Renty taught himself and his children to read when doing such a thing could get a person killed," she'd say. "He was a proud man! A good man!"

Every morning on my way to work as a probation officer for the state of Connecticut, I'd drop my girls at her house at 7 a.m. Mom would be waiting to receive them in her floral-covered armchair: I'd plop Megan in her lap and Shonrael would get busy baking a make-believe cake in her Little Tikes stove, set up near my mother's chair, alongside a miniature ironing board and a chalkboard easel where my mom taught both my girls to read and write. She'd tease them about all their toys, telling them the story of her beloved corn husk doll.

"One hot day, after returning from an errand to get the mail, I saw that I had left it outside and the sun had burnt it to a crisp," she'd say. "I've cried many times over that doll."

Every Christmas, as my girls tore through the wrapping on piles of presents beneath our tree, my mother would sigh and say, "Y'all don't know how blessed you are. When I was your age, we got one piece of fruit for Christmas, and we were happy with that."

She was happy too for all the blessings bestowed on her family. She also never complained about her upbringing—she was proud of it! I remember her describing the burlap underwear that her mother would cut and sew out of the feed sacks from cornmeal. "They were nothing like the Hanes we might wear today, but they served the purpose," she'd say. My mom shared that all too often you would see children playing and they weren't at all ashamed of their burlap briefs that bore an image of a corncob on their backside.

"Grandma, could you make Megan a pair of those?" Shonrael would joke.

As the girls got older, they both continued to sit in my mother's lap until their feet touched the ground. And though I was not there to witness it, I knew she was telling them the same stories. I didn't even know that Shonrael had been working with my mom on a family research project until she brought it home from school one day. It was a beautiful hand-bound book with a pink, yellow, and blue African-inspired print on its cover. It was similar in size to the Williams family history, and clearly directly inspired by it.

"DEDICATED TO MY LITTLE SISTER SO SHE KNOWS WHERE SHE CAME FROM" was typed on the first page, in all capital letters, followed by the title page: "From These Roots I Came" by Shonrael P. G. Lanier, Grade Five, Mr. Favello, T. W. Mahan School, Norwich, CT. May 3, 1996.

My heart swelled imagining how thrilled my mother was to help with this assignment.

"My roots grow deeper than slave times," this book begins. "Yet it is almost impossible to go further than the lonely, tough times of slavery. Regrettably, I can only tell you as far as my great-grandfather, Fred Thompson."

As I read my daughter's words, I heard my mother's voice speaking through them.

"Fred was born to the former slave Renty Taylor Thompson," the story continued. "Fred later recalls his father recanting a story when he, at age ten, was sold along with his mother to the Thompson Plantation. Renty was born Renty Taylor and after the trade assumed the name Renty Taylor Thompson. Renty later married a girl named Ophelia Murdock and to this union was born ten children."

The book includes the details, also learned from my mother, that Shonrael's great-grandmother Ophelia Murdock Thompson was of Cherokee heritage and made medicine from roots. These were all stories she had heard sitting on my mother's lap. She also shared my mother's journey—from her sharecropper childhood in Mount Meigs to entering Alabama State College in 1942 all the way to her moving to Connecticut and giving birth to me. She added that she, Shonrael, was Mattye's first grandchild, who got her middle name, Pearl, from Mattye's mother, my grandmother, her great-grandmother. Mattye's middle name was Pearl as well.

"Our names connect us," my mother often said.

The last page was particularly poignant. "I am deeply proud of my background. Unfortunately, I can tell you no more. All the records of the precious Thompson-Lanier family were destroyed in the Civil War. I have told you what I know of my history, and I am proud of it."

This was the first attempt at writing the Papa Renty story down. My mother was thrilled. But that did not stop her from telling these stories.

A few years later, when Megan was in fifth grade, I called home from work to check in. Megan answered.

"How is your day going?" I asked, as usual.

"Fine," she said. "I'm just listening to Grandma talk about slavery again."

That made me laugh.

My mother was so proud of her ancestors and wanted her granddaughters to be as well.

My mother had diabetes, which got worse as she aged and contributed to a decline in her health later in her life. A lift recliner with a tray attached to the arm replaced her favorite floral armchair. A walker replaced the mini-kitchen and easel. Instead of caring for my girls, now grown and in high school and college, I was stopping by daily to bring her new prescriptions, fix her lunch, and arrange doctors' appointments.

The diabetes created neuropathy in her feet, which made walking difficult. One day, as she was going out the front door, she slipped and fell. Both ankles broke, compound fractures, bone through the skin. She went to the emergency room, where they reset the bones, and from there she was sent to a nursing home for care. She was in her late seventies, and her care now consisted of brief and sometimes long-term stays in hospitals, nursing homes, and, on occasion, critical care.

I visited her daily. One morning I noticed that she was unusually preoccupied. I knew that she was anxious to go home, but she seemed burdened by something.

"Tam, you have to write our family story down," she said.

I promised I would, but to be honest, I was just saying that to comfort her. I was not sure how to do the genealogical research or where to even start. But she would not let me off that easily.

One evening I stayed with her in the hospital until very late. I finally went home to get some rest as I had to be at work at 7:30 a.m. the next morning. The following day, I went to see her on my way to the office.

When I walked into her room, she said, "Where have you been? I've been calling you!"

She was irritable and disoriented. My mother never got angry. Looking back, I think she knew that she was running out of time.

That broke my heart. I was already running on fumes—between my full-time job and making sure my girls had what they needed for school and that their homework was done, I was also at the hospital with my mom first thing in the morning and until I was kicked out at night. I was exhausted.

Another night, she called me around 2 a.m. to say she was having trouble breathing. When I got to the rehab center, she was agitated. I stayed with her until 10 a.m. and then called her sister, my aunt Sarah, who lived nearby.

"I need someone to come sit with my mom for a few hours while I run errands," I said.

It was Saturday, my one day to shop, and there was no food in the house.

She came to relieve me, and I then headed to BJ's. Walmart was next on my list, but I decided to check on my mom. "How's she doing?"

"She's just so restless," Sarah said. "Something is not right."

I went straight back to the rehab.

When I got there, my mother was tossing and turning in her bed. She was in need of immediate medical attention, so I marched into the hallway and shouted at the first nurse I saw, "My mother is in distress, you need to check on her!"

The nurse looked at me very nonchalantly and said, "I will be there in a few minutes."

"If you don't come now," I said firmly, "I'm calling 911."

The nurse followed me into the room and quickly placed an oxygen meter on my mother's finger—it was at zero. She was having a pulmonary embolism. I called my sister, Cynthia, and then followed the ambulance as it raced her to the hospital. My sister arrived just before I did and said that she saw my mom's eyes were rolled back in her head as they wheeled her into the hospital.

"I think she flatlined," Cynthia said.

We both were literally paralyzed with fear.

Our brother, Ennis, named after my dad, had died young, at the age of forty-six, from a stroke, just like my father. I was not ready to say goodbye to my mother. Doctors told me that they had put her on a respirator and when we were finally allowed to see her, I was not prepared for what that meant: The tube they had placed in her mouth was so big that it strained her lips to the point I thought they might crack. It was attached with straps to the back of her head that seemed too tight and dug indentations into her cheeks. There were needles attached to IVs stuck in her thumbs and both arms. I knew that these beeping and whirring machines were keeping her alive, but it all looked so terribly painful. Even worse, there was nothing I could do to comfort her.

We kept vigil by her bedside for the days that followed. The doctor confirmed that she had coded—and was fighting to stay alive. When another man on her care team suggested that her advance directive be changed from "full code" to "do not resuscitate," I was shocked: "No," I said, emphatically. "That's not her wish."

Thankfully, they did not push back.

A few days later, my mom was still in critical care and while still intubated, she had moments of consciousness. When she was awake, she would gesture that she was in a lot of pain and that the tube, which was stretching her mouth in a way that looked painful, was bothering her. One day, Shonrael was sitting with her, doing her homework, and my mother was conscious.

She pointed to Shonrael's pen, took it from her hand, and scribbled on her paper, "Take tube out."

Distressed, Shonrael called me to relay the news. I contacted her doctor and said: "You need to take the tube out now."

"That's not possible," he said. "If we take the tube out and she's unable to breathe on her own, we cannot put it back in."

"If she is strong enough to take a pen from my daughter's hand

and write 'Take tube out,'" I countered. "Then she is strong enough to breathe on her own."

I had been a probation officer for more than a decade by then. I went toe-to-toe with some of the most challenging personalities—but my biggest fights were with the hospital's medical staff, fighting for my mother's care. My mom survived the removal of the respirator and was able to breathe on her own with very little difficulty. She was a fighter!

The next time her doctor stopped by to check in, I told my mother, in front of him, that he had suggested we change her advance directives. She sat up straight in her hospital bed and looked him dead in the eye.

"I will go when God is ready to take me!" she said, wagging her finger at him, a gesture she found offensive. "Until then, you will do everything in your power to keep me alive—do you understand me?"

He remained silent, nodding in agreement.

My mom recovered and was in and out of rehab for the next few years. She even made it home from the rehabilitation center, but now needed dialysis. That was hard. I took her in for infusions, which lasted four to five hours, but her doctors would not let me or any other family member go into the treatment rooms with her.

"Hospital policy," they said.

So, when her doctor called me to say that she had coded during dialysis, I went into a full-blown PTSD panic. I raced to the hospital expecting beeping machines and another brutal intubation. I braced myself before entering her room, preparing myself for the worst.

Instead, I found her sitting up in her bed, waiting for me.

"Did you bring the tape recorder?" she asked, with a raspy voice.

"It's in the car," I said, my heart softening as I fought back tears.

I did not plan to record my mother that day. I often brought work home and would dictate my reports onto cassette tapes, which I would then give to the office secretary to transcribe. They could either be for a court report, restitution study, or presentence investigation. They were also warrants for people's arrest. But I knew recording my mother would make her happy, so I went and got it.

When I returned to her room, I pulled a chair up to her bed and pressed record.

She started to tell the stories: "Papa Renty worked the fields," she said. "He was the Black African. He taught himself how to read at night, after everyone else was asleep. He taught his children too."

I thought it was funny at the time because I knew all these stories, so I felt like she was not trusting me to remember them accurately. But I was also happy to do it. After so many touch-and-go incidents, I would do anything to comfort her.

After that scare, she was transferred home wearing two large orthopedic boots and needed assistance walking—at first with a walker, but ultimately was confined to a wheelchair. Part of her healing was telling these stories. I started sitting with her, asking her questions, and making these recordings. I was just going along with it to comfort her.

On my mother's deathbed, I made a promise to write these stories down—and to make a family tree for her father's side of the family like her cousin had done for Big Mammy. But truthfully, I did not know how or where to even begin. I remember one Sunday afternoon, before she got sick, I pressed her to explain something I didn't quite understand. I was visiting her at the rehab center, massaging her scalp and brushing her hair.

Often my mom would say, "You are African and Indian."

I knew that her maternal elders were Cherokee Indian but that afternoon I asked, "Weren't all enslaved people of African descent? What made Papa Renty any different?"

"I don't know now," she said. "All I know is that they called him the 'Black African.' "

After she passed, I was watching an episode of *Roots*. In one scene, Fiddler, the character played by the late Louis Gossett Jr., called Kunta Kinte, played by LeVar Burton, a "crazy African" because of his repeated attempts to run away. It was an epiphany! I knew that the Slave Embargo of 1808 prohibited the import of slaves, which meant that most enslaved men and women in the mid- to late 1800s were American-born. Like Kunta Kinte, Papa Renty was called the "Black African" because he was perhaps the last of the African-born slaves brought to the US.

"Mom, I figured it out!" I wanted to shout.

But she was gone.

2

Losing My Mom, Finding Papa Renty

The months following my mother's death were such a blur. Megan was in college, Shonrael was busy with her career, and I was trying to focus on my own work to keep me distracted. So much of my days had been consumed with my mother's care. I kept feeling that there was something I should be doing—refilling her prescriptions, calling her doctors. Fixing her lunch. But none of that was necessary anymore. She was no longer here to take care of, and I literally did not know what to do with myself.

I also could not shake the guilty feeling I had that I was not fulfilling my promise to document our family history. I knew that this was something I must do, but I just did not know where to begin.

It was 2010, which meant serious genealogical work would require trips to the archives, libraries, historical sites, or clerks' offices. The internet was not as broadly used then as it is today, and if there was a need, I could count on my girls to search the web. But this research would be a major undertaking. I had a few clues but did not know where or how to begin. And yet all I could think was how comforted my mother was in her last moments, trusting that this work would be done.

"Tam, you have to write it down."

One brisk March day, three months after my mother passed, all these thoughts were swirling in my head as I stopped by Rich Morrison's ice cream parlor and café in Norwich, where I often would go to pick up a salad for lunch. He was always behind the counter and had run that café for years.

"How have you been?" Rich asked. He was a frail man in his late seventies, with receding silver hair and unruly brows that masked his eyes. He was in his usual spot, standing behind the register. I shared with him that my mom had passed, and saw his smile deflate.

"I'm so sorry to hear that," he said.

I barely knew him, other than to say a friendly hello and share small pleasantries. But at that moment, something compelled me to bare my soul: I told him that I was burdened by a promise I made to my mom just prior to her death to document our family's ancestry.

"I don't know anything about genealogical research, and I don't know where to even begin," I said.

"I love this stuff," Rich said, his smile returning. "Write down what you know, and I'll see what I can find."

I was moved by his offer, but also thought, What does this elderly man know about the internet?

In 2010, your average senior struggled to find the power button, but Rich appeared to know what he was doing. I was not super savvy about anything online beyond email. I had also not yet heard of Ancestry.com or 23andMe. Rich seemed eager to help so I told him exactly what my mom had shared with me: that my great-grandfather was born Renty Taylor in South Carolina. He was later sold by the Taylor slaveholder and given the name Thompson. He was also the descendant of a man called Papa Renty, who was born in Africa.

"Whatever help you can offer, Rich," I said, "I appreciate it."

He jotted down all these various details, and to be honest, while touched by the gesture, I had little confidence that Rich would find anything meaningful or useful. As I walked out with my salad in hand, I thanked him again and didn't give the matter another thought until I went back a few weeks later.

As soon as I walked into his shop, he threw his hands in the air and exclaimed, "Where have you been? I found your Papa Renty on the internet!"

I was stunned. My first thought was, What's Papa Renty doing on the internet?

He was so excited that he tore a piece of paper off the receipt roller at the register.

"Write down your email address—I will send you what I've found."

I gave him my email address, and that same afternoon he sent me two documents. I decided to wait to get home before opening either of them. I was not even excited since it felt so implausible.

That evening, after dinner, I went to my bedroom, tired and ready for sleep. I saw my computer there on my desk and remembered Rich's enthusiasm. While I did not have any expectations, I decided to look at what he had sent me.

I opened the email and read his note, which said he had found a few things on the internet that he believed were about my Papa Renty.

The first attachment was a scholarly article published in the journal *American Art* in 1995 called "Black Bodies, White Science: Louis Agassiz Slave Daguerreotypes."

Intrigued, I began to read:

"Recent discussions of multiculturalism, ethnicity, identity, and race have raised many new questions about the nature of cultural difference. Some critics have derided 'political correctness' and challenges to Western canons of culture, while others have struggled to trace the genealogies of cultural oppression and to challenge normative structures of identity formation." It went on to talk about critical gaze and museums and asked the question, "Who represents? And who is represented? Whose voice will be heard? Whose stories will be remembered?"

I had no idea what any of this had to do with me or my family genealogy and almost clicked out of the document. But then I saw in the bottom corner of the first page a small box of information that read: "Renty, Congo. Plantation of B. F. Taylor Esquire."

My heart started racing.

I clicked to the next page and the picture that filled my screen took my breath away. A beautiful, regal dark-skinned man with short-cropped silver hair and chiseled cheekbones was staring at me. His eyes locked with mine, as if he had been waiting for this very moment.

"Oh my god," I thought. "It's Papa Renty."

It was not even a question: from the moment I saw him, I knew it was him. As I stared at this man's face, I was flooded with so much familiarity: the man I was looking at had the same features as my uncle Renty, or Bubba as we call him, and as my uncle Johnny, as my mother and me.

"Girls!" I shouted to my daughters. "Come see this!"

They came into my room and I said, "This is Papa Renty."

"Oh my god," they said in unison, staring into the screen.

"Mom, he looks like you!" Megan said.

"But he's so small!" Shonrael chimed in. "Based on Grandma's stories, I imagined a man ten feet tall!"

My daughters and I spent the next half hour just reflecting on every similarity: His high forehead and dramatic cheekbones. The soulful look in his eyes.

"Mom, you have the same eyes," Shonrael said.

"Grandma had them as well," Megan said.

It was true: his eyes were penetrating, so thoughtful and determined. I was immediately drawn to them: it was as if his eyes pierced my soul, he was talking to me, commanding me and demanding my attention. My body was flooded with so many emotions, excitement, and amazement. I felt like I was looking into a mirror. I stared at the photo a few more minutes, wishing my mother was alive to see it with me. I knew she would be thrilled by this discovery—an actual photograph! Of Papa Renty! And from the B. F. Taylor Plantation!

"Always remember we are Taylors, not Thompsons," I heard my mother's voice say. It all added up.

The girls went to bed, and I continued to read, now all the more intrigued to understand why Papa Renty was in this scholarly article. That was how I learned that this image was one of the so-called "slave daguerreotypes of Louis Agassiz, discovered at Harvard's Peabody Museum in 1976."

I paused—Harvard was less than two hours away from my home.

I pressed on and learned that Papa Renty was one of seven people whose images were captured in the fifteen daguerreotypes: "Here, the seated women calmly reveal their breasts, and the standing men are stark naked," the article continued. "But their attitudes are detached, unemotional, and workmanlike. In what seems to be a deliberate refusal to engage with the camera or its operator, they stare into the lens, their faces like masks, eyes glazed, jaws clenched. Fascinating and disturbing, these pictures raise compelling questions about the construction of—and the social investments in—the categories of 'race,' 'science,' 'photography,' and 'the museum.'"

The next paragraph sickened me: "The daguerreotypes, which were taken for Agassiz in Columbia, South Carolina, in 1850, had two purposes, one nominally scientific, the other frankly political. They were designed to analyze the physical differences between European whites and African blacks, but at the same time they were meant to prove the superiority of the white race. Agassiz hoped to use the photographs as evidence to prove his theory of 'separate creation,' the idea that the various races of mankind were in fact separate species."

I stopped reading. The joy I had experienced just moments before was radically stripped away by what I can only describe as a gut punch.

I looked back at the photo and Papa Renty's eyes once again locked with mine. We were just stuck there, staring at each other, and I realized that he was communicating with me. I felt his defiance, his opposition. It was a call to defend him. To stand up for him. To fight for him. As I stared at him, I felt his pain, his hurt, his frustration. In that moment, I knew I had to do something.

I read on and learned that Louis Agassiz was "the premier scientist of his time." As an agent of Harvard, he commissioned the photographer J. T. Zealy to capture nude images of Renty and other African-born enslaved men and women. Pointing to the stark physical differences, Agassiz concluded that blacks were a separate and lesser species, deserving to be enslaved.

The daguerreotype was a relatively new medium in the 1850s that predated photography as we know it today. Papa Renty's image was captured on a silver daguerreotype plate, an art form reserved for very wealthy family portraits at the time. Agassiz was a Swiss-born zoologist who studied comparative anatomy in France with Baron Georges Cuvier. His groundbreaking work was in classifying and ordering more than 500 fish species of Brazil and identifying 340 new genera. I continued to read and learned that Agassiz came to the United States in 1846 to take a post at Harvard University, which was where things turned dark. That was when he met Dr. Samuel Morton, a physician and anatomist based in Philadelphia who had published two books using human skulls to prove his theory that "races of mankind had been separately created as distinct and unequal species."

Recoiling, I turned away momentarily in disgust.

To summarize, Agassiz, influenced by Morton, commissioned the daguerreotypes to prove his own racist theories.

I looked at the image of Papa Renty again and interpreted the look in his eyes in a new light: everything about this felt wrong. I had a premonition, a feeling of urgency, a calling. I had to do something to right this wrong. All the stories of my Papa Renty proved the exact opposite.

There was a section of the article that quoted a letter Agassiz wrote to his mother after his first encounter with a Black man. "All the domestics in my hotel were men of color. . . . Nonetheless, it is impossible for me to repress the feeling that they are not of the same blood as us. In seeing their black faces with their thick lips and grimacing teeth, the wool on their head, their bent knees, their elongated hands, their large, curved nails, and especially the livid color of the palm of their hands, I could not take my eyes off their face in order to tell them to stay far away. And when they advanced that hideous hand towards my plate in order to serve me, I wished I were able to depart in order to eat a piece of bread elsewhere, rather than dine with such service. What unhappiness for the white race—to have tied their existence so closely with that of Negroes! God preserve us from such contact!"

As I was reading this, I felt the inhumanity of his words. Agassiz was blinded by his racism and only able to see the enslaved men and women through the prism of his "white sight" or "white privilege." His perception of my ancestors, of Renty and Delia, as nonhuman—as animals—was extremely cruel and abusive. And then he asked for God's protection! What about Renty and Delia?

"It was my enslaved ancestors who needed God's protection," I muttered to myself.

Above the overtly racist letter excerpt, there was a tableau of images: the profile of a European man next to a Native American next to a Negro and finally, a mixed-race man labeled "V. Hottentot." Beneath each drawing was the corresponding skull.

I was sickened but continued reading. The daguerreotypes were Agassiz's attempt to illustrate his support of the "polygenesis" theory. I learned from the article that in 1850, when the photo was taken, there was a belief among white Europeans that all people were descended from Adam and Eve. This was called monogenesis. Polygenesis was the theory of "multiple, separate creations for each race as distinct species that became the hallmark of the American School of Ethnology."

It was all so horrible. I was now forcing myself to get through the article when I came across a critical piece of information explaining that Agassiz went to South Carolina in 1850 specifically looking for African-born slaves "to gather evidence for his theory," and was introduced to several plantation owners there.

My heart once again started racing. I thought of Kunta Kinte, the crazy African. I thought of my mother saying, "They called Papa Renty 'the Black African.'" Both men embody the bravery, strength, and determination of men who had been stolen from their homes, beaten, tortured, torn from their families. And this man, Agassiz, was using them to prove that they were inferior. My Papa Renty! A man who taught himself and others to read when it was not only illegal to do so but could get a person killed. It was not only disheartening; it was also ironic.

The article mentioned fifteen daguerreotypes. Papa Renty's was the first image that I saw. The second one was of "Alfred Foulah, belonging to I. Lomas, Columbia, S.C." Papa Renty's portrait was face-on, and while he was naked from the waist up, it appeared he had cloth wrapped around his lower torso. Alfred was stripped naked. His image was so startling that I had to avert my eyes: it was a side view of an older man, perhaps in his thirties or forties, looking straight ahead, so the viewer only sees his profile. His stomach is slightly distended, his shoulders slumped. There was another image to the right of that, of his nude backside. I found it so violent and so upsetting to see this man, father, brother being viewed like a scientific specimen. I had to get up from my computer and walk around my bedroom to calm myself down.

I mustered the courage to continue reading and another note caught my eye: "Renty, (figures 12, 13) from the Congo tribe who also worked at the Taylor estate. Delia, (figures 14, 15) Renty's American born daughter, who also lived on the Taylor estate."

I flipped through the next few pages, seeing more beautiful Black bodies, all nude and being photographed as specimens, in the most humiliating and objectifying way—Jem, Gullah, belonging to F. M. Green; Jack, Guinea, Plantation of B. F. Taylor—and then I saw Delia. All the oxygen was sucked out of the room and my chest got tight. I could not breathe.

Delia looked to be in her teens and was, like Renty, naked to her waist. Her prepubescent breasts made me think, This is child pornography.

She too was sitting down, her waist also wrapped in material, her hands placed in her lap. She looked so sad. Trapped. Ashamed. I saw trauma emanating from her glassy, distant eyes as if she were mentally willing herself somewhere far away from the humiliation of this moment. They were looking through the camera, beyond it as well.

They were also brimming with tears. They were not streaming down her face. She was restrained and restricted. She could not rebel or refuse. It was clear that she was forced to take off her clothes, to sit for this portrait, and so the only way she could express her frustration and rage was through her tears, which no one could control. I saw her tears as an act of passive resistance.

I heard my mother's voice: "Papa Renty taught all his children how to read. Papa Renty was a proud man, dignified. He was revered."

My lungs felt compressed as I thought of my daughters, and what it would feel like to be in a room, watching them be treated in this way, and to have no power to stop it. Papa Renty's images were on the same page, beneath Delia's. His look was more defiant. Her visage was overwhelmingly sad. I felt the need to protect her, to cover Delia up, to bring her home with me.

Again I had to get up from my desk and walk away. It was too much. At the same time, I was drawn back to it, and wound up taking my computer into bed since I could not stop studying those images, trying to understand what this all meant. Agassiz commissioned those photos to prove the inferiority of Black people from Africa. But his theories were the exact opposite of everything I knew of Papa Renty! Of everything my mother claimed him to be and what he stood for.

Agassiz claimed that Africans had the intellectual capacity of a seven-month-old fetus, still in the womb of its mother.

My mother said that Papa Renty was a self-taught educator who had mastered Noah Webster's speller on his own.

Agassiz posited that Africans were submissive, obsequious, imitative.

Everything that I knew about my Papa Renty, and that I saw in that photo, was that he was obstinate, proud, and defiant.

Agassiz commissioned the daguerreotypes as evidence of an inferior race.

This photo of Papa Renty in particular, combined with all the stories I knew of him, was proof that he was the exact opposite.

As much as I wished my mom were there to see this picture, I also thought of how upset she would be to learn why it was taken. She would be hurt and heartbroken. That was when I knew that I couldn't let this narrative stand: Harvard needed to know that the man in this daguerreotype has a family who loves him, and an oral history that defines him—not as inferior, but as extraordinary.

I knew at that moment that I had to prove this to the world. But first I had to confirm what I already knew in my marrow and my heart: that the Renty in this image was my ancestor, Papa Renty.

3

Genealogical Trees Do Not Flourish Among Slaves

I stayed up late that night, poring through the article as well as the other links and documents Rich had sent me. I was surprised and amazed—that Rich, the ice cream shop owner, was also an internet supersleuth and genealogical whiz. What he provided was detailed and thorough. He included a crafty fan-shaped family tree with me at the center. Radiating outward, in concentric circles, were layers of my family: Ennis Lanier, my father, was to the left, and my mother, Mattye Pearl Thompson, to the right. Much of the information found about my maternal grandparents, Fred Thompson, born 1896, and Pearl Jackson, born 1900, was already known to me. The dates he added for my great-grandparents, Renty Taylor Thompson, born in January 1856, and his wife, Ophelia, born in 1858, also aligned.

I knew from our family's oral history that my mother's grandfather, Renty Taylor Thompson, had been born into slavery and that his father was also named Renty. I also knew that my mother's grandfather descended from an African-born enslaved man fondly known as Papa Renty.

But Rich's discovery revealed something new and profound: Papa Renty was one of the first enslaved people to ever be photographed and identified by name and place of birth. This was both overwhelming and emotional for me—it was also historic. This was my bloodline, I thought, and it was ensnared in something both good and bad. How fortunate was I to have a tangible piece of my African ancestry. But this was also my origin story—an image of my enslaved ancestor, depicted in the most objectified and vulnerable way, used as a tool to justify an illegitimate scientific experiment. I was conflicted and torn. I could not wait to reach out to the Peabody Museum, where the images were held, and to Harvard University!

Along with the family tree, Rich sent me a ten-page, single-spaced document titled "Ancestors of Tamara Lanier," in which he had compiled all the information he found on each family member, starting with my parents, and moving back in time from each findable date of birth and death to birthplace and occupation. I was floored by the breadth, depth, and detail of his research. He must have found my mother's obituary online too since it was also included verbatim.

As I scrolled through the pages, I saw the names of my parents, their parents, and their grandparents. Beneath each name, Rich cited the source where he found the information he had gathered. He included the 1880 US Census, which indicated that Renty Taylor Thompson was born in South Carolina in or about 1856, whereas the 1900 census stated that he was by then living in Precinct 21, Mount Meigs, Montgomery, Alabama, and in 1876 had married Ophelia, who resided with him. This all aligned with my mom's oral history, which was thrilling. I knew that my great-grandfather Renty Taylor Thompson was born a slave in South Carolina, but I did not know from which part specifically. My mom had always called that part of the family the "Carolina Geechees." I could also hear her say, "Remember, we're Taylors, not Thompsons."

The "Black Bodies, White Science" article also held several clues to where my ancestors lived in South Carolina, as it indicated that Papa Renty or Congo Renty was enslaved by Benjamin Franklin Taylor, from the Taylor Plantation in Columbia. This aligned with my mom's reminder, "We are Taylors, not Thompsons," and I now knew where the family name Taylor came from.

The article also supported another very painful story my mother often told: "Renty [Taylor Thompson] and his mother, Tena, were separated from their family and sold south."

She never explained what that meant specifically, but I knew from the history of slavery that it was the worst thing that could happen to an enslaved person, because the farther south you went, the more inhumane the experience was. To see this typed out, ink on paper, verified the oral stories my mother had remembered and passed down from her grandfather, who had been born a slave. Many would like to think that slavery was from a distant era, happening a long time ago. But my family's history refutes that. Rich's research made this crystal clear: I printed the document and wrote, "Born Renty Taylor, sold and became Renty Thompson," next to my great-grandfather's name.

Rich listed all of Ophelia and Renty Taylor Thompson's children included on the 1900 census, starting with Lena, who was twenty-one, and ending with Fred, who was then four. I knew Fred's full name was Frederick Douglass Thompson, but those who loved him all affectionately called him Fed. He was my maternal grandfather. I stumbled on Lena, as I knew this was an error. Fed's elder sister was named Tena after her mother. All the other information was correct, and so I assumed that this, like my mother's birth certificate, was one of many typos and errors I would find throughout my search.

These documents marked a beginning for me, a place to start the complicated work of piecing together my family's genealogy. I was amazed to learn, for instance, how important census records are for African Americans engaged in this work. In many states, it wasn't until 1870 that formerly enslaved people were recorded and recognized as human beings. That was why the 1880 census that Rich found Renty Taylor Thompson listed on was so significant. He was the first in my family to be counted as a person, and not as a slave.

Papa Renty was the first person whom Rich included in this packet. My mother's oral history aligned with his research, though one thing bothered me: in all the stories she told me, she'd never mentioned anyone named Delia. But there she was, both in the article Rich had found, and in the genealogy document he had compiled.

Why have I never heard of her? I wondered.

Then I thought about my great-grandfather Renty Taylor Thompson and his mother, Tena, being sold south. Perhaps they were forcibly separated from Delia, his aunt, as well as other family members? I knew that slavery ripped families apart. The cruelty was hard to imagine, and yet having just seen her in those violent and humiliating images, I also knew that anything was possible.

After a sleepless night, I called Rich to thank him.

"You found my Papa Renty!"

He was so gracious.

"Happy I could help," he said, and then shared that he had been doing his own family genealogy for decades. "I've traced my family back to New Hampshire and Vermont in the early 1700s. It is my passion."

I told him that was clear. He then asked me a lot of questions about Renty's Congo African origins, which he said were significant. I marveled that this was one of the first clues I gave Rich—that Papa Renty was known as the Black African. That piece of information was pivotal, as Louis Agassiz sought a "pure type" or African-born subject for his racist scientific experiment at a time when there were very few African-born slaves.

I was reminded of all the stories my mom shared growing up that connected our family to these African roots. For instance, she often talked about medicine her family used in the "old days," like John the Conqueror root. Shonrael, Megan, and I would tease her. My mom would wave her hand at us and insist that these traditional medicines worked just as well.

One night I decided to look up John the Conqueror root on the internet and was amazed to learn that the plant was named after an enslaved African prince from the Congo whose spirit was never broken. According to the folk law, the root had mystical and healing powers and many, including the great African American abolitionist and activist Frederick Douglass, carried it with them to ward off evil or other misfortune. It made sense that Congo Renty would practice traditions from his homeland—and pass them along to his children and grandchildren. These clues were like puzzle pieces to my family's history: I was still unsure of how to connect them into a cohesive narrative.

My mother also talked about the healing powers of the chrysanthemum tree, and how her great-aunt, Renty Taylor Thompson's sister, would bring the children with respiratory issues to this very tree and then scrape the bark and tell the kids to inhale. Again my girls and I thought that was bizarre—and again she was insistent that it worked. So I googled that and found that chrysanthemum was the cornerstone of American medicine for bronchial issues. When I shared this with my mom, she just smiled at me and said, "I told you that it cured your uncle Johnny!"

He suffered from asthma, as did other children in Mount Meigs, who were brought to this tree and healed as a result. This was just one of many discussions we had of African medicine. She also talked about how they used spiderwebs and soot to heal wounds instead of Band-Aids, and how people wore asafetida bags, which were small pouches filled with potent herbs that were worn like necklaces to ward off colds in the winter.

"The smell was horrible, much like rotten eggs," she said. "But it worked!"

I was so grateful to Rich—his research supported so many of my mother's stories. But I still had so many questions. Why were these images at the Peabody? Who found them? What was that experience like? And who are Jack and Jem and Drana? And what about Delia? Who is she and what happened to her? My mother had never mentioned her name in all the stories. Why hadn't I heard about her? I was haunted by how intensely sad she looked in those images and felt compelled to act. To do something!

I spent the following days immersed in documents and printouts. Rich had provided a treasure trove of information; it was voluminous and often difficult to follow. One such document was a 446-page dissertation submitted to Louisiana State University as a requirement for a doctoral degree in philosophy. The piece was titled "Rethinking Representations of Slave Life at Historical Plantation Museums," where the degree candidate, Julia Rose, explored how education in museums can impact social change.

Interesting, I thought, but how does this information relate to me? The document included slave narratives, one of which chronicles the life of a thirteen-year-old enslaved boy in the year 1800 from the Congo. His name was Renty; his father was Hector and his mother, Rose. His siblings were Stephany, Dick, Peggy, Basille, Michael, and Prince. Also noted were the names Caesar and Sancho and twins Adam and Eve. This document told the story of a stubborn little boy named Renty who was enslaved on the Magnolia Mound Plantation in Louisiana by the slaveholder Charles Norwood.

This tenacious little boy insisted that his enslaver provide him with a checked shirt, and his parents, astonishingly, limited the hours they would permit him to work. Echoed in these papers was my oral history, the stories of a proud and stubborn Papa Renty, but it was a bit sensational to me.

"Enslaved children telling their owners what to do?" It sounded a little embellished; I marked it "Little Boy Renty" and put it aside to revisit later.

Rich had given me an incredible head start with his research and I wanted to take it from there. That same day, while on my lunch break, I called the Connecticut Historical Society and spoke with their executive director, Kate Steinway. After I told her about my mother's dying wish and Rich's discovery, she exclaimed, "Wow! This is a great American story!"

She understood, as did I, that I was onto something huge.

I also decided to reach out to Harvard—I wanted them to know that Papa Renty was someone I had heard stories about my whole life! I wanted them to understand that he was not who Agassiz claimed him to be, but in fact the exact opposite. I wanted them to correct that story—not just of Renty and Delia, but also of the others in the daguerreotypes, Jack and Drana, Alfred, Fassena and Jem. It sickened me that they were still being objectified—on display to be looked at without more humanizing context.

One of the first people I reached out to was Henry Louis Gates Jr., as well as other professors who worked with him at the W. E. B. Du Bois Research Institute at the Hutchins Center at Harvard. I was sure he, of all people, would embrace and celebrate this news. This was 2010 and while Gates's PBS show, *Finding Your Roots,* would not air until 2012, he was known to be a premier academic authority of African American history. So I was surprised when he did not respond to my email. I tried again. No reply. I called the office and left messages. No return calls. So I kept trying. On one occasion his assistant answered the phone.

Finally! I thought, frustrated that it took so long to make a live connection. I introduced myself and explained why I was calling.

"I've received your messages and have given them all to Professor Gates," she said. "I will let him know that you are still interested in speaking with him."

When I did not hear back after that, I took it as confirmation that he was not interested in speaking with me. I found that perplexing but did not let that experience deter me. I was certain that I could find someone at the university to review my research. After all, Harvard was the world's premier academic institution. I just needed to find the right person there to help me find the missing pieces to confirm that Congo Renty was my Papa Renty, the man I had grown up hearing so many stories about. How could they not welcome and celebrate this news? I also wanted them to correct the narrative: my ancestor was the opposite of what Agassiz had theorized. Papa Renty taught himself how to read, using the Webster Blue Back Speller, at a time when it was illegal for enslaved people to be literate. I'd heard this story countless times growing up and knew how important that book was for the enslaved. It was originally published in 1783 by Noah Webster Jr., who's considered the "Father of American Scholarship and Education," as he sought to develop a way to teach children how to read using an orderly progression of words, rules, and pronunciations. At first he was mocked for trying to reform the King's English, but Webster traveled the country, specifically the South, circulating his speller as an inexpensive and more efficient way to teach children. This elementary approach to learning was embraced by all, including the enslaved, who seized the Webster speller as a vehicle for intellectual emancipation.

I was fascinated to learn Noah Webster was an abolitionist with lackluster convictions, describing slavery as an evil sin. In an 1837 letter he cautioned his daughter Eliza not to become too involved. Webster writes:

> My dear Eliza,
>
> I have seen your last letter to your sister Julia, in which, as in a former letter, you say that the spirit of abolition is among you. I am very sorry for this. The abolitionists are pursuing a course which, if not checked, will or may drench this country with blood. They are absolutely deranged. . . . The inference in that, remove the protecting force of the north and the slaves will rise and vindicate their right—this would sacrifice fifty or perhaps a hundred thousand men, women, and children—but no matter, the slaves would obtain their rights! Such appear to be their wishes.

Although a self-professed abolitionist, Webster appears to distance himself from the spirit of the movement by discouraging his daughter. This disassociation called into question all that I had ever learned about the Connecticut textbook pioneer, lawyer, teacher, and opponent of slavery. Webster continues:

> Eliza, slavery is a great sin and a great calamity—but it is not our sin, though it may prove to be a terrible calamity even to us in the north. But we cannot legally interfere with the south on this subject—and every step which the abolitionists take is tending to defeat their own object. To come to the north to preach and then disturb our peace, when we can legally do nothing to affect their object, is, in my view, highly criminal, & the preachers of abolitionism deserve the penitentiary.

In Heather Andrea Williams's book *Self-Taught: African American Education in Slavery and Freedom,* she writes: "The tool that African Americans used most frequently to decode written English was Noah Webster's *Elementary Spelling Book,* popularly called the Blue Back Speller . . . it was this little book that Frederick Douglass and countless other enslaved people used in the first steps toward literacy. And when slavery ended, adults and children, many of whom could not attend school, got a hold of the Speller and slowly taught themselves to read. The Speller accrued emotional significance as it helped individuals to decipher written language. 87-year-old John Walton expressed his sentimental attachment when he told an interviewer; 'I learn to read and write just since freedom. Us used Webster's old Blue Back Speller and I has one in the house to this day—I wouldn't take anything for it.'"

The Papa Renty stories I heard growing up said he studied well into the night, every night, until he understood and mastered the entire speller.

"If you don't know how to read, it's not easy to teach yourself," my mom said.

He then passed that knowledge on to his children, and anyone else who wanted to learn.

For Papa Renty and other enslaved men and women, the speller was an important first step in removing the chains of slavery. His self-taught literacy turned Agassiz's theory of scientific racism on its head. I could not wait to share these stories with both Harvard and the Peabody, the museum on campus where the daguerreotypes were held. I called to make an appointment to see them in person, certain the museum staff would be as excited as I was. For me it was more than historic: I thought of how many African Americans yearned to know, and have proof, of their ancestors. Having my mother's stories was a blessing, but a photo? This was rare for so many reasons.

I dialed the number on the museum website and was greeted by a very businesslike voice.

"Hello, my name is Tamara Lanier, and I've recently learned about the daguerreotypes in your collection," I said excitedly. "I have information that suggests I'm related to Congo Renty and I'd love to come see them in person."

"We can schedule a visit," she responded, in a voice devoid of emotion or enthusiasm.

I had to make an appointment since the Peabody, she explained, was an academic institution for scholars and writers interested in writing about the artifacts in their collection, and not a museum open daily to the public. My online research had also revealed that it was one of the oldest museums in the United States that focused on archaeology and ethnology. I did not even question why Renty and Delia were in this particular museum—I was just excited to see them in person.

Megan came with me on the day of my appointment, and as we were driving up Interstate 95 north toward Boston, we both marveled that after all these years of hearing stories of our extraordinary ancestor, he was trapped in a museum just two hours away.

It was August 2, 2010, and I was surprised at how difficult parking was. The museum was down a dead-end street and there was no dedicated lot, which meant I had to park at a street meter. It felt inaccessible. But I did not let that dampen my enthusiasm. I could not wait to see these images in person. To hold them in my hands.

I was a bubbly mix of nervous and excited as we walked toward the museum, which was housed in an austere Victorian brick building with narrow windows and wooden door entrance. It was a bright sunny day, and I remember entering through the tall doors and having to stop to regain my bearings. It was so dark inside that it took a while for my eyes to adjust. My excitement began to drain as the warm welcome I was anticipating was foiled by a woman at a security desk who asked me and Megan to leave our bags with her. I thought that was odd. Then a petite thin white woman with brown curly hair and glasses approached, holding paperwork for us. She introduced herself: Ilisa Barbash, Curator of Visual Anthropology for the Peabody.

She also was very businesslike and explained that we had to fill out these forms before we could proceed. I found the whole thing very off-putting. The whole experience reminded me of the prison guards I'd encountered visiting inmates in correctional institutions—very militaristic and curt. This was not at all what I had anticipated.

After we filled in the forms, Barbash said, "Follow me." She then escorted us to an even darker room, which felt like a storage area, where there was a table with a cover on top of it.

"I'll be back shortly," she said.

When she returned, she was holding a purple velvet cloth, which she laid down on the table. She then opened the cloth to reveal the daguerreotypes.

I was surprised by how small they were. Each was roughly three by four inches and could fit in the palm of my hand. The images were so hard to see in the darkened room that I could not make out who was who. Was that Renty? Or Jem?

Then our guide began presenting each artifact to us, in a very scripted manner. She was pointing to each as she spoke, and I remember wanting to hold them—to get a closer look—and may have asked if that was possible. It was not, she said definitively, explaining that the artifacts were so precious and fragile that even showing them to us was putting them in danger of further deterioration. I had driven two and a half hours to see and spend time with them—but it was becoming increasingly clear that neither was possible.

She then pointed out Renty and Delia, but it was like looking at a reflection in a river. Any visible image was fleeting, elusive, only appearing at certain side angles. I could never get the full image I now had seared in my brain. It was so far from the locking-eyes experience I had when I saw Renty on my computer screen that night in my bedroom, for the first time.

"I'd like to see his hands," I said, hoping there was a way to remove the frame so I could do that. In the picture in the article Rich sent me, Renty's hands were folded in his lap, just below the ornate frame. My uncle Johnny had told me often that Papa Renty had thick, dark, curved nails and I wanted to see if that was true.

"That's just not possible," she said.

The room had become increasingly claustrophobic, and I could not wait to leave this dank dungeon where Renty and Delia had been kept for too long. I wanted to take them with me, out of this horrible place. I learned later that the Agassiz Museum of Comparative Zoology was in another wing—which meant that my ancestors were housed in the same building as the skeletons of birds Agassiz had donated to Harvard when he founded that museum in 1859. It was all so inhumane to me. It made me feel like they were being kept in a zoo. Agassiz began that collection with twenty-five bird specimens, the museum proudly boasts on its website. And what of Renty? And Delia? They're not mentioned on the Peabody site. Why?

I knew it would be fruitless to ask Barbash any of these questions. She was for the most part silent during our visit, and I was so stunned by her lack of interest in me and my actual connection to two of the people depicted in those daguerreotypes, Renty and Delia, that all my questions I'd hoped to ask her that day stayed filed in my brain. Today was not the day to get them answered.

Before we left the museum, I handed her all of the genealogical information I had compiled to date, along with other corroborating research, which I had collected in a manila folder.

"I'd love to discuss my research with someone at some point soon," I said.

"Thank you," she said. "The museum is working on a project regarding the daguerreotypes, so if you find anything more, please send it our way."

As we made our way through the narrow dark hallways toward the entrance, it was difficult to hide my disappointment.

"That was a colossal waste of time," I said to Megan as we marched back to the car.

"Exactly," Megan said.

It was also foreboding. Everyone else I had shared my story with had been enthusiastic. Why was Ilisa Barbash so dismissive?

The very next day, I received this email from Pam Gerardi, the director of external communications at the Peabody. "Dear Tamara, it was a pleasure speaking with you the other day. What an interesting story you have, and I would be delighted if it does indeed connect to the Renty in the images we have here. I was hoping you would be able to write down for me the family line that leads back to Renty. There are literally hundreds of Rentys in South Carolina and Alabama. It would help if we had some names, dates, and places to help sort them out. (Though I did find Renty and Ophelia in Mt Meigs.) As I said, once we complete our plans for the project, we will probably bring in a professional to do all the family research on all the people in the images. Cheers—Pamela."

I found the whole exchange baffling: I gave the Peabody exactly what she was asking for. Did she even look at it? I wondered. It seemed that she was trying to distance me and my connection to Renty and Delia—instead of embracing it. I could not understand why this was so. Why would she not even want to speak to me about it? It made no sense. The overall feeling I got was that Harvard and the Peabody just wanted me to go away.

But then I heard my mother's voice, and I remembered Papa Renty's commanding look, which I interpreted as "Get me out of here!"

There was no way I was turning back now. I did not know how I would do it, but I knew that I would prove that Papa Renty and Delia were who I knew in my heart and bones to be: my ancestors.

4

What's in a Name?

Rich's research directly aligned with my oral history—but at that point in time, we were unaware of the historical significance, or the gravity of his discovery. I was still putting leaves on my family tree, building the genealogical research that my mom had wanted me to do—to write down the stories she had told me all those years. My promise to her.

But now my quest was bigger than that. I'd only ever seen Papa Renty discussed in terms of his invisibility, and the false myth that no one knew his background. I wanted Harvard—and the world—to know that Papa Renty was a proud man who taught himself and his children to read at a time when that was a risk to his own safety, and theirs. That alone debunked Louis Agassiz's theories, which Harvard clearly supported when the daguerreotypes were commissioned. Yet any time I read anything about the artifacts, back then in 2010, Agassiz was still being celebrated as Harvard's prized professor. In all the publications I had read about Agassiz, there was a blind worship of his scientific contributions—on glaciers, and fish, and birds—whereas his racism felt intentionally overlooked. I was astonished to learn that there were buildings on Harvard's campus named for him. This was a hateful man—why were they protecting and still celebrating him?

Meanwhile, my daughters were also probing the internet, searching for clues about their Papa Renty. Earlier that summer, Shonrael found a worldwide online petition to rename one of the tallest mountains in the Swiss Alps from "Agassizhorn," in celebration of the Swiss-born scientist, to "Rentyhorn" in recognition of the harms his racist theories have caused. The "De-mounting Louis Agassiz" movement was first started by Hans Fässler, a German historian who specializes in slavery and postcolonialism, and soon joined by Sasha Huber, the Swiss-born Haitian artist and activist who had launched the petition, which read: "On May 28, 2007, the 200th birthday of Swiss Naturalist Louis Agassiz (1807 to 1873) was commemorated in both Switzerland and worldwide. However, Agassiz was not only an influential glaciologist, but also an influential racist and a pioneer thinker of apartheid. To make this fact known, the campaign De-mounting Louis Agassiz has been launched suggesting taking the mountain away from him (thus de-mounting him) and henceforth to call the Agassizhorn (3,946 meters above sea level) on the boundary between the cantons of Wallis and Berne, named after him in the 1840s, to 'Rentyhorn.' Renty was a slave from the Congo on a South Carolina plantation whose daguerreotype was commissioned by Louis Agassiz in order to 'scientifically prove the inferiority of the black race.'"

My girls and I immediately signed the petition, and Shonrael reached out to Huber to let her know of our connection to Renty. Huber responded enthusiastically—that was the beginning of a deep friendship with our family. Within days we were Skyping between my home and hers, in Helsinki, Finland. Unlike Harvard, Huber never once questioned my claim; she only celebrated it. As she explained, "My mother is Haitian, and I'm descended from people who were enslaved. I relate to Renty's story and am so glad to learn more about him—through you."

Huber explained that she and Hans Fässler were part of a transatlantic committee rallying journalists, artists, historians, and scholars from Germany, Switzerland, the Democratic Republic of the Congo, Brazil, and beyond to expose Louis Agassiz as a racist separatist whose theories were used not only to support slavery in the United States, but also eugenics in Europe and by the framers of apartheid in South Africa.

"People don't understand how far-reaching his racism goes," Huber said.

I certainly had not, until I met her.

Even more astonishing was how many places had been named for Agassiz—more than fifty throughout the world, including mountains, lakes, and glaciers as well as towns, communities, and streets, from Antarctica to Argentina and all throughout the United States. Shockingly, he even has craters on Mars and the moon named for him.

In addition to the petition, Huber did what she calls a "Reparative Intervention" in August 2008 when she chartered a helicopter to travel to the peak known as Agassizhorn, where she placed a plaque with the following declaration: "The mountain you are standing on was named after the Swiss Naturalist Louis Agassiz. Agassiz however was not only a Glaciologist, Genealogist, and Zoologist but also an influential racist and pioneer thinker of apartheid. In 2007, the 200th year anniversary of Agassiz's birth was commemorated in Switzerland and worldwide. This gave rise to the de-mounting campaign which denies Louis Agassiz this mountain and has re-baptized it Rentyhorn, in honor of the slave Renty and other men and women who have suffered similar fates."

The world saw Renty as the face of American chattel slavery—

and now he had a place on one of the world's tallest mountain peaks. A photographer accompanied her and shot images of her placing the sign at the peak. It was Huber's artistic act, and petition, that helped bring global attention to Agassiz's racist past. I was interested to learn from Huber that Fässler was also an early reparations advocate who had written about why Switzerland, which prides itself on being a neutral country that did not colonize any countries, still made a tremendous amount of money in the slave trade, shipping human cargo to slave-owning countries—and therefore, Fässler argued, should participate in reparations. He, Huber, and their fellow committee members understood that the image of Renty symbolized all that was wrong and repugnant about enslavement. They also believed, as I did, that these stories had to be rewritten to begin to repair the wounds Agassiz caused with his horrific theories that have brought about so much harm in the world.

I shared all my Renty research with Sasha and she sent me *Rentyhorn*, a collection of essays that she edited that included the photos of her placing the plaque on the mountain. The opening essay was by Fässler, titled "What's in a Name? Louis Agassiz, His Mountain, and the Politics of Remembrance," which was followed by a piece called "Louis Agassiz and Adolph Hitler. Documents of Racist Mania," by Hans Barth. I read the book in one sitting, amazed at just how insidious and far-reaching Agassiz's impact was on humanity. His theories not only supported enslavement in the United States, but planted seeds for the Holocaust and apartheid. Agassiz's promotion of scientific racism has caused pain and suffering for untold numbers of people.

I found this upsetting and confusing. I had information about one of the people Agassiz had used for these theories—that disputed them. Harvard, the premier academic institution in the world, had a responsibility to sit and review my research. That is good scholarship. Instead they were protecting Agassiz and dismissing me.

Buoyed by all the brilliant essays in *Rentyhorn,* which deepened my own understanding of Agassiz and the daguerreotypes, I continued reaching out to academic institutions in the US that specialized in African American history, determined to find an expert who could help me confirm my findings. One such email, which I sent to several people at Yale's Gilder Lehrman Center for the Study of Slavery, Resistance, and Abolition, elicited two responses. David Blight, the director of the department and a professor of African American history wrote, "This is exciting news," and another woman, named Melissa McGrath, informed me that Yale University Press had recently published a book on the daguerreotypes called *Delia's Tears: Race, Science, and Photography in Nineteenth-Century America*—and that the author, Molly Rogers, was coming to Yale to talk about the book on February 23, 2011.

She also connected me with Rogers's editor, who gave me the author's email address.

I immediately wrote to Rogers, explaining my connection to Delia and Renty, and was so happy to receive her response: "Dear Tamara, many thanks for contacting me and for sending along some of your research. While researching and writing *Delia's Tears,* I long hoped to find a descendant of one or more of the men and women in the photographs—your news is therefore very exciting." The relief I felt was palpable—and fleeting: "I am sorry to say, however, that the documents appear to remain inconclusive."

I was taken aback by her certainty, which felt abrupt considering that she had not yet spoken with me about my oral history or any of the documentation I pieced together thus far. Instead she went on to point out what she considered discrepancies in census information: "The Renty Thompson listed in the 1880 census, was not recorded on the one taken in 1870," she wrote, adding, "This is not unusual as data was so often mis-recorded."

Overall, she said that I had to prove the connection between my great-grandfather Renty Taylor Thompson and the man known as Congo Renty in the daguerreotypes. While I knew that I had my work cut out for me, I was also struck by what felt like academic arrogance. It felt so dismissive, suggesting that scholarly research could annul ancestral accounts. This would become a theme, but then I was reminded of a popular slogan that the NAACP embraces, "There can be nothing about us without us."

Before she signed off, she wrote, "I wish you the very best of luck with your research."

I also understood how difficult it was to prove my connection. We arranged to talk on the phone, and in between I tried to read *Delia's Tears*. It was the opposite experience of *Rentyhorn*. Rogers's book reminded me of the article that Rich sent me: the very first pages talk about the subject matter in a very disconnected way, something to be studied. I understood that this was what academics do, but it also made me incredibly uncomfortable considering how intimate and violent these images are. Still, I was moved by the line "At the heart of this story is the question of what it means to be human." Another line that resonated was "History favors the keepers—the slaveholders, politicians, and others who made the documents we now use to write history. And even though Delia is at the very heart of the history of these photographs, she is nowhere to be seen." All true. And while Rogers states that "depicting Delia through the eyes of others repeats the repressive act that resulted in the photographs," she then begins the book with an admittedly fictional account of what Delia was experiencing as she was being photographed.

"*She was not supposed to be there,*" she wrote in italics, intimating Delia's thoughts. "*Nothing in her life so far had prepared her for this. All those years of working, sweating, laboring in the fields and later in the forge, none of it had so much as hinted at this.*"

As I read Rogers's words, my first thoughts were, How can we know what Delia felt? It was so invasive. It went on: "*Perhaps she had even seen a photograph, once, in the great house. But she herself was never supposed to have her picture made. This was no place for a slave.*"

This was a violation of Delia's space, a violation of her pain and privacy. Did Rogers, or anyone for that matter, have the right to step into that private moment of humiliation to project their thoughts? How could anyone know what Delia felt that day in the studio, or back at the Taylor Plantation? The next paragraph was more of the same: "*The sun beat down on her through the skylight, making her warmer than she had been outside in the sunshine a moment ago. . . .*" Then I got to the lines, "*but she had been told to hold still. Don't move.* Do not move. *He seemed a nice enough man, one who might be forgiving if she disobeyed, but everything was different here and so she did not trust her judgment.*"

I had to put the book down. It was too much. This passage was opposite the image of Delia, who was naked from the waist up, looking not at but through the camera. Her pain and humiliation were palpable in her face. She looked so incredibly sad to me. A transferal of Delia's victimization rippled through me—I experienced her trauma in a visceral way. To reenact this private, intimate moment felt abusive. If Rogers was going to step into this space with Delia, comfort her, I thought; console her by offering her humanity.

The very next chapter was about Renty. The first line read: "The moment his foot touched the floor, a spasm shook his body and raised the skin up on his arms."

It felt almost pornographic to me, that my ancestors were objects for Rogers to project her fantasies onto. I put the book down.

I knew that my story was an important American story, one the public would support. People wanted to know who Renty was, and I had information. I wanted Harvard to realize what an opportunity I was offering them and I knew that the only way I could get their attention was through press coverage. I also knew that February was the only time to get any interest in Black history. It was also when Rogers was coming to Yale to talk about her book, so I began reaching out to local papers and was thrilled when the *New Haven Register* agreed to do a story. "FAMILY TREE: African Slave's Remarkable Life Traced to Connecticut" was published on January 30, 2011. In the piece, there's a photograph of me holding a copy of *Delia's Tears.* The reporter Pamela McLoughlin did a beautiful job summarizing the oral history I had grown up hearing about my Papa Renty and so was the first instance of me fulfilling my mother's promise to write our story down. Then, on February 21, 2011, another local Connecticut paper, the New London *Day,* published a piece by Amy Barry titled "Norwich Woman Thinks Famous Photo Is Her Ancestor." In both instances, the reporters reached out to Harvard, which "declined to comment." Both articles mentioned my invitation to meet Molly Rogers on February 23 at Yale University.

Megan and Shonrael came with me to the event, and though neither had read *Delia's Tears,* both were interested to hear what Rogers had to say. We all feared that Delia and Renty's pain was being appropriated by the Peabody, Harvard, and other scholars to attain prestige and notoriety.

The talk took place in a large, stately classroom in one of Yale's historic buildings. We arrived early and introduced ourselves to Rogers and David Blight, who was hosting the conversation that evening. She was cordial, whereas he seemed a bit standoffish, which surprised me only because his first email to me had been enthusiastic. Something had shifted, as neither seemed all that excited that we were there.

Chairs had been set up in a circle in the classroom, with Rogers and Blight sitting next to one another at the head. My daughters and I took our seats as other people arrived. Of the thirty or so people who came, only a handful were students. David Blight welcomed everyone and introduced Molly Rogers, who began to read the Delia excerpt.

I heard Shonrael sigh, and Megan mutter beneath her breath.

Afterward, Blight led an informal discussion about the book, which meant people could ask questions throughout. Shonrael, Megan, and I all smiled when a middle-aged woman mentioned having read *Rentyhorn*. Another identified herself as a reporter from the *Journal of African American History*. She said she was writing a review of the book and had questions about Rogers's process, specifically how she found information about the men and women photographed against their will, and the ethics of photography in that moment in time, versus now. I was amazed at the authority with which Rogers spoke, as if her research about Renty, Delia, Jack, Jem, and the others was anything more than supposition. Yes, she had found census records and wills and other documentation to patch together proof that they existed, but anything beyond this was simply conjecture.

I waited patiently for an opportunity to introduce myself. I wanted to be respectful of Yale's program and was not sure how my story would be received. Toward the end of the conversation, I finally spoke: "Good evening," I said. "My name is Tamara Lanier and I'm the descendant of Delia and Renty."

Before I could utter another word, I felt all the energy in the room shift—to me.

It was so intense, to the point of feeling uncomfortable. People were riveted, hanging on my every word. I saw Shonrael and Megan scanning the room, surprised by the hunger the audience had to learn about me and my relationship to Renty and Delia. Grateful for the invitation and mindful of the program's purpose, to discuss Rogers's book, I didn't want to be a distraction. But by now I had the audience's full attention.

At the end of the event, I found myself suddenly surrounded by people with questions, three of whom were reporters—one from the *Yale Press*, another from the *New Haven Register*, as well as the woman from the *Journal of African American History*. They each asked me for my business card. Molly Rogers was signing books nearby, and two people asked me to sign *Delia's Tears* as well.

"No," I said. "It's not mine to sign."

I did not say then that I was working on my own book, but I had been keeping notes and a journal ever since my mother's death. At first I thought it was a family project, but since my visit to the Peabody I had realized this story needed and deserved a larger audience. This evening proved to me how necessary it was to "write it down"—not just to fulfill that promise, but to correct the record. The woman from the Connecticut Historical Society was correct: this was an important American story.

On our drive home, my girls and I talked about how scholars sometimes miss the mark by relying heavily on their research, often overlooking the value of African American oral histories. Historical records such as birth certificates, death records, and census information are documents written from a white perspective, which often fail to capture the essence of the Black experience. We talked about how this kind of approach discounts the stories that have been passed down in families like ours. We considered my mother, whose oral account of her age and date of birth was not sufficient. Although she celebrated June 8 as her birthday for her entire life, she was wrong according to the Montgomery officials and forced to accept the erroneous December 23 date they assigned to her. It's like they don't value and appreciate these oral histories as a meaningful way of recapturing a truer account of the African American experience. It was clear to us that we had to be Renty and Delia's historians.

I continued to write to other experts and heard back from Sheldon Creek, the assistant director at Harvard's Hutchins Center for

African and African American Research, who wrote that my story was a "missing link in history" and that it had "huge implications for reparations." Encouraging words, but no offer of assistance. Charles Ogletree, a law professor at Harvard, however, responded with an action plan. I had written to him on March 11, 2011, and shared my story. He wrote me back the next day and copied several people, some with Harvard.edu addresses, and one for the Cambridge branch of the NAACP, with the note, "I'm connecting you with some Cambridge sources and friends who know the Agassiz story." He also mentioned that there was a middle school in Cambridge originally named for Agassiz that had his name removed in February 2002 and was now called the Maria Baldwin Middle School, after the woman who was appointed principal of Agassiz Middle School in 1899—the first Black female to hold that position in the commonwealth of Massachusetts, and the entire Northeast. This was encouraging and reminded me of Sasha Huber's renaming campaign.

Ogletree also suggested that I connect with the NAACP's Cambridge, Massachusetts, branch. My family had a long history with the organization, as my mother was a charter member of the Norwich, Connecticut, branch and I am to this day affiliated with the New London branch, where we live the organization's creed, to "speak truth to power." The chapter investigated complaints against the Coast Guard and police unions and has been publicly critical of those entities that failed to hold police officers accountable for misconduct. In fact, it was after a complaint from a local officer that the first Black chief was hired in the port city of New London. President Jean Jordan and I have been seated on various advisory committees commissioned by local, state, and federal officials. The work of the NAACP is not for the faint of heart and certainly not for those reluctant to engage in the difficult conversations about race.

I knew what it meant to be affiliated with the NAACP and was therefore looking forward to the support of the Cambridge chapter.

In March, and after the urging of Ogletree, I drove two hours to meet with the general membership. I was the last item on the agenda, which I understood. I was a guest. When my turn came, I shared my story, and saw that several people were clearly interested, while others were unsure how they could help or what they could do. I was perplexed: if someone had come to our branch with an issue like this, our first order of business would be to send a letter to Harvard demanding that they meet with all of us. Instead they suggested that I alone write to Drew Gilpin Faust, then Harvard's president. As I drove the two hours back home, I felt even more disappointed than I had coming back from the Peabody. Why pass me back to Harvard? It did not make sense and felt like a colossal waste of time. They could have simply told me this over the phone.

Still, I followed their suggestion. On March 18, 2011, I sent a letter to President Faust asking her to please review the documentation I had gathered about my relationship to Congo Renty, and to share with me, his lineal descendant, how Harvard planned to use the daguerreotypes. I wanted them, at the very least, to know how Renty's oral history refuted Agassiz's claims. My visit at the Peabody had been so unsettling: I also wanted to know how those images of my ancestors would be shared with the world.

Dear President Faust,

The purpose of this correspondence is to formally request your assistance in a matter that has by many been deemed historically significant. Approximately thirty-seven years ago, a Harvard associate unearthed an amazing discovery. Found in the Peabody Museum were piercing and poignant images of the evils of slavery.

In 1850, Louis Agassiz commissioned the photographer J. T. Zealy to capture what he believed to be evidence of racial inferiority. The enslaved men and women depicted in these daguerreotypes have touched the hearts and conscience of people worldwide. Amazingly, I have historical and US Census information confirming that two of these slaves are in fact my ancestors. On numerous occasions, I have reached out to the Harvard academia and found them to be unresponsive. I have called the W. E. B. Du Bois Institute of African Studies; have left messages and forwarded emails almost to the point of ad nauseam.

I ask myself, why is Harvard, the keeper of such historically significant information, seemingly not interested in what has been described by the Connecticut Historical Society as a "Great American Story"?

Earlier this week I shared my plight with the Cambridge Branch of the NAACP and was encouraged to reach out to you. I do so for two reasons. Firstly, I would like to learn more about the slave daguerreotypes and how they have or will be used. Secondly, I would like a formal review of my documentation to reaffirm that Renty and Delia Taylor are indeed my ancestors. I anxiously await your response and would be willing to sit with you and discuss this further.

Sincerely, Tamara Lanier

On Friday, April 1, 2011, President Drew Faust responded.

Dear Ms. Lanier,

Thank you for writing and sharing your story with me. Subsequent to receiving your email I was glad to learn that you have also been in touch with Ilisa Barbash and Pamela

Gerardi at the Peabody Museum and that you have had an opportunity to view the daguerreotypes you mentioned in your email. I understand that the Peabody Museum is involved in projects regarding those daguerreotypes and that Ms. Barbash and Ms. Gerardi have agreed to be in touch with you if they discover any new relevant information. I hope you will also do the same. As a historian, I recognize the significance of this study, and I very much appreciate your offer to be of assistance.

With my best wishes,

Drew Faust

I was stunned by her evasive response. This was a moment for Drew Faust, the first female president of Harvard University, to stand on principle, to live up to its motto: *Veritas*. To tell the truth. Instead, her response felt disconnected from the humanity of my request. That upset me the most: regardless of my personal connection to the subjects of these photos, Harvard did not seem interested in rewriting the story, that Louis Agassiz was a renowned scientist who used Renty and Delia to prove white supremacy, and Black inferiority. Faust's response strengthened my resolve: using Renty, a literate man who was an educator, dispels the narrative in its entirety. I thought they'd at least be willing to tell that part of the story. Harvard's response: silence.

They had already silenced my ancestors. I was not going to let them silence me.

5

De-Mounting Agassiz

I stayed in touch with Sasha Huber, who invited me and my girls to visit her in Grindelwald, Switzerland, the summer of 2012 for an exhibit related to the De-mounting Agassiz movement at the Grindelwald History Museum called *Gletscherforsher Raccisst: Louis Agassiz (1807–2012).* In the lead-up to the event, Huber put me in touch with Hans Fässler, the event organizer. He had also written a book, published in 2005 titled *Reise in Schwarz-Weiss,* on Swiss participation in slavery as the Swiss banks played a huge role in the transatlantic slave trade. Hans told me that he had requested permission from the Peabody to use the Renty image for the exhibit and they had said no.

"They did not like the content of our exhibition," Fässler explained. "So they refused to let us use that image."

I was not surprised. It reminded me of their refusal to let me use the images the previous summer when I sent a request for Renty and Delia for the book I was working on. After going to the Molly Rogers event, I realized that the story I promised to "write down" for my mother was much bigger than our family genealogy. It *was* a great

American story. A woman named Jessica Desany Ganong, the imaging services coordinator at the Peabody, replied: "Thank you for submitting your image request form. I notice that you do not yet have a publisher and date of publication for this request. We would be happy to consider your request once these are in place. Please know that due to the sensitive nature of these images, your request will be reviewed by a committee and may take up to five weeks to process."

That was a slap in the face. I had only just begun writing this book—and at that time was considering self-publication since I did not have an agent or any connection to the publishing world. I thought, Don't they know how extremely difficult it is to secure a publisher?

Once again I was being dismissed and denied. It bothered me that they treated me like I was someone who had no right to use the images. Their response should have been more compassionate. I decided that I was not going to ask them for permission ever again. From that moment on, if I wanted to use Renty's image, I would!

Hans Fässler was equally upset that they would not let him use the images for his exhibition, and the *Boston Globe* wrote about the controversy on June 27, 2012. Mary Carmichael covered the story, reporting, "The museum's curators say they denied the Swiss group permission to reproduce the images because of the Peabody's blanket policy against the display of exploitative images of naked people."

When I read that, my first reaction was, "So dishonest!"

There were dozens of examples where Harvard allowed the images to be reproduced—including Molly Rogers's book, which had Delia on its cover. Granted, her image was cropped from her shoulders up, but it was still obvious that she was naked. And you could see—and feel—her humiliation in her eyes. How was that okay? But my and Hans Fässler's requests were not? It was becoming abundantly clear to me that the university wanted to control how the image was used—and Fässler had the emails to prove it. He shared one with the paper, in which an employee from the "Harvard Art Museum" wrote, "Some of the language in your exhibition materials, although interesting, are aggressive towards Agassiz, who was a very influential figure at Harvard."

Fässler pushed back and the director of communications, Daron Manoogian, responded to say that he could use the images, and that the email was "sent in error by a 'very new, temporary employee.'" The whole interchange infuriated Fässler, who understood my own exasperation with the university. He opted against using the images and instead Sasha Huber made silhouettes based on them for the exhibition, which my girls and I were excited to go see. It was my first time traveling out of the country, so I was not sure what to expect. We were going to the Swiss Alps; would I need to pack for cold weather? Instead it was the summer, and 100 degrees. Once we arrived in the small mountain town, we were treated with such open arms. I was immediately put at ease. It was also wonderful to meet so many interesting people—from all over the world—who had also come to see the exhibit. They were all there in support of renaming Agassiz's mountain after Renty.

Then Hans and Sasha asked me to address the crowd and explain my relationship to Renty. I was not prepared and had never spoken publicly about Renty before, so I was incredibly nervous. As I took to the podium, I remembered the interest people had at the Molly Rogers event, but that was an intimate crowd! And they all spoke English! This was different: there were dignitaries from the Democratic Republic of the Congo; journalists from Switzerland, Germany, and Italy; a professor from Brazil; and so many young people! That encouraged me the most—that students in their teens and twenties were interested in retelling the Agassiz story from Renty's point of view. That was, after all, what Hans and Sasha were proposing with this exhibit and de-mounting movement.

I drew a big breath to remind myself that these people wanted to hear what I had to say. Then, as I exhaled, I tapped into my mother's passion and commitment to our family history.

"I am descended from Congo Renty," I began. I talked about my mother, and how I had grown up hearing stories of this extraordinary man, our Papa Renty as we lovingly called him in my house. I knew Renty as a community leader, someone who valued education and was unafraid to teach anyone interested in learning. I explained how these stories, which I'd heard my whole life, led to me finding Sasha, and to standing before everyone at this precise moment. That if it were not for my mother telling me the stories that her grandfather told her, I would have never made the connection that I was related to the man that Rentyhorn was being named for.

"Renty's own story survived as a result of that generational love," I said.

Shonrael and Megan were sitting in the audience, beaming. Everyone else was too. Some people were nodding their heads; others began to clap. The crowd was so enthusiastic throughout the entire presentation. I felt deeply supported and encouraged. I scanned the audience, marveling at how many people from different countries were there, and how they all knew who Renty was. That they too were moved to act, to give him his power back that Agassiz had attempted to strip him of. I thought of how proud my mom would be of this moment and once again wished she were there with me, to witness it.

The exhibit was very moving and included a film of Sasha's reparative intervention. The first helicopter company refused to take her once they learned what she was doing. It was too controversial, they said. The second one agreed, and Sasha herself marveled at how daring it was to land on a mountainside and hike up to the peak to place the plaque. This piece is described in the foreword of *Rentyhorn*, by Pirkko Siitari: "Huber's chosen method is that of social intervention. Taking action for change. She stages a performance or event, documents it and finally transforms it into an installation. . . . *Rentyhorn* deconstructs racist power relations, both past and present—by revealing how a place name is never neutral. It makes us see our environment in a new light."

For this intervention, Sasha took photos of the plaque after she installed it in the mountain, and then she removed it since the range is a UNESCO site. Part of this exhibit includes the letter she wrote to former UN secretary-general Kofi Annan, then a member of the patronage committee at UNESCO, to ask permission to permanently install a bronze plaque renaming the mountain to Rentyhorn. She sent the petition along with the request to Annan as well as to the mayors of Grindelwald, Guttannen, and Fieschertal, the three villages that surround the mountain peak, and the two presidents of the territories that flank it, as well as all the other members of the UNESCO World Heritage Site committee. It also includes their responses. Whereas all the political figures declined her request, a representative from Annan's foundation wished her luck in her future endeavors.

Sasha and Hans both consider this event a success in that it began a necessary conversation about Agassiz that made people wrestle with his legacy. "We shined a light on what had been buried," Sasha said. "Agassiz's racism is undeniable. He was one of the worst and most effective racist thinkers of his time. This is well-documented. Why are we celebrating him?"

These were my questions too, and here, in a small village in Switzerland, I felt like I'd found people who finally understood my confusion at Harvard's refusal to acknowledge me. The exhibit also included the emails from Harvard about the *Boston Globe* controversy, and a map of all the places that had been named for Agassiz. This was where I learned that Agassiz named Agassizhorn after himself, back in 1840, before he came to the United States to teach at Harvard.

"Until the lions have their own historians . . ." Shonrael began.

"The history of the hunt will always glorify the hunter," Megan said, finishing a line the girls often quoted when talking about their Papa Renty.

After the festivities ended, the girls and I decided to take a train to Milan since we were close to the Italian border. As we were making our way back, I noticed three white police officers interrogating a young Black man in his twenties. I assumed he was African, as we had noticed quite a few African migrants when we got off the train in Milan. It was a stark contrast to our experience in Switzerland, where we were among the only Black people, other than the representatives from the Congo, at the exhibition.

Likewise, we were the only other Black people on the train, and I suddenly felt incredibly vulnerable witnessing this man's exchange with the police. Would we be next? I did not speak German, French, Italian, or Dutch. Even more unsettling, I did not know the laws in Switzerland.

This incident interrupted an otherwise pleasant trip. I went from being a tourist visiting Italy for the first time to fearing a police encounter.

Louis Agassiz made the stigma of being Black a crime all over the world. No one else on that train seemed to give the incident a second thought; they were completely unbothered, almost as if it was a regular occurrence. I found the whole thing unnerving.

Back in Switzerland, as we were saying our goodbyes, I exchanged emails with many of the dignitaries who had come for the event. Roger Buangi Puati was one of the representatives from the Congo who invited me and my daughters to come visit him there.

"Come, my country would love to have you!" he said. "There you would be treated like a queen!"

6

Praying for a Breakthrough

I returned to the United States invigorated. I understood that Renty's story was not contained to one country: he was a global symbol. His stoic gaze was a call to action to rewrite history, and to balance the scales. The community of activists I met at the De-mounting Agassiz event also made me realize that I was not alone.

Since Harvard refused to acknowledge me, I also understood, thanks to Sasha and Hans, the power of the media. I became laser-focused on getting a national media outlet to tell my side of the Renty story—and force Harvard to respond.

I wrote to a reporter with the *Boston Globe,* suggesting that their readers might be interested to know this story. He asked me to call him.

"Very interesting story," he said on the phone that same morning. "But I'm not sure there is anything here for us to investigate."

I may have sighed.

"Besides, what makes you think you can challenge the most powerful academic institution in the world?" he added.

Surprised by his lack of interest and annoyed by his blind defense of Harvard, I quickly interjected to say, "It's not might that makes right."

I think he heard in my voice my disappointment as I continued, at this point talking over him: "It's right that makes might and I firmly believe that I am on the right side of history."

I was beginning to understand Harvard's far-reaching influence. This reporter had no interest in seeking the truth and reporting it. There was no neutrality. He was siding with the university, assuming they knew more than I did about my own ancestors—which was what Harvard thought as well.

Harvard refused to respond to any press requests. In the few stories that had been written about me and Renty, whenever the reporters reached out to Harvard for comment, they either declined or they maintained that I could not prove my claim. This was gaslighting, as the university was injecting doubt into the very people whose jobs it was to uncover truth. This was a consistent theme with news organizations, which inspired my mantra: "Might does not make right. Right makes might."

Powerful people use their influence to control the narrative, but it's the grassroots efforts that tell the story. So I continued to look for ways to make my story relevant. I scoured the papers daily, looking for stories with similar themes and threads, and then read about Mr. Fortune, a man who had been enslaved by a prominent Connecticut doctor who dissected his human remains following his death and preserved his skeleton for scientific study. Mr. Fortune was finally being given the dignity of a proper burial thanks to the children of the Waterbury school system, who petitioned the Mattatuck Museum, where the remains were gifted.

I was so moved by his story that I decided to attend the memorial event on September 12, 2013, at the state capitol in Hartford. More than three hundred people came to attend his funeral service, which was led by Amy Wellin, the rector of Saint John's Episcopal Church on the Green, the parish in Waterbury where Mr. Fortune had been baptized in 1797. She quoted scripture that spoke to the ills of slavery, then ended the service by saying, "It is with restored dignity his bones will be buried. . . . We bury Mr. Fortune not as a slave but as a child of God who is blessed. . . . We must refuse to give in to the forces that seek to diminish us."

I happened to be sitting next to a woman who I later learned was Gabrielle Foreman, a professor of English literature and African American history from Penn State. She had written several books on the Black activist movements in the nineteenth century. I'm not sure why, but I shared Papa Renty's story with her. Moved, she took me by the hand and said, "Come, let's go to Fortune's casket and pray."

We walked together up to the casket, which was covered in a regal deep purple velvet cloth with a large burgundy cross. Together we placed our palms on it, and bowed our heads.

Mr. Fortune, I am sorry for your suffering. May you rest in peace knowing the world now knows your story, I thought quietly to myself. And please, dear God, help me find a reporter who has the courage to tell my story so the world will know who my Papa Renty really is as well.

At that very moment, a reporter named Rick Hartford with the *Hartford Courant*, the largest newspaper in Connecticut, approached and asked us our names, and for permission to use a photo that was just taken of us.

"Would you mind sharing what you prayed for?" he asked.

"A breakthrough," I said.

He smiled and said, "For what?"

I told him about the unwillingness of many news networks to tell my story after Harvard kept saying that I could never prove anything about my relation to Congo Renty of the famous Zealy daguerreotypes. I told him that I wanted to find a major media outlet with the courage to run the story—that I was related to one of the first enslaved people ever to be photographed—despite Harvard's refusal to acknowledge me.

An Associated Press photographer named Jessica Hill had taken that photo, which was published the next day in multiple newspapers. Rick Hartford from the *Courant* followed up and said, "We'd like to run a feature story on you—and your connection to Papa Renty."

Look at God, I thought, answering prayers in real time. I was grateful for all the miracles, signs, and wonders poured into my life. This was yet another divine intervention, another example of God placing special people in my path. Two of the *Hartford Courant*'s best investigative reporters were assigned to my story and I learned through them the paper had done its own investigative piece on itself. As one of the oldest, longest-running newspapers in the United States, it had published ads for runaway slaves in the eighteenth and nineteenth centuries. It also ran a story about how Aetna, the Hartford-based insurance company, had insured slaves for the people who owned them—in the 1850s, when enslavement was illegal in Connecticut.

Aetna, the global leader who dominated the insurance industry and made Hartford the insurance capital of the world, was prompted to issue a public apology in March 2000 for insuring the lives of slaves. Aetna referred to this chapter of the company's history as "deeply disappointing."

Two of the *Courant*'s journalists, Anne Farrow and Joel Lang, and editor Jenifer Frank won a Pulitzer Prize for their reporting on that story, which led to the book *Complicity: How the North Promoted, Prolonged, and Profited from Slavery,* published in 2006. This was a team that was unafraid to challenge Harvard or question the North's role in the history of enslavement in the United States. I was in excellent hands.

Nancy Schoeffler was reporting my story with Rick Hartford, so I gave them all the information I had gathered thus far and connected them with Kate Steinway from the Connecticut Historical Society, as well as Rich Morrison from the ice cream shop. They did what I had hoped Harvard would do originally: comb through all that research and ask me thoughtful questions and help me zero in on what was still missing.

"Have you found any proof of your relationship to Congo Renty?" Rick asked. "Any way to connect your great-grandfather Renty Thompson to the man in the daguerreotypes?"

This was the recurring question, and I knew I needed a professional genealogist to help fill it, someone with credibility to give me and my mother's oral history credibility.

Shonrael shared this quest one afternoon with her coworker, who said, "I know the best genealogist in the world, Chris Childs. He works with the New England Historic Genealogical Society in Boston and did Barack Obama's family tree. I'm certain he will be willing to help."

On January 5, 2014, Shonrael gave me the email for Chris Childs, whom I wrote to that same day: "Hello, Chris, my name is Tamara and we have a great friend in common." I gave him all the background about my reason for emailing and included links to the local stories that had covered it. By the end of the day I was talking with him on the phone. Once again, I could not believe my good fortune. This was yet another example of God's intervention, placing important people in my path. Chris immediately saw the value and importance of what I was trying to do, and he was captivated by the story.

"I'll reach out to the Mormons in Utah," he responded. "That's where we will find the slaveholders' will and the slave index."

He must have sensed my confusion, or maybe I even blurted out, "What on earth do the Mormons have to do with my Papa Renty?"

He explained that the Mormons believe they can posthumously

"baptize" relatives if they can prove a familial connection, which was why they began collecting all the genealogical data they could find. As a result, they have the largest database of genealogical documents in the world. Chris also explained that the only way to piece together my enslaved ancestors' whereabouts was to look at the slaveholders' documents. I knew that proving my lineage was particularly challenging since the births and deaths of enslaved people were rarely if ever documented. What I did not know, until I spoke with Chris, was that the slave owners kept indexes and inventories of their property—which, he warned, included slaves along with farm equipment and animals. I had seen wills of slave owners that often named enslaved people as part of their inheritance, but never these inventories. What Chris helped me realize was that to learn anything about my enslaved ancestors, I needed to first find the wills and slave indexes of the people who had enslaved them. What a demeaning process: for white researchers looking for their ancestors, they have the privilege of searching easily accessible and well kept government documents. The Black experience is so very different.

On January 9, 2014, Chris sent me a wealth of information, including Colonel Thomas Taylor's handwritten probate will and slave index, dated 1834. He was the father of Benjamin Franklin Taylor, the man who had supplied Louis Agassiz with Renty and Delia for his scientific theories.

These documents were written in nineteenth-century cursive, which made them difficult to read. The first one I pulled up on my desktop was a scan of the original document that had the title "Inventory and Appraisement of the Estate of the Late Col. Thomas Taylor" written across the top of the page. I was reading it on my desktop, which was frustrating since I didn't have the luxury to zoom in and enlarge it, and trying to make out the loopy and slanted penmanship was like deciphering a coded language.

Chris had explained that the slave index was a document within that inventory that listed all the slaves as property belonging to, in this case, Colonel Thomas Taylor, who had died. They were listed as property to be distributed, as per his will, to his heirs.

There were three columns of names, each followed by a number that I quickly surmised was their worth in dollars. On the right, my eyes were immediately drawn to the name Renty, written with a big loop on the *R*, proof that he existed. And next to it the number 300. I felt ill—the inhumanity of placing a value on a person's life. What would that mean to put a dollar amount on my life? This was another example of Black people being reduced to chattel.

Beneath him was Hector, 600, and Caesar, also 600. Delia was listed beneath them as worth 250 and July only 100. Another person named Richard, who was listed as a cook, was valued at $1,000, whereas Bill and Peter, described as carpenters, were listed at $1,000 each as well.

In the second column, I saw another grouping that included familiar names: Jack and Tena. That hit me like a ton of bricks: Tena was my great-great-grandmother, Renty Taylor Thompson's mother. These were my direct ancestors; I had no doubt in my mind. This was proof. But Tena was also listed in the same family grouping as a man named Jack. Could that be the same Jack who was captured in the daguerreotypes, along with Renty and Delia? He was also from the Taylor Plantation. Jack and his son Little Jack are the only Jacks listed in this index. This suggested to me that Jack and Tena were related, which would mean that I was his lineal descendant as well.

Then in the third column I saw "Big Renty," who was listed at $400. I assumed that was Papa Renty. That the first-mentioned Renty must have been his son and my great-grandfather Renty Taylor Thompson's father.

On another page, I saw more names of people listed with number values, intermixed with "Rhone Mare," 100; Bay Horse, 75; and mules, 150. I may have let out a gasp, or a sigh. To see the names of people I immediately recognized as my ancestors alongside livestock was sickening. I was so hurt by the way they were listed, and thought as I read, Why? How did they value each person? Why was Papa Renty, who was older, worth $400? Whereas Delia was worth only $250? Were the cooks worth more than the field hands? What was the rationale for assigning dollar values to these people? I couldn't help but think how devaluing it was to Black life.

And yet, seeing these names in writing was another powerful affirmation—it was proof of their existence. Here is my family, together in this document. When I saw a slave named Fed mentioned, it was another match. My grandfather, Renty Taylor Thompson's son, was Fred, named after Frederick Douglass, but went by Fed. These are uncommon names—and more proof to me that they were my ancestors.

As I continued to study this document, I recalled the naming traditions and heard my mother's voice in memories: "Black folk gave everyone the same name because families were so often violently separated during slavery," she often said. "This was how kinfolk could keep track and later find one another."

Renty, Tena, Fed. These were all names in my family. This was my family.

I spent hours poring over each and every recognizable name, focusing on the family groupings and wondering how they intersect.

Sancho, Renty, Eady, Hector, Molly, Caesar, Delia, July, Stephany . . .

Then it occurred to me, these family groupings were remarkably similar to the "Little Boy Renty" document provided by Rich over four years earlier, which detailed a defiant young child who insisted on wearing a checkered shirt. I knew that the nexus between the two slave indexes could not be ignored. I now believed that I had insight as to how Papa Renty arrived here in the US. He didn't travel the middle passage alone—his entire family was kidnapped along with him. I was overcome by the inhumanity that my ancestors had endured, that they were not seen as people—and were so powerless over this institution of slavery that they could do nothing to change their circumstances. The hopeless despair they must have felt was all-consuming. It certainly was for me.

Once again, I was struck by this false notion that slavery was so long ago—but my great-grandfather was enslaved. My mother lived in the household of at least one person who was born a slave—and I assumed lived in the same community as many. This happened in her lifetime.

Another vital piece of information that Chris found in Utah was Benjamin Franklin Taylor's will. That was as chilling to read as the slave index. It was also written in cursive, and in tight, small sentences that I had to strain to make out. Item 5: "I also give and bequeath unto my said wife the following slaves: Lewis and Eliza, Sam and Betty and their children (except Marian, a negro girl hereto given to Mrs. Mazyck) also all my household and kitchen furniture and my horses and carriages."

The cruelty of enslavement summed up in one sentence. It was almost unbearable, unimaginable, and yet there it was, written down in ink. Marian, a young girl, split from her family. I could not shake the idea of a child being ripped away from her loved ones. The violent fracturing of families was a trademark of slavery.

Item 6: "I will and direct that all my negroes (except those herein specifically bequeathed), be divided equally among my five children: Thomas Taylor, Benjamin Walter Taylor, Virginia Green, wife of Halcot P. Green, Annie W. Mazyck, wife of Wm St. J. Mazyck, Sally Coles Taylor, to them and their heirs forever."

Again, another wave of queasiness washed through me. The finality of it. The hopelessness and helplessness. To be kept in such a barbaric institution. Granted, this was a legal practice in the United States at the time—but so inhumane. They were not property—these were people. Being treated as an item on an inventory list.

When I was able, I continued to read. Item 9 stopped me cold: "To my daughter, Annie W. Mazyck, I give and bequeath the following Slaves and their increase: Marian, Tena, Betsy and Nora."

I was flooded with a whirlwind of emotions. There was Tena. My great-great-grandmother. Renty Taylor Thompson's mother. Benjamin Franklin Taylor had hundreds of slaves—and only names a few in his will. One of them was Tena. As odd as this sounds, I thought, How fortunate am I? This was another confirmation of my oral history. I now knew that she was not sold—but "bequeathed." Again, this was evidence of the devaluing of Black life to an object that could be sold or gifted—both evidence of an evil institution. Still, this helped me piece my family back together. God was placing information at my fingertips.

As for Renty, her son and my great-grandfather, I had another clarifying realization: "Her increase" meant any children she gave birth to. My great-grandfather Renty Taylor Thompson was not yet born, yet he was already enslaved. More proof of how violent this practice was: Tena, like Marian, separated from her family. So heartless and cruel.

That line of investigation would be my next pathway. I also saw the names of two other slaves in Benjamin Franklin Taylor's will: Hannah Thompson, Prince Thompson. While I had no idea where the surname Thompson came from, I felt like that was another important clue.

Shonrael, Megan, and I spent several days going through all the documentation Chris had found, which both correlated with the information that Rich had sent—and all of my oral history. I wrote Chris a very heartfelt email: "Chris, thank you so much for forwarding me the probate information! This is very emotional for me! I say this because I have dedicated the past four years of my life looking for something to corroborate what my mother told me."

I remember thinking how amazing my mother was, not only for

remembering all the details her grandfather told her but for doing so with such accuracy. I even have a recording of my mom talking about Tena, Renty Taylor Thompson's daughter, whom he named after his mother. She was known as the bossy aunt—as she told all her brothers what to do and when. I noticed that she was misidentified as Lena in the typed version of the 1900 census that Rich had sent me early on, but if you look at the handwritten census, it clearly spelled Tena with a *T*. Her grandmother, whom she was named for, was also misidentified as "Rena" in George Thompson's death record, the document that the Connecticut Historical Society sent me.

It was clear that getting their names right was not important to the record keepers. There was no interest in accurately documenting Black lives. But I also knew that she was named after her grandmother, who was the Tena I saw in Thomas Taylor's 1834 will. As I combed through documents that Chris sent me, trying to decipher the tiny script handwriting, I saw all my family names repeating: Renty, George, Sarah, and "Fed"—not even Fred, but Fed! That really stood out, since that was the same name my grandfather went by. Several years before my mom died, she told me his given name was Frederick Douglass Thompson. All I had ever known was he was Fed Thompson. Seeing a Fed listed in both Benjamin Franklin Taylor's will, and in Thomas Taylor's will, was all the proof I needed.

I told Chris that the *Hartford Courant* was doing a story on my quest and that I was sending the reporters all the information he had uncovered through the Mormons, including the probate will. I ended that email with, "Almost as amazing as the story of an African born 164 years ago is the fact that his great-great-great granddaughter now has documents to validate that story. Words cannot express how grateful I am right now!"

When Chris and I got on the phone to review all the information he had found, my head was swimming. There were so many details to sort out! The will was very long, and our main focus was items 5,

6, 7, 8, and 9 in Benjamin Franklin Taylor's will. Chris explained that the will was in a probate box with lots of documents.

"Unfortunately, some key pages are missing," he said. Still, this was where he found so many of my family members named.

I kept thinking, Of the more than three hundred people Benjamin Franklin Taylor enslaved, my family members are mentioned. It again felt like a miracle. He also included a line, in item 13, that really struck me as odd: "In the division of my negroes among my children as above provided I desire that, as far as practicable, families be kept together and that the old and infirmed negros be permitted to go with their families and be kindly treated."

Everything else in that document was so inhumane, this sudden moment of kindness stood out. How could he separate a child from her mother and father, but then ask his heirs to treat the elderly with kindness? I was puzzled by that.

The *Hartford Courant* published a major front-page feature story on February 17, 2014, titled "In Search of a Truer Papa Renty." The reporters did an excellent job, including the history of the Blue Back Speller and the significance of knowing that Papa Renty had taught himself how to read, and his children as well. They also interviewed Chris Childs and included the difficulty of making these connections: "Childs is still researching Lanier's family line to conclusively put Lanier's great-grandfather—Renty's son, also named Renty, who died in Alabama—on the same plantation where the elder Renty had been a slave. Pages are missing from the documents Childs has been able to download, and a trip to South Carolina where the original documents are kept might allow Lanier to follow her family members after they left the plantation."

The article helped explain the difficulty of doing African American genealogy.

"The records for enslaved African Americans prior to 1865 in the South as well as for emancipated African Americans afterward in the late 19th century can be minimal," Childs cautioned. "Some of these items may be quite difficult to find—sometimes no longer surviving or never recorded—and we are perhaps left with some paper evidence combined with oral traditions to tell the story."

It also included my belief that the names in the Taylor will were all the evidence I needed. And clearly it was enough to allow the reporters to publish the story, which the Associated Press picked up and circulated. I was suddenly inundated with messages from people—most of which were overwhelmingly supportive.

"This is the next *Roots*!" more than a dozen people wrote.

This proved my theory that anyone who saw those daguerreotypes, and learned about their origins, wanted to know more about the enslaved men and women in those images.

Every once in a while, someone would chime in with a hateful message.

"Get over it!"

"Slavery was a long time ago!"

Shonrael and Megan were ready to respond to each and every taunt, but I told them to just ignore them, and not give such ignorance any oxygen.

7

Looking for Renty, Finding Rose

I started scouring the internet, looking for any information I could find on Benjamin Franklin Taylor and his children. The irony of having to look for my broken family by finding the still-intact families who once enslaved them was incredibly painful. It was also necessary. I needed them so I could begin piecing my family back together—to learn how my great-grandfather Renty Taylor Thompson wound up in Alabama.

I started searching on genealogical websites and quickly found all kinds of historical documents about the prominence of the Taylor family. A blog on the American Revolution in the South had an excerpt about Thomas Taylor, calling him "one of the most influential men" in South Carolina, and then citing his accomplishments. He served as a captain in the Revolutionary War before serving as governor of South Carolina and then was a commissioner who was responsible for planning the city of Columbia. In this illustrious list, there's only one mention of the people he enslaved. "Of Mrs Taylor, it is said she bore all the responsibilities of the family while he was away in the field," that the British "carried off her slaves," and that "her provisions and stock were stolen." The language throughout the entire piece was carefully chosen to protect and glorify the Taylor family, whereas my loved ones were clumped together in one objectifying word. It was all so unsettling, and inhumane.

I was searching for any acknowledgment of my ancestors and the role they played in the greatness of this family—and found nothing, other than another fascinating coincidence: I started seeing the names of the slaveholders were George, Benjamin, John, Mary, William, and Sarah. These are also names of my own family members, for generations. Renty Taylor Thompson, for instance, named his daughter Tena after his mother, and his other daughter, Annie, after the woman who had enslaved him. This struck me, as she was born after emancipation. This was another clue to me that all of the people in the Taylor slave indexes—including Renty, Delia, Fed, Tena, Hector, Caesar, George, and even more—were my ancestors, as I saw these names repeated there as well.

Through this research, I learned that Colonel Thomas Taylor married Ann Wyche and they had a dozen children, including Benjamin Franklin Taylor, who had not only enslaved Renty and Delia, but offered them to Louis Agassiz to be photographed as proof of their inferiority. Every single passage I read about the Taylor family pointed to more privilege and glorification versus the marginalization and erasure of the very people who were directly responsible for creating that family wealth through Black exploitation and violence. Benjamin married Sarah "Sally" Webb Coles and they had six children: Virginia Eliza, Thomas, Sally Coles, Ann, Eliza Rebecca, and Benjamin Walter Taylor. When he died, he divvied up his slaves and gave them to his children. I wanted to know where each of these children went, as my hunch was they each took my family members with them, wherever they wound up settling. Those were the places where I would focus my research—and hopefully find evidence of how my great-grandfather Renty Taylor Thompson wound up in Alabama.

I knew from my mother's oral history that he and his mother, Tena, had been separated from their family and "sold south." Chris provided me with the probate wills, which helped me understand that they were not sold but given to Benjamin Franklin Taylor's daughter Annie at the time of his death. As item 9 in the probate will states: "To my daughter Annie W. Mazyck, I give and bequeath the following slaves and their increase: Marian, Tena, Betsy and Nora."

Tena was my great-great-grandmother Renty Taylor Thompson's mom. I realized that she must have been pregnant with him at the time of Benjamin Taylor's death, or close thereafter. Hence her "increase" was my great-grandfather, the same man who told my mother so many of the oral stories she had passed on to me. The timing made sense, as Benjamin Taylor died in 1851 and Renty Taylor Thompson was born shortly thereafter. I had his death certificate, which the Connecticut Historical Society had found for me. It listed his date and place of birth as Charleston, South Carolina, in 1854, and his death as Mount Meigs, Alabama, in 1945. The 1880 US Census was another vital clue, as my great-grandfather was listed on it as Renty Thompson, age twenty-six, residing in Montgomery, Alabama, with his wife, Ophelia Murdock Thompson, and their two children, William, age four, and Tena, age one.

Still, both Chris and I were baffled as to why Charleston was listed as his place of birth, since Benjamin lived in Columbia. I was on a mission to figure this out. Through all my Taylor family research, I saw that they moved between Virginia and South Carolina, Mississippi, Louisiana, and Alabama and my premise was that my own family members, while never officially accounted for, would go back and forth with their slaveholders. This meant that wherever the slaveholders landed at the end of slavery was where my ancestors laid their roots. I also deduced that those who were newly emancipated knew where their family members lived—and would travel long distances to reunite with them. That meant that Renty moved to Mount Meigs, Alabama, from Charleston, South Carolina, not because he was sold, but because he had family there. The 1870 census listed Renty as married to Ophelia Murdock. Lee and Peter Murdock are also listed in the Taylor slave index, so I deduced that Tena stayed back in Charleston, where she had other children, and that her son Renty Taylor Thompson moved to Alabama with Ophelia and her family members. This was where they raised their family, since their children Tena and William—my mother's aunt and uncle, both of whom she grew up with—are listed in the 1880 index too.

This was 2015, and genealogical groups were becoming popular on social media platforms—I found one Facebook group dedicated to families from Columbia, South Carolina, home of the Benjamin Franklin Taylor Plantation, where Papa Renty and Delia had been enslaved. I noticed a woman named Rose Shiver was very active on the site and decided to send her a message, introducing myself, and I included a link to the "Finding Papa Renty" story that had just been published in the *Hartford Courant*.

She responded the following day with this note:

> What a wonderful story, would love to help as much as I can with your research. I had an opportunity to meet Edmund Taylor, descendant of the Taylor family about two years ago; he invited me to his home to tell me more about the Taylor's. We talked about everything except the elephant in the room. THE AGASSIZ PHOTOS. When I brought it up, he said B. F. Taylor was very much interested in science, so he allowed the photos. He went on to say [that the Boston politician Daniel] Webster visited South Carolina and saw how "well" the slaves were treated and it changed his opinion on

> slavery. . . . He also mentioned a slave named Sancho who was the only slave buried in the Taylor cemetery. He said he could read and write, and he was a minister. Going back to Colonel Thomas Taylor's Will he leaves Sancho to his wife and after her death he would go to Benjamin Franklin Taylor. The Taylor family had plantations in South Carolina, Mississippi, and Alabama. So perhaps that's how he (Renty Taylor Thompson) wound up there. On the 1870 census, it showed Edmund (my 3X grandfather) had a son born in Mississippi. . . .

I was stunned. I had been interviewing historians and working with a world-renowned genealogist, and in one interchange this total stranger gave me more useful information than anyone had in all my years of searching. It was as if she already knew my story and so where to look for clues. There was so much information to process in that letter: To begin, she had found a Taylor descendant, and had already spoken with him! This was major news, as was the news that the Taylors' dynasty stretched into Mississippi and Alabama. I knew that they lived in these states but did not know, until this moment, that the Taylors had plantations there.

Plus, the name Sancho stood out as I had seen his name listed with Congo Renty in both the "Little Boy Renty" document and Thomas Taylor's slave index. It was all clicking. I wrote her to say as much, and asked if I could call her. She agreed, and when we spoke later that same day, we bonded almost immediately.

"I'm looking for any information about the Taylors," I explained on the phone.

"I'm descended from an enslaved person from the Taylor Plantation too!" Rose interjected.

That was our common thread, and passion: she was the linear descendant of a man named Edmund who was originally owned by

Thomas Taylor and then given to Benjamin Franklin Taylor. By then I'd spent so much time poring through the slave indexes that the name Edmund was familiar. I asked Rose to hold on for a moment and went to get Benjamin Franklin Taylor's slave index. Sure enough, Edmund was listed there, along with Hector, Jack, and Caesar. These were all names that kept repeating alongside my family members in wills and indexes.

Layered in goose bumps, I said, "Rose, it is very likely that we are related! Or at the very minimum, our families knew each other and were friends!"

Of all the people I had reached out to, from world-renowned historians to genealogists—no one offered the kind of insight or information that Rose had. She still lived in Columbia, where her family had stayed after the abolition of slavery on November 13, 1865, and she was also bitten by that same genealogical bug. We shared that same energy and drive to find out more about who our people are, and where we come from. For Black people doing this work, searching for our ancestors is not done out of curiosity; it grows out of a sense of enormous loss. It's about reconnecting something that was violently detached. The process of trying to piece it back together is painful, and necessary.

For Rose, like me, this work was deeply personal. She was able to recall plantations, their specific locations, names, and which Taylor family member ran each. My heart skipped a beat when she mentioned that one of Edmund's sons had traveled with William Taylor to Mississippi—proof of my theory that the slaveholder's children took members of their family to other parts of the country, breaking up the Black family unit in the process.

Rich and Chris both understood the difficulties of doing African American genealogy—how you must go to obscure and often painful places to find clues to piece your history together. They knew that there was scant documentation, often misspelled, or not dated or poorly recorded. But they did not understand it in the way that Rose did. They knew there were dead ends—but their cautions could not prepare me for the painful despair or disappointment associated with this work.

We started off talking about white supremacy and how enslavement consciously broke up Black families. We commiserated on how hard it was to do genealogy since the slaveholding families refused to keep track of our ancestors. And we marveled at the resilience of our families and Black communities for their commitment to telling oral stories and making sure that they were passed down from one generation to the next. Rose and I wanted to honor those ancestors by finally writing these stories down.

That day, Rose and I talked for two hours. Toward the end of our call I said, "Rose, I need to talk to Edmund Taylor."

"Agreed," she said. "Let me find his number for you."

The irony hit me hard: Rose's great-great-grandfather Edmund may have been named for the very man who might be the greatest resource for me. There were so many parallels between Rose's family and mine—including the naming patterns. Before I hung up the phone, I told Rose how grateful I was to be on this journey with her.

"I feel the same, Tammy," she said.

That evening, I had found a friend and comrade.

A few days later, Rose called me.

"Tammy, I found his number," she said.

It was a Sunday afternoon. I'd just come home from church and was finishing up my housework before settling into my "Renty research," which was how I spent most evenings.

"Are you going to call him?" I asked.

"I'm not going to call him, you call him," was her witty and quick reply.

This man's ancestor had not only enslaved Papa Renty but clearly thought Black people were lesser beings, as he had offered him and

Delia to Agassiz as proof that African-born Black people were inferior to white people. How had this family's attitudes about Black people changed in the last 150 years?

But then, in my mind, I saw Renty's eyes and heard my mother's voice, both commanding me to keep moving forward. This man could be key to helping me solve so many mysteries. I hung up with Rose and immediately dialed the number. As the phone rang, I wondered, What the heck am I going to say?

For the last two years of my life, I had devoted countless hours to searching and consuming every piece of information I could find on the Taylor family and now I was only moments away from the answers. I had to be careful in how I presented myself: I didn't want them to think I wanted anything beyond information.

I was still figuring out how to introduce myself when I heard a woman's low, soft-spoken voice say, "Hello?"

"Good evening," I said. "You don't know me, but my name is Tamara Lanier and I received your contact information from a close friend."

I went on to explain that I was researching my family history and that for years I had been searching for the descendants of Benjamin Franklin Taylor.

There was a pause and unnerving silence.

I kept talking.

"I'm a descendant of the enslaved man Renty Taylor and my family was separated just after the death of Benjamin Franklin Taylor, sometime before the Civil War," I continued, amazed at how steady my voice was. "I was hoping to find someone who might know the Taylor family history. And would be willing to share it with me."

"You would want to speak to my father but he's ninety-eight years old and hard of hearing," the voice replied. "Tell me what you'd like to know and I'll pass it along to him."

I shared with her what my mother had shared with me:

"My great-grandfather Renty was born Renty Taylor and our oral history says that he and his mother, Tena, were sold and became Thompsons." I was speaking slowly and methodically, trying not to have any emotion in my voice. The woman remained quiet on the other end of the line. I was worried I might lose her.

"I believe that Renty had a unique relationship with the Taylors because he named all of his children after the Taylor children," I continued. "My mother was called Mattye but her legal name was Mary."

"Oh my goodness," the woman said, opening up for the first time. "My name is Mary too, also after my ancestors."

That was the icebreaker.

"We have Williams, Benjamins, Sarahs, and Simons in our family," I said. As we chatted a bit longer, I felt compassion in her voice. I noticed that she was speaking slowly and loudly, and asked if her father was in the room with her.

"Yes," she said. "And he'd like to speak with you."

Moments later, Dr. Edmund Taylor's voice crackled through the phone.

"Delighted to hear from you," he said in a thick southern drawl and a voice shaky with age.

"Likewise," I said, relieved. This was going better than I ever imagined. I told him about Renty and realized that while he was familiar with the Agassiz daguerreotypes, he didn't realize that Papa Renty had become the face of them.

"I'd love to have an opportunity to talk to you in further detail," I said. "I'm trying to piece together my history and think you may have helpful information."

"I'd love to meet with you in person to discuss," he replied cheerfully.

My heart skipped several beats. "Just say when and where, and I'll be there!"

"Why don't you come to visit us here in South Carolina?" he said.

I had just hoped to speak to him, so the prospect of a visit was unexpected—and thrilling. I imagined how powerful that would be.

"That would be great," I responded.

The date he offered happened to be the same day as the Woman of the Year Award, which was being presented to me by the Connecticut General Assembly's Commission on African American Affairs. It was a big honor. I was being recognized for my work in criminal justice reform. A big ceremony was planned at the capitol—yet this was more important. I'd ask my girls to accept the award on my behalf. I was not going to miss this opportunity.

I told Dr. Taylor about the event, and he also thought that was important—a good sign. He suggested another date that coincided with his granddaughter's graduation—but he insisted this was more important. I was touched by that. He was nearing one hundred years old, so I also knew I was working against time. I shared my research with him on that call that led me to conclude that Renty did not have an adversarial relationship with the Taylor family, summing up a line in Benjamin Taylor's will that stood out to me: "In the division of my Negros amongst my children, I desire that, as far as practical, families be kept together, and that old and infirmed Negros be permitted to go with their families and be kindly treated."

"Yes," Dr. Taylor said. "That is important."

I could tell he was proud, and decided to save my questions for when we met in person. For instance, how else could the same man who offered Renty and Delia to Agassiz as examples of an inferior race say such a thing? This was his dying declaration and it made me wonder if he had an attack of conscience as he neared the end of his life.

As soon as I hung up, I ran out to the hallway and called my girls. Each popped her head out of her bedroom.

"We're going to Columbia, South Carolina, to spend the weekend with the family who enslaved our ancestors!" I announced excitedly.

Shonrael was standing in the doorway of her bedroom and Megan was down the hallway. The expressions on their faces quickly went from intrigued to disbelief.

"Is this a joke?" Shonrael asked. "I'm not going! Seriously, Mom, you are joking, right?"

"Mom, this is too much," Megan chimed in, shaking her head.

"I am dead serious. I am going to spend the weekend with the Taylors and you are welcome to come if you like," I said.

"Mom, you don't know these people!" Megan said, walking toward me.

My girls thought I was crazy, but it was also obvious to them that my mind was made up. They knew that I was stubborn! My mom always talked about how determined and persevering Papa Renty was—my girls and I are convinced that these were traits I inherited. I was not going to let their apprehension about the trip deter me. I immediately called Rose and told her the news.

"Rose, I'm counting on you to be there!" I said.

"Absolutely," she replied.

After I hung up, I assured them that it would be a safe and uneventful trip. I think they both knew. They had seen that determined expression before: there was no use in trying to convince me not to go.

"This is too much," Megan said, still shaking her head.

"This is the only way we can find information about our ancestors," I said. "This is good."

"*Good* is not a word I would use to describe any of this," Shonrael said. "But we also understand why you have to go."

I booked a flight and a hotel room, and the day I arrived, Rose picked me up at the airport.

She's a tall, beautiful woman who was dressed in a floral print dress. That was our first time meeting, but it was like reuniting with a long-lost family member. She's equal parts witty and thoughtful—

and a fountain of knowledge. She was also direct, and not one to mince words. We fell right in together, two kindred spirits.

She first drove me to my hotel so I could get changed, and then we both drove to the Taylors' residence together—not the plantation where Renty and Delia were enslaved, as that home no longer existed, according to Rose, who promised to take me on a tour of Columbia after lunch.

Dr. Taylor lived in a historic colonial on a beautiful piece of wooded property with a huge lake in the backyard. I felt like I was walking into a time capsule, with its antique furniture and portraits of ancestral family members hanging on the walls. Mary welcomed us and brought us to the living room, where Dr. Taylor and his wife were waiting. He was frail, but not feeble, and as alert and engaging as he was on the phone. His wife was quiet but seemed supportive and kind. We were all sitting in the living room, making small talk, when the doorbell rang.

"I want you to meet Dr. Rudy Wise and his wife," Dr. Taylor announced as a couple in their forties entered the room. "He's also a descendant of the Taylor Plantation."

I wasn't expecting anyone else and was pleasantly surprised to meet another descendant. I saw this as another opportunity for more information-gathering. Dr. Taylor also said that he encouraged and supported Rudy's decision to pursue a medical career. While generous, I couldn't help but think that Dr. Taylor was setting a stage for me to see what good work the Taylors had done to atone for the sins of their ancestors.

We headed into the dining room, where a beautiful mahogany table was set with burgundy napkins, fine china, and silver goblets that matched the forks, knives, and dessert spoons that were laid horizontal on the place mat above the plates. There were two small bouquets of white gardenias that perfumed the room set on either side of an antique china soup tureen in a brown and peach pattern. It was all very formal, yet I also got the feeling that this was how the Taylors always ate.

We all took our seats, Dr. Taylor at the head of the table, his wife at the other end, and Rose and me next to one another. Dr. Wise and his wife sat across from us. There was some small talk—about the history of Columbia, and Dr. Taylor's daily swim in the lake—and then lunch was served.

"I hope everyone likes grits," Dr. Taylor announced as a delicious egg, cheese, sausage, and grit casserole was served on plates that matched the soup tureen centerpiece. "I'd also like to point out that we're eating from the dishes once owned by Benjamin Franklin Taylor."

I marveled that this family had heirlooms that were more than 150 years old.

"And the table and chairs that you are sitting on were all carved by the Taylor family carpenter," he added.

Dr. Taylor continued to talk, but I was paralyzed in thought, unable to see, hear, or say anything. I was fixated and focused on the Chippendale-style chairs with their elegant back splats. They matched the magnificent dining room table and sideboard. I did not know until that moment that my ancestor was responsible for such artistry. Prince Thompson was listed in the will as the family carpenter—in the same family grouping with Hector and Renty and Rose.

I was suddenly filled with pride and amazement: I was sitting in a chair hand-carved by my enslaved ancestor; it was as if he were embracing me. I felt so blessed to have the opportunity to sit on something that my ancestor made. This was yet another moment where I had to pause and give thanks for the many miracles, signs, and wonders that had been revealed to me. I had Renty Taylor Thompson's walking stick, the only ancestral heirloom I had ever imagined until this moment: my body touching something that my ancestor's hands had made 170 years ago. There was something so poetic about how this piece of furniture could lift and support me.

After we finished eating, Dr. Taylor announced that he wanted to read a narrative about the Taylor family and slavery that he had written for the University of South Carolina, which is also in Columbia. He had already told us that Columbia was the capital, versus the better-known Charleston, because the Taylors had donated so much land to the city. Again I noted his pride in his family's generosity. He began to read: "Colonel Thomas Taylor, an American Revolutionary, owned many slaves."

I was impressed by how straightforward he was in the telling of his family history. He continued in his slow, shaky voice: "One was named Sancho and he was probably the Colonel's personal servant. When Colonel Taylor died, he left Sancho to his son Benjamin Franklin. When Benjamin died, he in turn gifted Sancho to his son Captain Thomas Taylor, who fought in the civil war. Sancho died at the age of 72 and his tombstone is in the small Taylor plot at Trinity Cathedral. He was a minister and preacher in Columbia showing freedom of actions. He must have had very close personal relationships to all three of his Taylor owners for him to be buried in Trinity Church in their plot. He is the only negro in that graveyard. I believe his desire to be buried by his masters and their desire to have him there too and the tone of the epitaph manifests a high mutual respect for each other and a Christian relationship."

Several things ran through my mind as he read this story: To begin, Sancho was a name Rose had mentioned in her first exchange with me, and one I had recognized, as I had come across it several times in my research. It was always listed in the same groupings as my family members, confirmation that they knew one another and were, perhaps, even related. I did, however, find it very hard to believe that Sancho "desired" to be buried with his masters.

Dr. Taylor continued to read: "Below is his epitaph, which Sancho wrote himself: 'Servant of Thomas Taylor died July 6, 1864 at age 72 years. During a large portion of his life, he was a member of the Columbia Baptist church and for many years a preacher of the gospel. He was humble and laborious and strove faithfully to serve both his heavenly and earthly master in all his relations of his life, as a servant, a Christian and a preacher.'"

Dr. Taylor paused to let that piece sink in, before continuing: "He wrote this himself. He enjoyed the respect and confidence of all who knew him. He was particularly dear to his colored brethren. And now he has been called to his rest in heaven. Among them by placing a stone over his grave."

After he finished reading, I had so many thoughts swirling in my mind. The line "serving his heavenly and earthly master" in particular poked at me. Dr. Taylor must have sensed this as he added, "Those were Sancho's words."

In my head, I reasoned that Sancho had to play the game. He knew that he had to appease his master. I also thought it was ironic that the Taylors celebrated the fact that Sancho could read and write. If Sancho was a learned man, like Papa Renty, I thought, why would the Taylors support Agassiz's theories by supplying examples of what they must have thought was an inferior race? It was all so confusing. I was puzzled. If the Taylors knew about enslaved people's literacy, how could they support Agassiz's theories? The whole purpose was to prove Black inferiority, and this story that Dr. Taylor had just shared did the opposite. This reconfirmed that supplying people he had enslaved to Agassiz as subjects was not about proving Black inferiority: it was about the promotion of slavery.

"They were so fond of Sancho," Dr. Taylor continued in his trembling voice, "that they buried him in the family plot, at the time where no slaveholder would do such a thing."

Dr. Taylor went on to explain how his ancestors had traveled throughout the South establishing Christian churches. He also said that the Taylors and those they enslaved were one family who worshipped together. He unabashedly explained that this Christian approach to slavery captured the attention of northern politicians and changed the hearts and minds of many abolitionists—including Daniel Webster.

No relation to the textbook pioneer Noah Webster, Daniel Webster was born in New Hampshire in 1782 and lived in Massachusetts as a constitutional lawyer, member of Congress, United States senator, secretary of state, and purported abolitionist. He was also a man who would be president. In 1839 Webster declined the nomination for vice president; but President William Henry Harrison died one month after his inauguration. Webster would have ascended to the office of the United States president had he accepted the nomination. He was a dominant political figure in the North, and he was also the invited guest of the slaveholder Benjamin Franklin Taylor in the South. Dr. Edmund Taylor explained that his ancestors were "benevolent Christians" who treated their enslaved with "dignity and respect." That politicians from the North would travel great distances to visit the Taylor Plantation to bear witness to what Dr. Taylor described as one Christian family. In his memoir, Dr. Edmund Taylor writes:

> The Taylors established Christian churches in Columbia and always supported them. Religion exerted a strong influence on their attitudes and practices towards their servants. Colonel Thomas Taylor's son, Benjamin Franklin, sheds light on the question and apparently was in the middle of the slavery issue of the day, dying in 1852. Daniel Webster is said to have visited his plantation, EdgeHill, to study slavery

and after which he ceased to speak against it in the United States Senate.

"Dr. Taylor," I asked, "do you think these Massachusetts scholars, scientists, and politicians all traveled to South Carolina to study slavery? Or to witness the benevolence of the Taylor family? Or perhaps they were looking to use EdgeHill as political propaganda to protect their financial interests?"

Dr. Taylor stressed that they were God-fearing Christians whose "benevolent" approach to slavery was studied by Harvard professors and Boston politicians. I suspected something more sinister; this was not scholarship, this was a northern aggression.

Lunch was over, and as we got up from the table, I asked Dr. Taylor if I could take some photos of the beautiful woodwork.

"My research suggests that my ancestor was the family carpenter," I explained.

"Of course!" Dr. Taylor said, delighted.

I got up from my chair and went to pose in front of the mahogany sideboard that Prince Thompson had also made, which matched the table and chairs, beaming in amazement at the level of skill and sophistication. In that photograph, Dr. Edmund Taylor was on my right, his wife, Mary, on my left, and I was in the middle, glowing with an ancestral pride that I think only I in that moment understood. A portrait of a woman named Sarah hung behind us. It was painted in the mid-1800s, around the same time Prince and Renty lived and worked on the Taylor Plantation. As I smiled for the camera, I thought to myself, Imagine having an image of Papa Renty in my dining room? Or a chair that Prince Thompson had carved? Imagine being able to say, These are the plates my ancestors ate off? The furniture they made? Imagine.

It was truly an amazing afternoon, and before we said goodbye to Dr. Rudy Wise, he gave me an envelope full of his genealogy and Dr. Edmund Taylor likewise shared a packet of information about his ancestors for me to take. Afterward we took a tour of the Taylor property and a trip to the site of the former EdgeHill Plantation, which was now a subdivision. Even though the plantation house was no longer there, I still felt like I was standing on sacred space. Being with Rose on the same land where our ancestors had toiled was powerful.

We rode in the car with Dr. Taylor, who pointed out all the land that the Taylor family had donated to the state. That resonated with everything I had read: this was a prominent family who had significant wealth. What remained unsaid was how that fortune was accumulated. I kept thinking of my ancestors toiling on that land, stolen from their own, made to work for their indentured keep. Sad.

After we said our goodbyes to the Taylors, Rose took me on her tour of Columbia. She showed me Arthurtown, the land her family bought from the Taylors in 1872, which has since been developed into a community. She next drove me to the Taylor family cemetery, where Sancho was buried alongside the Taylor family members. Rose and I got out to look for his headstone—I imagined it to be carved in marble or limestone, like the other family members'. However, we were unable to find anything with Sancho's name or epitaph written on it. Disappointed, we got back in the car to drive through downtown Columbia. There I noticed a large Confederate flag flying at full mast.

"Rose, what on earth?" I said, flabbergasted to see that symbol so prominently displayed in the downtown area.

As we neared, I was even more taken aback: it was erected in front of the State House.

"Rose, stop the car!" I shouted.

As a state employee, I was disgusted.

"Your tax dollars pay for this building and its grounds," I said.

Rose just shook her head and said, "It will never come down. There have been ongoing fights and, as a compromise, the state erected a monument of an enslaved man somewhere in the back of the building to offset the symbol of hate."

I snapped a photo, still unable to believe what I was seeing.

"As a taxpayer, we should not be paying for insults," I said, now seething. "You are paying to be marginalized and trivialized. It is wrong."

"Tammy, you are preaching to the choir!" Rose said.

I knew that was the case, but I was also tired of having to face the blatant racial assaults and accept the marginalization.

The next day, Rose drove me to the airport. As we hugged goodbye I said, "This is just the beginning."

Upon returning home, I could not wait to get into all the genealogy and other documents Dr. Edmund Taylor gave me; I was sure I'd find interesting overlaps. Amazingly, after reading the information provided by Dr. Taylor, it was apparent that what I had, what I was witnessing, was the intersection of two family histories. The same stories, told from two very different points of view: one from the enslaved man Papa Renty, and the other told by the slaveholder Benjamin Franklin Taylor.

Dr. Taylor shared that the Taylor family operated a branch of the Underground Railroad to Ohio, where many of the enslaved Taylors were set free. My mom was recorded saying that Renty's children fled to Ohio by way of the Underground Railroad and were also set free.

Dr. Taylor shared that the Taylors traveled the South establishing Christian churches and acknowledged that some of their slaves could read and write and preach the gospel, specifically referencing Sancho Thompson. My mom was also recorded saying that Renty could read and write and would preach the gospel. She also told the story of her enslaved ancestors being forced to attend the white

Christian services but later they would "steal away and worship as they pleased."

Mama or *Papa* before an elder's name is a term of endearment, an African tradition passed down through the generations. Many of my ancestors were fondly referred to as Papa Renty, Papa Jake, and Papa Simon. The women were called Mama Ophelia and Mama Tourie. It was not lost on me that Dr. Edmund Taylor remarked fondly of an enslaved woman, Mama Lettie, who worked as a nurse in the Taylor family medical practice. These two family histories, told from very different points of view, were the same. I was certain of that.

The following week, I was back home in Norwich when I saw the news: on June 17, 2015, a white supremacist man named Dylann Roof went to a church meeting in Charleston, South Carolina, and killed nine people.

Less than a month later, on July 10, the flag was removed from the State House.

8

The Truth Is in the Ground

Early one Saturday morning that fall, I received a text from Laura Lillian Best, or LLB as I call her, that read, "Holla at a Sista." I called her to find that she had learned of an event at the Prudence Crandall Museum in Canterbury, Connecticut, later that day.

"Let's go!"

I met Laura Lillian at our local chapter NAACP meeting and we bonded immediately. We had a similar interest in social justice, and she was, like me, a lover of Black history. She also lives in Norwich, not far from where Sarah Harris was born. In 1832, Harris was one of two Black young women to attend Prudence Crandall's Female Boarding School in Canterbury, making it the first integrated school in the United States. The community outrage was so swift that Crandall closed the school and reopened in 1833 solely to teach Black students, many of whom came across state lines for the opportunity. Connecticut lawmakers at the time responded by passing a "Black Law" barring African Americans from other states to attend school in Connecticut. This led to Crandall's arrest and detention.

The same evening that the trial ended in a hung jury, a mob attacked the school, smashing windows and setting the structure on fire. Fearing for the safety and well-being of her students, Crandall decided to close the school and ultimately left the state.

I admired Crandall for her courage, and was intrigued to learn that the Connecticut General Assembly had voted to pay her an annual pension of $400 in 1886 until her death as a formal apology—and reparations—for their actions.

Today the Prudence Crandall Museum is in Canterbury, not far from Norwich, where Laura Lillian and I drove together to attend a lecture by Warren Perry, professor of archaeology and anthropology and codirector of the Center for Africana Studies at Central Connecticut State University. He's also the director of archaeology at the eighteenth-century African Burial Ground, the site in downtown Manhattan that was discovered during a construction project in 1991. The discovery halted the work—because the remains of 419 men, women, and children of African descent were found, many with artifacts from Africa in their wooden coffins. It is thought to be the oldest African cemetery ever excavated in an urban area in the United States and was declared a national monument in 2006.

Perry's mission was to unearth the history of slavery in New England through excavation. Throughout his presentation, he said again and again, "The truth is in the ground."

This struck me: he was referring to the artifacts unearthed through archaeology, and how they told the story of the people who lived on that land. I kept thinking how I might apply this to my own research—not so much about artifacts, but cemeteries themselves. Where were my ancestors laid to rest? Where was Papa Renty buried? And Delia?

My mother had shared so many stories of Antioch Baptist Church in Mount Meigs, Alabama, her family church and one of the first Baptist churches in the state. I knew that my great-grandfather

Renty Taylor Thompson was buried at the church cemetery, as were many of my relatives. Who else was buried there?

I began to focus on cemeteries, which was how I came across a woman named Denise Hardin, who was one of a group of volunteers fighting to preserve the neglected African American cemeteries in Montgomery and the surrounding area, which included Mount Meigs.

I reached out to Denise via email in September 2015, and she responded immediately with information that resonated: "In addition to genealogical research, I am involved with cemetery transcription and preservation efforts," she wrote. "The Taylors, the Harpers, and the McLemores all came from Virginia and the Carolinas to spread the gospel of our Lord, Jesus Christ. They settled in Montgomery, Alabama, in 1818 and established the four cornerstone Baptist churches: Old Elam, Bethlehem, Rehoboth, and Antioch."

Denise was a descendant of the McLemores and through her I learned that the Antioch Baptist Church was founded as a white church, and then became mixed when an enslaved man named Caesar Blackwell was asked to be the preacher. His name struck me as familiar—"Caesar" was listed in the Taylor slave indexes that Chris Childs had sent me in the same family grouping with Papa Renty's children: Renty, Delia, and Hector.

Denise was also a treasure trove of information. She pointed me to a genealogical website called Find a Grave, which had just been bought by Ancestry.com two years before, in 2013. It was originally founded by Jim Tipton, who began it as a hobby in 1995 to record the cemetery information of celebrities. He understood that the information chiseled into tombstones—names, dates of birth and death, and often family relations—doubled as records of the people buried beneath them. Tipton started an interactive website where people could upload photos of tombstones and other valuable information. Denise was an early contributor to the crowdsourced site.

She began "reading cemeteries," or going into neglected graveyards and recording all of the information on the headstones, in 2008 and uploaded that information, with pictures, onto the Find a Grave website.

"A hobby became a passion and mission," she explained.

She got her start in a Black cemetery in Montgomery called Lincoln.

"I had visited Lincoln out of curiosity back in 2008 and was upset to see how poorly maintained it was," she explained. "The grass needed mowing, and there was garbage scattered everywhere. And then I saw a tombstone for a man named James Streety."

Denise got quiet on the phone, and I could hear her struggle to maintain her composure.

"I could tell that he was a tall man," she said, holding back tears. "His entire skeleton was exposed."

She said she was so distressed that she sat down by his grave and cried. "This was somebody's son, husband, and father."

Once she pulled herself together, she took a picture of his marker and went home to see what information she could find about the life of Mr. James Streety. Born in March 1864, he married Henrietta Goldstein, who was also buried in the same cemetery. After she uploaded this information onto Find a Grave, she decided to record and upload all of Lincoln cemetery, which was originally allocated to hold seven hundred graves. By the time Denise was done, she had uploaded 6,892 markers.

"People were buried on top of one another," she explained. "It became my mission to make sure if anyone was looking for their family members, I could be helpful."

These were enslaved people and their descendants, so to me this was another example of the devaluing of Black life. The neglect of recordkeeping and recording was an erasure of their lives as if they did not exist. Denise was doing the necessary work of beginning to repair the harms caused by enslavement to these families.

Within a year of sharing Mr. Streety's information, someone reached out to Denise from Houston, thanking her for finding their ancestor. Since then Mr. Streety has been properly buried thanks to her efforts and the community attention it drew to the Lincoln graveyard.

Antioch's cemetery is much smaller, and similarly in disrepair. Denise's campaign was featured in the local newspaper, the *Montgomery Advertiser*. The story was accompanied by a photo that made my heart hurt: it was an image of Denise standing in Antioch Cemetery, which looked more like an overgrown forest. In between the thicket of trees, I could barely make out the moss-covered tombstones as they had been taken over by weeds. All I could think was, This was a sacred space where so many of my enslaved ancestors are buried—they deserve the dignity of a decent burial ground.

Denise explained that Antioch was a mixed church until the Civil War, after which the white members left. This history aligned with what Dr. Taylor had told me over lunch, and I was not surprised to learn that while he reveled in the fact that his family helped establish so many churches, he did not boast that he also came from one of the largest slaveholding families in the United States as plantations and work farms were established alongside these churches.

Denise was yet another person I found on my journey who gave me insight. She introduced me to Find a Grave, which became a helpful tool in my genealogical search. I logged on and, as Denise had indicated, I quickly found Taylors in Louisiana, Georgia, South Carolina, and Alabama. I loved this interactive tool because it had hyperlinks. If I went to Benjamin Franklin Taylor's page and clicked on his wife's name, it took me to her page, where it had her relevant information—date and place of birth and death. Rather than go from one genealogical website to another, this was an interconnected web of information. One-stop shopping.

I shared all this news with Rose, who introduced me to Sonya Hodges-Grantham in South Carolina, another woman dedicated to preserving the burial grounds of African Americans. Sonya's focus was on slave cemeteries in South Carolina and, like me and Rose, she had a personal connection since she was Sancho Thompson's descendant. He was the enslaved man whom Dr. Edmund Taylor had told me about at lunch. He also had given me the document of this history, which refers directly to Sancho being "the only Negro" in the Taylor graveyard. On the Find a Grave website, I saw photos of all the Taylor tombstones, many of which were marble monuments. I expected something similarly respectful for Sancho, considering the epitaph that Dr. Taylor had read to us over lunch. The last line again, was, "To show their respect for his virtues and their gratitude for his labors, the Taylors placed a stone over his grave."

So I was shocked to learn that it was indeed a stone, a rough-hewn boulder. When we could not find it the first time we looked together, Rose later sent me a photo of that slab. There was no epitaph that I could see. You would not know that Sancho was buried there.

Dr. Taylor had said many times over lunch that "Sancho was the only Negro in their family plot," so when I realized that his grave was not marked in the same way as the other family members', I thought, He was marginalized in life and death. And he would have been better off buried with his family members, people who truly loved him.

Sancho was also listed with Papa Renty in all the Taylor indexes, as was Edmund, Rose's ancestor, and Caesar, the first Black preacher at Antioch. I know in my heart that our ancestors knew one another—and likely there was also a kinship between them.

Through Denise, I learned that Jesse Peter Taylor, the brother of

Benjamin Franklin Taylor, was born in South Carolina but migrated to Mount Meigs, Alabama, with the Thompsons and the McLemores, from whom Denise was descended. I also knew from the wills I had already secured through Chris Childs that Benjamin Franklin Taylor owned enslaved people with the surname Thompson: they included Sancho, Hannah, Prince, and George. I believe this relationship between the Taylor and Thompson families explained how my great-grandfather Renty Taylor Thompson's surname was changed from Taylor to Thompson.

Prior to my mother's death, I recorded her saying that Renty Taylor Thompson had a brother named George Thompson. I had his death certificate—it was one of the first pieces of information I received from the Connecticut Historical Society—back in 2010. I wondered if I could find more death records, and if that information might somehow help me find where more of my ancestors were buried. I was particularly focused on Delia. What happened to her? Where did she wind up? Could I possibly find her resting place?

One Sunday evening in late 2015, Rose and I were texting one another as we did regularly since we met. I was now looking for burial records and wrote, "I need to find Delia's final resting place."

Rose was sharing with me all the information she had come across in her quest to help me find more leaves for my family tree. In that conversation, out of nowhere, she shared that she had come across a document in her South Carolina research naming George Thompson.

I quickly acknowledged, "That's a match! I have George's death certificate."

"Send it to me," Rose replied.

I texted Rose a copy of the death record that the historical society had sent me back in the summer of 2010, months after my mom died.

She immediately responded: "Oh my god."

I replied, "Oh my god, WHAT?"

Not able to wait for her answer, I called Rose and asked, "Oh my god, WHAT?"

Rose explained that George Thompson, according to the record, had lived and died in the community of Arthurtown in Columbia, South Carolina, and that his place of burial is the Child's Cemetery.

This was one of the sites she drove me by when I visited her.

"Yes!" I replied. "And?"

"The Child's Cemetery and Arthurtown are parcels of land previously owned by the slaveholder Benjamin Franklin Taylor," Rose continued.

"Oh my god, oh my god, Rose!" I exclaimed. "How do you know this?"

"My family purchased the land from his widow and established Arthurtown in 1872," she said.

I was trembling when I asked, "Rose, how can we prove this?"

"I have the deed."

Within moments, she texted it to me.

In a miraculous discovery, George Thompson's death certificate reveals that he lived and died in Columbia, that his mother was Tena, and that his father was Renty, the son of Papa Renty. But most remarkably, the certificate determines the domicile of the decedent as "Arthurtown," which, prior to 1871, was land owned by Sally W. Coles Taylor, the wife of Benjamin Franklin Taylor.

This for me was one of the biggest oh-my-God moments in my journey. George Thompson's death record was the answer I had been looking for. It undeniably linked me to the family of Benjamin Franklin Taylor. This death record points to a kinship between the Taylor slaveholder and the Thompson descendants, but even more incredibly, this record places my ancestors not only in Columbia, South Carolina, but on land owned by the slave owner Benjamin Franklin Taylor. George Thompson's death record is proof that my ancestors lived, died, and are buried on Benjamin Franklin Taylor's land.

Of all the millions of people I could have met on social media, no one but Rose could've made that connection. Arthurtown was land that was owned by the slaveholder Benjamin Franklin Taylor. Rose's family bought that land from his widow.

That was it for me. I put my ancestors on the slaveholder's land. I had nothing else to prove to Harvard, or anyone else. I now had the documents to confirm what I always knew to be true.

I thought of Harvard's insistence that I could not prove my ancestral ties to Congo Renty. How upsetting that was considering the violent nature of slavery, how it broke up families. I thought of Tena and her "increase," my great-grandfather, the third of five Rentys being "given" to Benjamin Franklin Taylor's daughter. The inhumanity, the outrage. Yet my ancestors persevered. They found one another despite that violent undoing. They made families. They told stories so that we could remember where we came from. In doing this research, I felt like an adopted child trying to piece her family's history together. Many times I wished that I could have one more conversation with my mom so she could help me fill in the blanks. But there was a part of me that always believed that she was with me, leading and guiding me in the right direction.

9

The Hubris of Harvard

By now Shonrael was building our family tree on Ancestry.com, adding new leaves, finding information in the website's vast database, adding to what we already had collected. I was also using the site to do research and found all kinds of useful information that supported my mother's stories, including a crisper copy of George Thompson's death certificate than the one the Connecticut Historical Society sent to me, which was a photocopy and difficult to read. I printed that out and placed it in my ever-expanding three-ring binder, receipts that proved Papa Renty was my ancestor. I was also delighted to find a record that listed my great-grandmother Ophelia, Renty Thompson's wife, on the "Wallace Roll of Cherokee Freedmen, 1880 to 1892," which backed up my mother's claim that she was Native American.

I no longer felt that I had to prove my ancestral ties to anyone. All the names in the Taylor family wills and slave indexes were enough for me. I knew that Congo Renty was my ancestor, but I did want to learn more about Delia. Everything about her facial features suggested trauma, and a tragic life. I wanted to know what happened to her, and I hoped that I might find more information, somehow, somewhere. I also wanted to continue to flesh out our family tree and thereby fulfill my promise to my mother: to write our oral history down before it was forgotten. Every document—whether a death certificate, land deed, or even a slave index—was a confirmation and validation of my mother's stories.

Still, I found it disturbing that Harvard only allowed the daguerreotypes to be used as the subject of scholarly articles and books *they* deemed appropriate—and it appeared to me that it was only for those that were *not* critical of Louis Agassiz. I was still holding out hope that the university would come to its senses and meet with me to start correcting the narrative: Congo Renty was not invisible. He has a rich oral history and a family that reveres and loves him.

I had also become active on Facebook, where I joined Rose's Columbia County genealogical group and found an online community of people like me, interested in slave histories, and genealogy specifically in South Carolina. I filled my timeline with Papa Renty stories, posting every newspaper article that detailed my journey as well as photos I took along the way—of me with the Taylors, with Rose, at academic panels and more. I was also often tagged in posts sharing interesting articles or upcoming events. I learned on Twitter that Harvard Law School was being scrutinized over their logo, which depicted three enslaved people carrying baskets of wheat beneath the word VERITAS, which means "truth" in Latin. It was the family crest of Isaac Royall Jr., a Harvard alumnus from a large slaveholding family who endowed the law school in the 1930s. I was astonished at how deeply entwined Harvard was with the institution of slavery, though it made me feel like I was not alone in my struggle with the university around these issues.

Harvard law students had demanded that the crest be replaced, and at first the university resisted, so the students led a protest.

When the campaign gained national attention, Harvard finally relented and agreed to change the crest. Drew Faust made a public announcement: "We do so on the understanding the school will actively explore other steps to recognize rather than to suppress the realities of its history, mindful of our shared obligation to honor the past not by seeking to erase it, but rather by bringing it to light and learning from it."

I found the quote so hypocritical. If they felt this way, then why, as the premier academic institution in the world, were they not interested in Congo Renty's true story? It was confounding! Yet I saw the power the students at Harvard had to get the administration to listen, so I decided to reach out to the *Harvard Crimson*, the student newspaper, to share my story, as I felt it directly related to the law school controversy. I hoped they would see the connection between this issue and my own struggle with Harvard to recognize me as Congo Renty's descendant.

On March 30, 2016, I received a lovely invitation from the assistant managing editor at the paper to come to the university to do an interview in person. "Tamara, thank you so much for your phone call and sharing your story with us. . . . We would really like to include your story in the feature I mentioned about troubling histories at Harvard, potentially even do a video if you are comfortable with that."

By then I had also learned that Harvard was planning a major event to announce its decision to replace the old law school logo with a new one, and installing a plaque to commemorate four enslaved people—Titus, Venus, Bilhah, and Judah—who had worked for two of the university's past presidents, Benjamin Wadsworth and Edward Holyoke. I had found this promising and decided to write to Drew Faust, first reminding her who I was, and then asking to attend the event: "I was made aware of what many feel is a change of heart as it relates to Harvard and its ties to slavery; I was also made aware of an upcoming event on April 6th. I am writing to inquire about the event and express my interest in attending."

When she did not respond, I called her office. Her assistant said an invitation was not possible. I had also learned that the iconic John Lewis was going to be at the event, which I found problematic: John Lewis shed blood, sweat, and tears to earn his civil rights legacy. He was a true hero in the fight for racial equity in this country, and I felt that Harvard simply wanted to capitalize on that.

In the meantime, the *Harvard Crimson*'s associate managing editor wrote to me again, this time copying six people at the paper: "Thank you for your call last week to our newsroom and telling me your incredible stories about how your ancestors' daguerreotypes are in the Peabody Museum as relics connected to Agassiz's research on racial superiority, and that Harvard rebuffed your desire to have their full stories included in the exhibit." They understood immediately—not only my ties to Papa Renty but that Harvard was attempting to silence me. I was invited to come to the campus any time before April 10 to do the interview in person as well as a video diary. I decided to go up on April 6, the same day John Lewis was scheduled to be there, in the hope that I might see him. I first met the Georgia congressman, who died in 2020, at a Congressional Black Caucus conference in 2013. He was hosting a workshop on voter rights that I attended. I made my way up through the crowd to introduce myself and showed him a picture of my Papa Renty. He was immediately familiar with that image and was so interested in my story that he gave me the name of someone in his office who handled his schedule.

"Make sure she gets you on it," he said.

She was hesitant to schedule a meeting since I was not one of his constituents, but I persevered and wound up visiting him in Washington, DC, on April 14, 2014. I knew that the Native American Graves Protection and Repatriation Act had been signed in 1990 and thought that we needed federal legislation protecting the relics of slavery as well. In talking with him, I shared that he bore a strong resemblance to my uncle John, and even showed him a picture. I felt certain if I saw him at Harvard, that he would remember me.

While I did not see John Lewis that day, I still felt hopeful: the young people understood the importance of my point of view. How I was giving an authentic voice to Congo Renty, based on years of oral history passed down from one generation to another, versus the academic supposition that Harvard was engaging in. There was a lot of back-and-forth between me and the *Crimson* staff—fact-checking calls, and requests for photos, which I gladly sent. Then, on May 5, 2016, I received the following message from the assistant managing editor:

> Dear Tamara,
>
> I hope this email finds you well. I wanted to reach out first and foremost to thank you for all of your help and time, from sending me documents to traveling up to Cambridge and speaking with our reporter. Unfortunately, we have ultimately decided that we won't be publishing excerpts of your interview because of concerns the Peabody Museum has raised and because recent events on campus have caused our own story to focus more on the Harvard Law School. I am very sorry that we won't be able to include your words but thank you again for all of your help and cooperation.

My thought in that moment was, Wow. What about the freedom and autonomy of the press? By now it was clear to me that Harvard was actively trying to silence my story and Papa Renty's legacy. Their claim to view the university's ties with slavery through the prism of humanity was just rhetoric. I was gutted, but I was not going to give up on the students just yet. I saw in them the zeal and compassion that I knew were necessary to get Harvard to change their tune.

I continued doing my own research for the book I'd started writing right after my mother died in 2010. Back then it was a family project and a promise kept. Now, six years later, I wanted to set the public record straight about who Congo Renty was. What started with a five-page genealogy chart was quickly becoming an American epic.

In that search for validation of my family's oral history, I began doing deep dives on the history of enslavement in nineteenth-century South Carolina, hoping to find more clues that would help me figure out what happened to my ancestors: Where did Delia wind up? How did my great-grandfather Renty Taylor Thompson get to Alabama? A Facebook friend tagged me in another post about a panel discussion being held on Monday, October 10, 2016, at the University of Connecticut Law School on the history of slavery and race in South Carolina, featuring Manisha Sinha, a history professor who had just published *The Slave's Cause: A History of Abolition*. Also speaking that evening were Jim Bowers, who as a student integrated the University of South Carolina in the 1960s and then returned to become the first African American law professor at his alma mater; and Eric Foner, a renowned historian of slavery, the Civil War, Reconstruction, and nineteenth-century America at Columbia University.

My girls were busy that evening, so I wound up going by myself and decided to wear my "Free Renty" shirt, which was bright red and had the Congo Renty image on the front, with his name written below it. Ever since the Peabody informed me that I couldn't use the image for my book project, I decided to use it however and whenever I wanted. Shonrael, an excellent graphic designer, made the shirts as well as business cards with my contact information, as people often asked for it at events—especially if I was wearing my tee. I found that it had a profound impact on people: they wanted to know who Renty was, and I was happy to tell them.

I had no idea if the daguerreotypes would even come up in conversation that night, but I knew that it would be powerful to wear Renty on my chest. Sure enough, they were discussed, since it is hard to talk about enslavement in South Carolina without mentioning these historically significant artifacts. These were among the first photographs ever taken of enslaved people; they had become symbols of everything that was wrong about the abhorrent practice. I waited for the appropriate moment to stand up in the packed audience and say, "Renty is my enslaved ancestor."

This was during the formal question-and-answer portion, toward the end of the evening, and once again I could feel the energy in the audience shift, just as it had at the Molly Rogers event.

Afterward I approached the stage along with the other audience members who had follow-up questions for the panelists. That was where I had a very interesting conversation with Manisha Sinha, who was shocked and amazed to learn that I was related to Renty. She shared with me that she had been chosen by Harvard to be a part of an international committee to research and explore how the daguerreotypes should be used. She said she had been meeting with historians and scholars for several years and never once had Harvard mentioned knowledge of Renty's lineal descendants.

This must be the project Pam Gerardi mentioned, I thought to myself, annoyed. I also remembered that Drew Faust promised in her email that she would keep me abreast of anything related to the artifacts, but I had not heard anything more on the subject. So I was shocked, and disappointed, to learn that they were doing something on this scale—enlisting historians from all over the world, but not even bothering to accept my offer to share Renty's rich oral history with them. It just didn't make sense!

I could tell by the look on her face that Professor Sinha was as confused as I was. She said that Harvard had commissioned academics and historians to construct narratives about who these people were.

Why didn't they ask me? I wondered.

Manisha may have read my mind.

"Never has Harvard ever said they had any knowledge or connection to any descendants of the people in the daguerreotypes," she said.

I came to this event to learn more about the history of slavery in South Carolina so I could continue piecing my story together. To learn that Harvard was creating their own narratives about Renty and Delia was beyond frustrating: once again I was confronted with academic arrogance. Why was Harvard willing to pay historians to create these narratives when they had me, a living descendant, who could share stories of at least one of the subjects photographed? I had reached out to them multiple times to share Renty's rich oral history. By dismissing me they were dismissing him, his legacy, his story.

To add insult to injury, I soon learned that Harvard was hosting an international conference on "Universities and Slavery: Bound by History." Again a friend tagged me on Facebook about the event with the simple question, "Did you know about this?" I did not. It was March 1, 2017, and the event was taking place on March 3. I immediately wrote Drew Faust to request two tickets since Shonrael wanted to go with me.

Faust's assistant responded that the event was "oversubscribed" and there were no tickets available. Disappointed but not dissuaded, I called the Harvard president's office. When her assistant answered, I said, "I have an email from Drew Faust saying I was going to be kept apprised about anything pertaining to the daguerreotypes. I understand this panel will be talking about universities, their ties to slavery and reparations—and assume that will include mention of these artifacts?"

She asked me to forward the email, which I did. That prompted her to give me one seat.

"I need two seats," was my reply.

After a lot of push and shove, I received confirmation the morning of the event that Shonrael and I had two assigned seats. We made the now-familiar drive to Cambridge, and as we were walking toward the Radcliffe auditorium, we noticed a group of students with posters gathered near the entrance. As we drew closer, I realized it was a protest—and I was amazed to see Papa Renty's face on the literature the students were handing out.

"That's my ancestor!" I said, as a white woman in her early twenties handed a flyer to me. "What are you protesting?"

She explained that they were protesting the conference since the students did not like the way Harvard was not being fully transparent about their involvement in slavery.

"We'd love to hear what you have to say about it afterwards," another student said. "Come find us. We'll still be here!"

They had scheduled an event for 6 p.m. after the conference to demand that the university do more than pay lip service regarding reparations. I was intrigued—what else would I learn today?

Shonrael and I went to sign in at the Radcliffe auditorium. Radcliffe College was the all-women's school that Elizabeth Cabot Cary, Louis Agassiz's wife, founded.

"Why here?" I wondered.

It made me uncomfortable. There we were once again handed a program—with Renty's face on it.

"What the heck is going on?" I asked Shonrael. My hackles were up, as were hers.

"I have a bad feeling about this," she said as we made our way into the auditorium.

As soon as we entered, we both stopped dead in our tracks: Papa Renty was staring at us from a movie-size screen that spanned the width of the stage and hung behind the podium. His face was the backdrop to this conference. His eyes locked with mine and all the oxygen was sucked from the room to the point I felt an intense pressure on my chest. As all the other attendees were busy finding their seats and chatting excitedly among themselves in the crowded auditorium, I remained paralyzed. He seemed to be speaking to me with his eyes. I felt his indignation and rage.

"Mom, Papa Renty looks mad," Shonrael said.

"As he should be," was my response.

By the time we found our seats in that overcrowded room, I felt beat up. Why did Harvard insist on using his image? Knowing full well that I claimed him as my ancestor? They knew that I was coming—and they were billing this conference as a discussion about reparations and slavery and the exploitation of enslaved people—only to continue actively exploiting Papa Renty. The program was a slap in the face, followed by this gut punch of the looming image. It was too much.

As we waited for the conference to begin, I flipped open the pamphlet and read the introduction by Lizabeth Cohen, the dean of Radcliffe.

"Welcome to Radcliffe, Harvard's Institute of Advanced Study, for this conference exploring the complicated relationship between institutions of higher learning and the institution of slavery," she wrote. "The man you see on the program's front cover, Renty, lived and worked as a slave in South Carolina in 1850, when his photograph was taken for the Harvard professor Louis Agassiz as part of Agassiz's scientific research. While Agassiz earned acclaim, Renty returned to invisibility. His photograph remained buried in an attic drawer at the Peabody Museum until its rediscovery in 1976."

My blood was now boiling. I wanted to stand up and scream, "He is not invisible!" He had a family who loved him then, and loves him now. I was so incensed. How dare they water down Agassiz's "science" and not name it for what it was: violent lies that fueled Jim Crow, the Holocaust, and apartheid as well as the systemic racism that to this day kills people of color.

I could not read any more. I felt ill. I wanted to leave but I decided to stay to at least hear the acclaimed journalist Ta-Nehisi Coates speak. He had published a famous essay in the *Atlantic* in 2014 called "The Case for Reparations," and I wondered if he had any idea about me or my relation to Renty.

Just then the lights in the auditorium dimmed and there was a ripple throughout the crowd as Lizabeth Cohen took the stage. She introduced herself and then went on to describe the conference as a place to discuss the recent role universities have played in grappling with their own dealings with enslavement. She cited Brown University and their decision to look at their own history vis-à-vis slavery in 2003, and also mentioned Sven Beckert, who started teaching a course at Harvard on that same history at this university.

I was intrigued by the setup: Were they going to do the real work of acknowledging the harms their interactions have had on people of color? Then Cohen said, "Let's begin by looking at the cover of your conference program."

Once again I was overcome with a feeling of dread.

"The program cover features a portrait of a man named Renty, who was born in Africa, kidnapped, and sold into slavery in the United States in the first half of the nineteenth century."

My heart started racing. Congo Renty was not only the backdrop to the symposium, but he inspired it. So why was I not officially invited to this conference, especially after Faust's assurance that I would be kept apprised of any developments? And why did I then have to practically beg for two tickets?

"This image was taken in 1850 when Renty was a slave on Edge-Hill Plantation near Columbia, South Carolina. Portraits were chiefly reserved for the well-to-do in the nineteenth century. So who took this image and why? It turns out the portrait was taken for Louis Agassiz, a Harvard professor and world-renowned scientist in his day. He was one of the inaugural professors at the Lawrence Scientific School, the precursor today of the John A. Paulson School of Engineering and Applied Sciences here at Harvard. Some of you, in fact, are watching from Agassiz House, our overflow space, where we will all gather later today for a reception after the conference. That building was named for Elizabeth Cabot Cary Agassiz, herself a teacher, president of Radcliffe College, and Louis's wife."

Cohen's choice of language describing Agassiz was disturbing, as was the fact that a conference about reparations was taking place in a building named for a man known as the father of scientific racism worldwide. It was cognitive dissonance.

"Louis Agassiz was a proponent of a scientific theory that was regarded as one of the most cutting-edge ideas of his day. The theory of polygenesis. That theory denied that all humans shared common ancestry and instead posited that different races were actually distinct and unequal species."

Again, her language was not in the least bit critical of the damage this theory caused not just to my family members directly but to all of humanity. Worse, by using such detached clinical language to describe Agassiz's work, she continued to treat Renty as Agassiz had, as an object, something to be studied.

"In 1850, Agassiz traveled to a South Carolina plantation to gather evidence for polygenesis. He observed enslaved workers there and long after his return to Cambridge he studied portraits taken of five of the men and two of the women. Agassiz classified and cataloged those men and women by their physical characteristics in much the same way that he classified and cataloged species of animals earlier in his career."

I flashed back to walking through the dark, dank halls of the Peabody Museum where all of Agassiz's specimens were stored. Ever since that visit, I had wanted to free both Renty and Delia from the macabre zoo where they had been kept since Agassiz commissioned those images. My mind was racing, connecting all these dots.

"The image of Renty that you see on the cover of your program and here on the screen is one of those images."

"Here we go," Shonrael said, under her breath.

I braced myself for the slight I knew would follow.

"To Agassiz, Renty was a specimen to inform the Harvard teaching curriculum and to contribute to the development of the academic discipline of comparative anatomy and anthropology. Renty's cataloged biological characteristics were what interested Agassiz. Today it is Renty's personal story that interests us."

"His personal story?" I said to Shonrael, shaking my head. This was outrageous.

"Exactly what I expected," Shonrael said. "I took time off work for this?"

"So what do we know about that story? The historical record tells us that he was a member of the Congo tribe. The historical record tells us that he spent his days laboring. The historical record tells us that he was a father. His daughter Delia also worked on the Edge-Hill Plantation. Renty was surely much more than either Agassiz's list of characteristics, or the bare facts revealed in the conventional written historical record. Much of his story remains unknown or pieced together by conjecture because so much has been erased from that written record. But that does not mean that we should stop trying to know more."

At this moment, I wanted to get up and scream. They were gaslighting not only me but in fact the whole world, since the conference was being broadcast globally. They had evidence that Renty does have an oral history: there had been newspaper articles about it. Why were they pretending otherwise? Again, rendering me mute as Agassiz did to Renty. This was dishonest and disingenuous on a new level!

"We have in fact hosted two seminars here at Radcliffe on the Agassiz images, one in 2012 and another in 2015. You can read about one campaign to elevate Renty, literally, in my note in your program."

De-mounting Agassiz was referenced in the pamphlet, relegated to a few sentences, which I thought was interesting. Yet there was no mention of me or my family or my claim.

"For many years, the Agassiz images remained hidden in an attic here at Harvard, until the Peabody Museum staff rediscovered them in 1976. Similarly, the historical tie between universities and slavery has remained buried for years. But that relationship could never fully disappear any more than Renty's photograph truly vanished even when it was out of sight. Now we must comb through the attics and open the disturbing drawers of our university's past no matter how difficult. As we do, I trust that we will grow to appreciate more and more how an image like Renty's has significance far beyond the EdgeHill Plantation in Columbia, South Carolina, where he was enslaved. Thanks to our distinguished speakers assembled here today and through all our efforts, we will, and we must, continue to unearth this history today and commit to ensuring that it informs our work moving forward."

The welcome speech was the ultimate dismissal of me, and of Renty. Harvard had no interest in his story. They rejected it, and instead hired historians to create a narrative about him. I felt the transference of Renty's trauma course through me like molten lead. He was being objectified all over again, treated like a slave at a conference that was supposed to be addressing and undoing harm.

Drew Gilpin Faust was the next person to take the stage and by then I could not take in another word. It all became blurry. She introduced Ta-Nehisi Coates. As he took the stage, I knew in my heart that he had no idea that Renty's descendants were among the academics and writers in that crowd. Instead he named a few of the scholars in the audience who had informed his work and gave an exceedingly warm thank-you to Faust for her work as a historian.

During his speech, so much of what Coates said aligned with my experience.

"We talk about enslavement as though it were a bump in the road," he said. "I tell people, it is the actual road!"

Then he spoke about all the ways it still impacts us today, using the concept of plunder, which enslavement was based on. He urged universities that are pursuing this study of enslavement not to limit it to enslavement.

"Enslavement is the originating system of plunder, but it birthed all sorts of systems of plunder that haunt us to this very day," Coates said.

He went on to define plunder as "taking from somebody else to benefit another group of people. It is the act of taking and putting people into a box so you can more efficiently rob them," he said, and this time, instead of feeling ill, I understood the reason I felt ill. Harvard was continuing to plunder Renty and Delia, and now me and Shonrael, at this very moment.

He said so many things that helped me articulate my feelings toward Harvard. "Enslavement was a system. It was not about being nice. It was about structures, the way things were set up to benefit one class of people to the detriment of another," he said. "It is very important to understand the intentionality of it, and to not speak about it as though it were outside our hands."

Then he said something that jolted me: "I think every single one of these universities needs to make reparations. . . . I don't know how you get around that. I don't know how you conduct research that says your very existence is rooted in a great crime, and you just shrug, and at best say, 'I am sorry,' and walk away," he said. "I think you need to use the language of reparations. To use that word to say that something was done."

Faust had opened the conference with a discussion of the debts society owed because of slavery—with Papa Renty glaring at all of us from behind her. It was so manipulative. If they were going to truly embody the mission of that conference, they would talk about the harm caused to Renty—instead they caused him further harm. In all my interactions with the university, they have never once taken responsibility for the harm they caused him, or Delia, or any of the other people captured against their will in those images. Seeing Renty used in this way was the opening of an old wound. Agassiz continued to be spoken of as "a great scientist" who was also a "man of his time," whereas Renty remained invisible.

"When you stand on the backs of other people who have been exploited, you have to, in a moral sense, in any institution that is teaching young people about morals and ethics, you have to do the right thing and try to make amends for that," Coates said. "I just don't know how you get around it."

I did not either.

About an hour into the conference, Shonrael said, "Mom, this is a waste of our time."

I agreed. I was ready to go home. By then Shonrael had gone on Twitter, where she found a live international discussion about the conference. Participants worldwide were tweeting their remarks using the hashtag "Unislavery." Frustrated by Harvard's refusal to acknowledge our family story, Shonrael tweeted: "Renty is not invisible. He has a family in the audience right now who loves him."

Suddenly her phone started to light up: people were liking and responding to her tweets.

"Mom, look!" she said. "You have to start tweeting too."

I posted the *Hartford Courant* story with the line "The Real Congo Renty."

That also got several likes. Emboldened, I tweeted the photo of me with Dr. Edmund Taylor along with the caption "Sons and daughters of former slaves with sons and daughters of former slave owners," an ode to Martin Luther King's "I Have a Dream" speech.

That elicited even more likes and comments, like "Amazing!" and "Wow!"

We noticed someone in the row in front of us looking around as if she was scanning the audience—for us.

"Keep going," Shonrael said with a smile. "We're hijacking the conference's live feed!"

Shonrael was doing the same, sharing pictures, news articles, and snippets of our story. We decided if they were not going to tell Renty's story from the podium—we would tell it for them—from our seats.

"Keep tweeting," Shonrael said.

"We are Renty's descendants," I tweeted. "We know his personal history: he was a loving father. A learned man."

We felt the energy in the room shift. Cohen and Faust were right: people do want to know Renty's history. Our question was and is, who gets to tell it?

About two hours into the event, there was an intermission. We went to the lobby, where a woman walked up to us.

"Are you Renty's descendants?" she asked.

We said yes, and she added, "Why didn't Harvard acknowledge you or your story?"

We just shook our heads. Soon we were surrounded by roughly ten more people who had seen the tweets and were actively seeking us out, including a history professor named Robert Hall. He was visibly upset when I told him our story and said that he knew Sven Beckert, one of the forum organizers.

"I'm going to write to him directly," he said.

The event was about to start up again when Shonrael said, "Mom, I think we have been beaten up enough."

I agreed and said, "Let's go."

The very next day, I received the email Professor Hall promised to write:

> Dear Professor Beckert,
>
> I am a historian who retired from the faculty at Northeastern University effective December 31, 2016. I am also a Harvard alumnus (Class of 1969) and was both a member of the Ad Hoc Committee of Black Students (which negotiated with the Rosovsky Committee for the creation of the Department of Afro-American Studies) and a member of the editorial board of the student-run *Harvard Journal of Negro Affairs.*
>
> I attended yesterday's conference at the Radcliffe Institute for Advanced Study and enjoyed it very much. Thanks for your lead role (with Evelyn Brooks Higginbotham) in organizing the conference.
>
> Were you or anyone involved in managing the conference aware that there were two descendants of Renty (from the Congo) in the audience during at least part of the conference? They live in Connecticut and have done much to flesh out the life story of Renty Taylor. The most vocal and visible of Renty's descendants is Tamara K. Lanier, a Chief Probation Officer with the Connecticut Judicial Branch; Criminal Justice Chair, Connecticut State NAACP; and Vice

President of the New London, CT branch of the NAACP. Ms. Lanier appears to have made some efforts to bring the rest of the story of Renty to the attention of people (someone . . . anyone) at Harvard to little avail thus far.

Ms. Lanier (who attended yesterday's conference with her daughter) can be reached by telephone or email and I hope that you will get in touch with her or refer her to someone at Harvard who may be interested in what else has been learned about Renty beyond what was rendered in Liz Cohen's "A Message from Radcliffe Dean Lizabeth Cohen" in the printed conference program.

Sincerely yours,
Robert L. Hall
Associate Professor Emeritus of African American Studies & History, Northeastern University

I so appreciated this gesture—and, once again, never heard from Harvard.

10

The Aha Moment

At first Harvard's treatment felt dismissive, but now it was becoming abusive. The conference on "Universities and Slavery" made it clear to me that Harvard was not interested in the truth about Renty. I was completely puzzled by their resistance but continued researching and building on my already compelling documentation. That was how I came across a paper written by Yxta Maya Murray, a law professor at Loyola Marymount University, that explored the plight of Carrie Mae Weems, an African American artist who had visited Harvard's Peabody Museum to see the slave daguerreotypes in the early 1990s. Weems signed a restrictive contract agreeing not to capture, record, or use the likenesses of the enslaved men and women, but was so moved by what she saw that she photographed them during her visit anyway and used those images in her art exhibit titled *From Here I Saw What Happened and I Cried.*

For the series, she enlarged four of the daguerreotypes into photographs ten times the original size and then tinted them a dark red that gave the effect of being drenched in blood. "A Negroid Type" was emblazoned across Renty's chest in a white font in one piece, and in another she used the side view image of Delia and the painful play on words "You Became a Scientific Profile." Jack's image was branded "An Anthropological Debate" and his daughter Drana is labeled "& a Photographic Subject." In an explanation of her work on the Museum of Modern Art's website, where I found it, Weems states, "When we are looking at these images, we are looking at the ways in which Anglo-America—white America—saw itself in relation to the Black subject."

It hit me then that these images were both among the first photographs ever taken of enslaved African people as well as the first documented examples of racial profiling. Photography was a new medium in the 1850s, and Agassiz used it to present these Black men and women not for who they were, but for who he wanted them to be. These were also the first mug shots. A negroid type. An anthropological debate. Agassiz hired Zealy to take pictures—not to portray who Renty was, a self-educated religious man, but who Agassiz wanted him to be, a sinister, subhuman species, racially inferior to white people. The images were used as propaganda to poison people's imaginations and devalue Black lives, the point of Agassiz's racist fantasy. These original false narratives made me think of the many Black men who complained to the NAACP alleging racial profiling, and of the many more who were arrested, prosecuted, and found guilty of crimes they did not commit. Or killed, like Trayvon Martin, who was shot on his way home from a 7-Eleven, with Skittles and an Arizona Iced Tea, because he looked "suspicious." Or thirteen-year-old Tamir Rice, shot by a police officer for playing with a plastic gun in the park.

Racial profiling is the through line that points to the inequity in the criminal justice system, which finds Black people incarcerated in state prisons at nearly five times the rate of white people. I saw this firsthand in my work with the NAACP and through the Connecticut

Racial Profiling Prohibition Project, an advisory committee established by the Connecticut General Assembly that I had been part of since its inception in 2012. In 1999, Alvin W. Penn submitted legislation prohibiting the practice of racial profiling after he, a Black state senator from Bridgeport, Connecticut, routinely got pulled over by police officers in Fairfield County. The law requires data reporting for all traffic stops and collecting and analyzing all racial disparities. I was appointed to be a member of the committee due to my role in the NAACP. Racial profiling has always been a cause I have embraced—I have dedicated much of my career to eradicating it. How ironic that my enslaved ancestors were possibly victims of the first incident of racial profiling in the history of this country. It all begins with these daguerreotypes.

Weems's artwork *widened* a wound that I'd already experienced when I first saw "Congo Renty" in the article Rich sent me. It also made me understand that Harvard was not interested in knowing who Renty, Delia, Jack, and Drana are. Just as Agassiz wanted to tell the story of who he thought they were back in 1850, Harvard continued to tell the story of who the university and select academics wanted them to be today. Neither version has anything to do with the truth. And every time Harvard tells that story—or anoints someone to do so—Renty and Delia and Jack and Drana and all the others forced to sit for those photos are stripped of their dignity, their heritage, and their legacy.

Harvard's "only-we-can-tell-this-story" approach had always bothered me—but then I read that the university threatened to sue Weems, claiming that she had freebooted their copyrights to the images. According to Murray's essay, Weems knew that she didn't have a legal leg to stand on but believed that there was a greater moral argument: that became part of the art piece. In her response to the lawsuit, Weems famously said, "I think your suing me would be a really good thing. You should. And we should have this conversation in court." She basically welcomed a free and open debate as to Harvard's claim of ownership of the daguerreotypes.

That emboldened the question stirring within me: What legal right does Harvard have to these images?

Instead of suing Weems, Harvard purchased the rights to her images and would go on to collaborate with her, using these pictures in future books and exhibits. Reading that stopped me cold, just as seeing Renty as a backdrop in the Radcliffe auditorium had: it occurred to me in a flash that nothing had changed since the 1850s, when these photos were taken. It also made me ponder the question Murray asks in her essay, "Who owns the rights to the violent events of the past?" Just as Ta-Nehisi Coates's presentation helped me understand that the daguerreotypes were the plunder of slavery, Murray articulated the legal issue that had been nagging at me since the conference: "More fundamentally, did Harvard indeed own the daguerreotypes, which would clinch their copyright and contract claims? And if they did, should they own images of enslaved people that Agassiz won through violent coercion? Or should we regard these relics as cultural property belonging to African-Americans, which should be returned to the descendants of African-born enslaved people?"

Most compelling was her argument for restitution: "People committed serious crimes in the course of taking these photographs. . . . If Agassiz and his cohorts wrestled enslaved people's property from them through violence or the threat of violence, then the daguerreotypes are the proceeds of robbery. . . . And, if the images cannot be separated from the pictures, as indeed they can't, then the daguerreotypes themselves are the fruits of taking through fear of force. Consequently, a commitment to nonviolence—or even common sense—militates that Harvard should not now own these objects."

That passage hit me like a freight train.

I had to stand up and walk around to process the emotions

coursing through me: in several sentences, she articulated what I had been feeling with every slight, every dismissal.

Prior to the March 2017 conference—and so seven years after my mother died—I was willing to work with Harvard to tell Renty's story in a way that memorialized him as the great person he was. But when I left Cambridge that day, I understood, thanks to Coates, that a crime was committed when the images were taken—their likenesses stolen—from my ancestors, who had no choice but to sit for those pictures, which was evidence of plunder. Because of my work as a probation officer, I was well versed in the concern of restitution and victims' rights. One of the first things I learned as a trainee was that property wrongfully taken must be returned, and that the victim must be made whole. Throughout my twenty-seven-year career, I'd conducted countless restitution studies and presentence investigations, where I made recommendations to the court as to how to best meet the needs of the crime victim. A criminal act was committed when Renty and Delia were forcibly photographed. What would make them whole?

Murray's essay made me question, again, why Harvard felt they could control this plundered property—on what ground? She writes, "Under what legal doctrine could we transform legal title in properties made by enslaved people, driven by the concern that these properties are the fruits of illegal force? Should we employ the tort of assault and battery, which could feasibly garner the victims' heirs' damages? Or should we turn to restitution in crimes? . . . Wrestling the daguerreotypes from Harvard and placing them back in the custody of descendants or appropriate institutions would not succumb to a myth of cultural purity and authenticity, but rather recognize a history of abuse and theft that Harvard currently would rather keep quiet."

As I read these words, the energy and excitement building up inside me were so intense that I felt like I might implode. Suddenly it all made sense. Taking the images in the first place was a crime, committed by Agassiz, who was employed by Harvard at the time. The victims deserved to be made whole again via restitution, or in this case reparations. There are similarities between the two. Restitution and reparations both seek to make a victim or victims whole, but they are applied in different contexts and have distinctly different meanings: While restitution is more about compensating individuals for a specific loss, reparations seek to right a historical and systemic wrong—as in the case of the descendants of American chattel slavery. Murray articulated my pain and frustration in a way that cut through all of Harvard's gaslighting behavior. In that revelatory moment, I was reminded of the great Roberta Flack song "Killing Me Softly," where she sings, "Strumming my pain with his fingers."

That essay changed my life as Murray's legal analysis helped me understand why Harvard refused to acknowledge me as Renty and Delia's descendant. If they did, then I would have legal standing to claim the artifacts. I knew the daguerreotypes were priceless, and that Harvard enjoyed the academic prestige of controlling how they were used and by whom. But Murray's essay helped me understand two profound truths: Harvard does not have good title to the artifacts, which are in fact the proceeds of a criminal act. Property appropriated from Renty and Delia does not belong to those who stole it from them. It should go back to the victims, or their descendants.

The daguerreotypes don't belong to Harvard—they belong to the descendants.

This was an aha moment for me. A revelation! I suddenly understood why Harvard had been so steadfast in dismissing me—and I immediately started looking for an attorney. I wanted to know what my legal rights were. The few local attorneys I spoke with offered thoughts and condolences. And they all made one thing clear: Harvard was a beast. Taking them on felt impossible. I needed a courageous and resourceful legal mind, one who was not afraid to speak truth to power.

That April, I went to a criminal justice workshop hosted by Al Sharpton in New York City. I'd been once before, and I decided to go again as it so directly aligned with my probation work. Benjamin Crump happened to be speaking that day. I knew him as the civil rights attorney who represented the family of Trayvon Martin. When the all-white and female jury acquitted George Zimmerman after he shot and killed Martin on his way home from getting candy from the store, people took to the streets in protest and the Black Lives Matter movement was born. Ever since then, Ben Crump had become the spokesperson for Black social justice—representing the families of Michael Brown and Tamir Rice, among many others who lost their lives to racial profiling.

Hearing Crump speak that day helped me understand his power. He speaks from the heart and has the air of a Baptist preacher. When he started talking about two systems of justice in America, it resonated with so many of the racial incidents I witnessed, and fought, as a probation officer—and through my work with the NAACP. Then, as I listened to him, it occurred to me: *He* would not be afraid to go up against Harvard. And he would understand the historical significance of this case!

As soon as Crump finished speaking, I began to make my way through the packed auditorium. I had to speak to him! I was among dozens of people who felt the same way. As I started to weave my way through the crowd, squeezing between people who were also vying for his attention, I was working up my nerve. What could I say to grab his interest? I imagined that every single person swarming him at this moment also had a case they wanted him to represent. All I could think was, How can I sum up my story?

I had my contact card with Renty's face on it that Shonrael had made in my hand and when I finally made it to the stage where he was posing with people for photographs, I passed my phone to a stranger and said, "Will you take my picture?"

This was my moment. As we were both smiling for the shot, I took a deep breath and said, "I have a case that I know you would be interested in. I'm in a fight with Harvard over images of my enslaved ancestors. They have created this false narrative that denies them their heritage and dignity."

He turned toward me, intrigued. That emboldened me.

"This is a reparations case," I added. "And it's historic."

I could tell by his expression that I had his attention. I gave him my business card, and he handed me his. I left the event encouraged and hopeful.

Two or three days later, my cell phone rang.

"Ms. Lanier, this is Attorney Ben Crump," his cheerful voice boomed through the receiver. "I haven't been able to think about anything else but your story since we met."

My heart was pounding with anxious excitement. Was he calling to say this is an impossible case? Or to say that I didn't have a legal leg to stand on?

No, Crump was quick to say, "This is about reparations."

He understood how historic this case was, as I prayed he would.

"This could be a landmark case," he continued. "But first I have to go back and sell it to my partners, many of whom are white and conservative."

I knew that if anyone could sell this story, it was him. He said he wanted to meet with me to look over my documentation, and so we arranged to meet up in Maryland a few weeks later as he was planning to go to the NAACP national convention, as was I, with Jean Jordan, our New London branch president. By then my three-ring binder was bulging with newspaper articles and genealogical research. Still, the morning I was planning to meet him in Maryland, I was sick to my stomach with nerves. I'd gotten Crump's attention. What was I asking him for specifically?

I wanted to be clear: A terrible thing happened to Renty and Delia when Agassiz commissioned those images. Harvard employed Agassiz at the time, and so supported him in his research and work—and they continue, to this day, to profit off that plunder. Renty and Delia were brutalized in that moment—and are still being victimized and terrorized every time their likenesses are used by Harvard. As was I, their descendant whom Harvard refused to acknowledge.

I believed all of this to my core, yet I was so nervous. What if Crump asked for an astronomical amount to even sit down to talk with me? He was the most famous civil rights lawyer in the world. He would deserve that—but I did not have it to give him. And I certainly did not want him to think I did not value him or his expertise. Then he arrived at our meeting spot and his warm smile put me immediately at ease.

His first words were "Let's pray."

The peace that came over me was immediate and profound. Once again I felt my mother's presence. I felt she played a part in this moment. We found a quiet corner at the conference hall. I took the binder out of my bag and began to tell him my story, starting with my mother's oral history and the promise I made her on her deathbed. I told him about Rich, and then showed him the research I had amassed thus far—from the "Black Bodies, White Science" article that set me on this journey to the slave indexes and Taylor wills that Chris Childs found in Utah to Murray's extraordinary essay that helped me understand that I had legal standing.

I wanted him to understand not only that Renty was my ancestor—but also that we had a historic case.

He was floored.

"This is about reparations," he said with a serious look and a nod of his head. "Now I just have to go back and convince my partners."

A few days later, my phone rang: "Ms. Lanier," Crump's voice boomed through my receiver. "I sold it to my partners. Now I have to find a Connecticut attorney who's willing to challenge this as a two-hundred-year-old slave reparations case."

I was overcome, with both joy and hope.

"Thank you!" I said, holding back tears.

"This is about reparations," he said again. "And I have faith that we can prove it."

"And I have faith in you."

11

The Reichlin Letter

After twenty-seven years working at the Connecticut Judicial Branch in Norwich, I decided to retire as chief probation officer on September 30, 2017. The timing felt right. My mom used to say, "Anything worth doing is worth overdoing," and now that I had Attorney Crump interested in helping me, I was ready to direct all my attention to my case against Harvard.

On my last day of work, I was doing my final handoff to my colleagues Vicky and Maureen. Over the course of my career, I learned the importance of documentation. As my very first supervisor, Ethel, always said, "If it is not documented, it didn't happen." In my home life, I had always saved things, for nostalgic purposes. But in this line of work, I had to be prepared with supporting evidence to testify in court at a moment's notice. My last item on my to-do list before I walked out of City Hall once and for all was sharing situational templates I had made with Vicky and Maureen, who would be responsible for managing the office after I left. Basically, I had a binder of potential scenarios: "If this situation happens, here's how you would handle it." As we were wrapping up and about to head out for my retirement lunch with my entire staff, Maureen said, "Tammy, by the way, Brittany says there's a letter for you."

My office was on the fourth floor, and before I made my way downstairs to Vicky's office on the first floor, I handed a stack of letters to Brittany, the office secretary. I was certain it was all inmate correspondence. During my tenure, I instilled a new practice of sending a letter to every client at their sentencing detailing the conditions of their probation, since it was their responsibility to reach out to their probation officer as soon as they were released. These letters were proof that we notified them—as often many would not follow up and we'd have to track them down to begin their probation period. Since I was the point of contact, that meant I received lots of letters from inmates, especially those with long sentences, who would often write to me with questions or concerns about their cases or where they might live or work once they were released.

"I know the letter she's referring to," I said. "I believe it's inmate correspondence."

"No," Maureen said. "Brittany says it's about your Papa Renty."

The last thing I wanted to do was walk back up those stairs—ever again! I was done. I almost told her to not worry about it, but something inside me said, Go get it.

When I reached the fourth floor, Brittany was waiting for me with an envelope in her hand.

"I went through all the things you passed on to me," she explained. "But this one seemed personal."

I opened it and saw that it was from a Dr. Seymour Reichlin in Green Valley, Arizona. I recognized that name immediately. In all my research about the daguerreotypes, the name Ellie Reichlin was mentioned only once or twice as the Peabody employee who had discovered the daguerreotypes at the museum in the summer of 1976. I found it odd that in every other piece I'd read, she was only ever referred to as "the Harvard associate," so much so that I'd been looking for any reference of her name ever since. I spent hours scouring the internet trying to track her down since I had so many questions for her, starting with "What was it like to see the daguerreotypes for the very first time?"

I started reading the letter: "Ms. Lanier, I have just found out that you have traced your great-great-great-grandfather to the man pictured in the infamous Peabody Agassiz daguerreotypes as Renty. I write now to tell you that it was my wife, Ellie, who discovered these photos at the Peabody, and who tracked down the circumstances under which they were taken."

My heart was racing so fast that my hands started trembling: I found her! Or rather, she found me! This meant I was going to have an opportunity to speak with her and ask all my questions, like "Where did you find them? What was that like? Who did you tell? How did they respond?" I wanted to learn every moment from her point of view and continued reading:

"Sad to say, she died six years ago, and did not live to see the extraordinary conclusion to this history."

"Oh my god," I uttered out loud.

It was as if I had been punched in the chest—all the hope that had accumulated in a matter of seconds disappeared in a flash. All my questions for her would remain unanswered and my joy was quickly replaced with despair. I immediately thought, If Harvard had not fought me so hard, I may have gotten the chance to meet Ellie. I did not explain this to Brittany, but instead kept reading, hanging on every word.

"Whoever hid them at the time must have understood that they were too embarrassing to show, and too important to throw away. I suspect, with no proof, that it may have something to do with the fact that Louis Agassiz's son donated [a large amount to] the Peabody and was its honorary director for 20 years."

This information was too much to process at that moment—though I did realize that this letter was full of important clues. More than anything, I could not wait to speak to Dr. Reichlin! I saw that he had included his home address and email and I felt a bit disappointed that I could not call him that moment. I would have to wait until I got home to reply.

In the last paragraph, Dr. Reichlin wrote: "In the newspaper [article I read about you there is a photo of you carrying] a copy of the book by Molly Rogers called *Delia's Tears*. Have you or anybody else tracked down the fate and descendants of the other people pictured? It is sad but hopeful that from sadness, some good can finally come. Sincerely yours, Seymour Reichlin M.D."

He was talking about the piece that had run in the *New Haven Register* back in 2011 and I realized that he too had been following the news about the daguerreotypes, looking for anyone related to the people in those haunting images. I could tell from the tone of his letter that he cared deeply about Renty and Delia, and all the others photographed. And that they haunted him as I was sure they had haunted Ellie. I folded the letter carefully, along the same lines he had, before slipping it back in its envelope and placing it in my handbag. Before I made my way back down those stairs for the final time, I said a grateful prayer that I was compelled to walk back up those stairs.

Dr. Reichlin's letter was another star pointing me in the right direction.

From there I went off to my goodbye lunch, where my local senator gave me a special citation and my whole staff wished me well. It was all very lovely, but I was distracted. I could not wait to get home to respond to Dr. Reichlin. As I began to make my way from the restaurant, my mind continued to race, connecting all these dots that led to this chance encounter: Dr. Reichlin said that Ellie had died in 2011, the year after I had reached out to Harvard. That meant he continued to look for any news about the daguerreotypes, just as I had been doing all these years. Had Harvard been more open to sharing my story, Dr. Reichlin may have found me earlier and I may have had a chance to meet Ellie. That reignited my frustration with Harvard: Why were they so determined to control the narrative of these artifacts? And why were they protecting Agassiz over the people he violated?

As soon as I got home, I went straight to my computer.

"My dear Dr. Reichlin, words cannot begin to express how touched and moved I was after receiving your letter." I was typing as fast as I was thinking. "Believe it or not your wife Ellie has been in my heart and thoughts for months now and it was a great disappointment to learn of her passing. I recently completed a small draft book where I thank God for her. And I so would have loved an opportunity to talk to her. And to let her know that from the bottom of my heart I thanked her.

"Since learning of this amazing discovery in 2011, I've reached out to Harvard and made them aware of the probate and US census records that link me directly to the images. I have been ignored and they have resisted my requests to learn more about the daguerreotypes. To be honest, if they had been open and transparent about me and my story, I feel I may have had the chance to meet your wife. I feel sad about that.

"If you are willing, I would love to know more about Ellie. Not much is written about her. Often she is referred to as the Harvard associate or the Harvard staffer. To me she was so much more.

Please consider giving me a call."

I clicked send, and then said a little prayer that he would respond quickly. Periodically, throughout the afternoon, I'd check my email. Nothing. I checked once again, right before I went to bed. And there it was, waiting in my inbox, a message from Dr. Reichlin.

My heart fluttered as I opened it up:

"Dear Tamara, your letter brought me to tears. There is a three-hour difference between Tucson and Connecticut, so I will call you tomorrow."

I barely slept that night in anticipation of our conversation. I kept running through all my questions in my head, starting with "What did Ellie do at the Peabody? Where did she find the daguerreotypes? And why is she never mentioned in any of the reporting?" That last piece truly perplexed me.

The next morning, I answered my phone on the first ring.

"Tamara?" a kind, gentle voice asked.

"Yes! Hello, Dr. Reichlin! What a thrill to get to speak with you!"

I told him how moved I was both by his letter and by his wife's discovery.

"If it weren't for Ellie, I would never have found my Papa Renty," I said.

He replied, "Now, you're making me cry!"

We spoke for hours that day. I was in awe of his many medical accomplishments; of his world-renowned leadership in the field of neuroendocrinology, and that he was the University of Connecticut School of Medicine's first medical director in 1969. I told him about my mother's dying request, and my first chance encounter with Rich Morrison, which led me to finding Renty in the first place. He shared with me his memories of Ellie coming home from work the day she found the daguerreotypes.

"She was rattled," he explained. "Soon thereafter, she brought home copies of the three-by-five-inch images that a colleague was able to blow up into eight-by-ten-inch prints. She was very ambivalent about even viewing them. She found it all very painful."

I knew from the way he spoke about her that she was a kindred spirit, someone who understood in an empathetic way how degrading these images were. Dr. Reichlin said that she became determined to find out who the people were in those photos, and why they were stashed away at the Peabody. He also shared that Ellie's boss at the time did not want her to do this research, which was ironic since he was the person who asked her to catalog all the museum's holdings, and that was how she discovered the daguerreotypes in the first place.

"So, she took it upon herself to do the research on her own time and dime," Dr. Reichlin said.

He explained that it was very much in character for Ellie, who had graduated from Sarah Lawrence College as an anthropology major and had spent a summer living with a First Nations tribe in Vancouver, British Columbia, where she became friends with the chief's daughter, a young woman her age named Rosemary Thomas. They remained close friends for the rest of their lives. After she and Seymour got married, they moved to Rochester, New York, where he became a full professor at the medical school and she enrolled in a PhD program in cultural anthropology. Then, when they lived in St. Louis, she worked in a museum on the archaeology of the tribal artifacts of the Mississippian tribes. This all led up to her getting a job at the Peabody Museum, where her official title was Acquisitions Curator. She was specifically interested in working with marginalized groups—her inner calling was about repairing harm.

As Dr. Reichlin regaled me with stories of his extraordinary wife, I could not help but think of all the people to discover the daguerreotypes, and thank goodness it was Ellie. She immediately saw the humanity in those images. Another person may not have. In fact, Ellie's assistant, Laura Condon, was the one who first found the photos in a file cabinet in the museum's attic. She showed them to Ellie, who was shocked by the discovery and immediately set out on a mission to learn as much as she could about how they wound up at the Peabody. Though there were no formal acquisition records, there were clues: she contacted a daguerreotype expert who dated them as pre–Civil War, for starters. Then each person photographed was identified by name, where in Africa they were from, and what plantation they were from, and "JT Zealy, Columbia, South Carolina" was also printed on the images. Another scholar whom Ellie contacted was aware that Louis Agassiz had been in South Carolina pursuing theories about race, and with that she started to research Agassiz's full biography. At one point she was connected to a scholar on slavery named Peter Wood, who had written a book called *Black Majority: Negroes in Colonial South Carolina from 1670 Through the Stono Rebellion,* which appeared in 1974 and was a National Book Award finalist.

Dr. Reichlin was laughing when he told me this small-world story: "Peter wrote back and asked, 'Are you the Ellie Reichlin who gave me a mug when I was a little boy?' "

They had only been married a year when Dr. Reichlin, now a world-renowned neuroendocrinologist, started his residency at Washington University; the chairman of medicine was Barry Wood. He invited Ellie and Seymour to their Christmas dinner that year and Ellie painted several mugs as gifts for his children. Peter Wood was nine years old and still remembered that moment and Ellie twenty-five years later! He had since become a foremost expert on slavery and is now a retired professor living in Colorado, still giving lectures about racism.

Ellie compiled her research and findings into an article for *American Heritage* magazine in June 1977 called "The Faces of Slavery: A Historical Find," which detailed her discoveries.

"It was such major news that the *New York Times* picked it up," Dr. Reichlin said, with such pride. That was when it dawned on me that we were both still working through our grief—his for Ellie, mine for my mother—by picking up their torches, where they left off. What he was doing for Ellie by continuing to follow the story about the daguerreotypes was the same kind of healing work that I was doing for my mother.

Just as I had questions for him, he had many for me.

"How did you know that Congo Renty was your ancestor?" he asked.

"I felt it in my bones when I first saw that image," I explained. "But I also knew from my oral history that everyone in my family called Papa Renty the Black African. I had the assistance of a wonderful man who offered to help with the genealogy and gave him that clue along with all the others that my mother had shared with me, and that was how he found the *American Art* 'Black Bodies, White Science' article. From the moment I saw Renty Congo, I knew that was my Papa Renty."

I also shared with him the cold reception I'd received at the Peabody and heard him sigh through the receiver.

"That does not surprise me," he said. "But it does upset me. I'm so sorry to hear that you and your daughter were treated that way."

While it was difficult to say goodbye, we promised to stay in touch.

Within days, his daughter sent me a copy of the *American Heritage* article that Ellie wrote, and I was as emotional reading it as I was reading the article Rich had sent me seven years earlier. This was my only opportunity to hear Ellie's thoughts about the daguerreotypes in her words—to connect with her. I also realized how crucial she was in breaking a historic story that Harvard had kept under wraps for decades: that Louis Agassiz was not just a celebrated botanist and zoologist when he arrived from Switzerland in 1846 to start working at Harvard University as a professor. In this article, she pieced together his background and learned that he had become greatly interested in the work of anatomist Samuel Morton, who wrote *Crania Americana* in 1839 and *Crania Aegyptiaca* in 1846, which compared ancient and modern skulls to argue that mankind was not one species, but several. Agassiz was famous for his work identifying and classifying fish, but in the United States he seized on Morton's theories to further the absurd and racist theory of polygenism.

In her meticulous piece, Ellie reported that Agassiz made a declaration in 1850 at a meeting for the Advancement of American Science in Charleston, South Carolina, that the races were "well marked and distinct" and did not originate "from a common center . . . nor from a common pair." This was before the Civil War, so the southern states pounced on the esteemed scientist from Harvard's theory of polygenesis. They saw it as proof of racial inequality, and in support of enslavement.

During our conversation, Dr. Reichlin had said that he and Ellie were particularly disturbed by the images because they reminded them of medical textbooks. In her *American Heritage* piece, Ellie reported that Agassiz hired the photographer J. T. Zealy to take studio portraits, reserved for the wealthiest families, but instead of capturing images of women and men in lacey bespoke finery, the men and women Agassiz selected to prove his repulsive theories were stripped naked and made to stand, feet apart, arms rigid and outstretched by their sides. In some images their chins were resting on a tripodlike apparatus to help them stay still, presumably while Zealy got the lighting just right before taking a shot of their backsides.

Ellie wrote of "posing each one nude to point out the anatomical details in which the scientist had shown special interest and finally, labeling each with the subject's first name, tribe and owner."

In all the reporting I'd read about the provenance of the daguerreotypes, there was mention only of "a Harvard associate" doing the original research, which gave the impression that they sponsored and supported it. I now understood that they had in fact appropriated Ellie's work—without giving her proper credit! It was more proof that they were trying to cover their own culpability in how these images came into existence.

Compelled to prove his theories, Agassiz traveled to Columbia, South Carolina, to meet with the naturalist Robert W. Gibbes, who took him to several plantations where Gibbes had identified several men who were African-born—Agassiz wanted "pure types" not yet mixed with American blood. Ellie points out in her article that this was not easy to find in 1850, since the importation of slaves was made illegal in 1808. She even noted in her piece that "some of those who Agassiz examined must have been smuggled into America as part of the illicit trade that continued until the Civil War."

This was another moment where I was overwhelmed by the power of my own oral history. Papa Renty was called the Black African. Louis Agassiz wanted a pure type. I knew, on so many levels, that the man in the picture was my ancestor, but his African origin was the ultimate confirmation. My ancestors proudly held on to that defining piece of information and passed it down from one generation to the next. My mother often said that the Africans were respected and revered among the slaves, and that was why they celebrated Renty's African origins. Referring to him as "the Black African" was a term of endearment and makes me proud of the legacy that my family has retained and cherished.

At the end of her article she writes, "Agassiz's theory was discredited by the mid-1860s, but the daguerreotypes survived; and it's ironic that these pictures, made to demonstrate the inferiority of their subjects, instead conferred a kind of immortality on the men and women we only know as Renty and Delia, Jem and Jack. It was no consolation for the humiliation they endured both as slaves and objects of scientific curiosity, but a rare gain for those who now encounter these people as memorably real survivors of a painful epoch."

That last line made me so incredibly emotional. I wanted to hug her—for so many reasons, but especially that paragraph. I had never thought of Renty and Delia as survivors—until Ellie put it that way. We talk about the survivors of the Holocaust, but not of slavery. I would also expect that kind of elevated understanding today—but not in 1977. It was so courageous. Her tenacity and humanity drove her to piece together this story—to reveal Louis Agassiz for who he really was. It was also my opportunity to hear Ellie's voice.

Meeting Dr. Reichlin was revelatory. To start, I thought Harvard had done all the research on the daguerreotypes, so learning that it was Ellie's original research was an epiphany. I also started to see a pattern in Harvard's ruthlessness. Why did they try to prevent Ellie's work? And then attempt to cover up her true role in the story by never naming her?

Once again, all of this made me so frustrated—for Ellie, and myself. I was not the only person whom Harvard has dismissed when it comes to these historical artifacts. But just as my mom's passing was not the end of her campaign to find my family's roots, Ellie's passing was not the end of hers. She passed the baton to her husband, and in his endless searching for more stories about Renty and Jack and Delia, he found me.

That summer, Dr. Reichlin traveled from Arizona to Connecticut to visit me. He brought his daughters and grandchildren. Megan and Shonrael were there too. Meeting him and learning about Ellie's crucial role in Renty and Delia's story gave me the boost I needed to keep going. Now that I was retired, I had time, and so if there was ever anything being presented about Renty or slavery, I would go.

That was how I wound up driving to Yale during a blizzard in February 2018 for a lecture that Harriet A. Washington was giving on her book *Medical Apartheid,* in which she discusses the daguerreotypes as an early example of dehumanizing Black bodies in the name of science. New Haven is a forty-five-minute drive from my home and what started as a light dusting of snow turned into a whiteout—the drive took two and a half hours and thank goodness my friend Laura-Lillian Best, or LLB, went with me! It was treacherous, and I was glad to have company and a comrade.

We arrived during the last ten minutes of the discussion. Afterward I went up to Harriet and introduced myself as a descendant of Renty.

She is a Black woman, and responded warmly, "How fascinating!"

But Randi Epstein, the white woman who had interviewed Harriet, looked on inquisitively, and I felt that she needed convincing of my claim. I was used to this kind of scrutiny by now and continued to share snippets of my own story, including that I'd recently connected with Dr. Seymour Reichlin.

"He's the widower of Ellie Reichlin, who discovered the daguerreotypes in the Peabody and was responsible for doing the research of how they came to be," I explained.

"I know Seymour Reichlin," Randi Epstein said, as if she did not believe me. Then I remembered that I had photos on my phone from the visit with Dr. Reichlin and his family. In one he's holding a framed photo of Ellie and I'm holding one of my mother. We're in my living room, surrounded by our children, everyone beaming. When I found it, I showed it to both women.

Finally, she believed me.

It turned out that she too was a professor of English and public health at Yale and had recently asked Dr. Reichlin to review a book she had written on hormones. I turned my attention back to Harriet, who said she had to fight with Harvard to use the image of Renty in her book. Her perseverance paid off and she was finally granted permission.

"At first, I fought with them too," I explained. "But then I decided that I was not going to ask them anymore, and just started using the image."

Harvard only seemed to allow use of the images if Agassiz was not referenced in a negative way.

Seymour and I have since become very close friends, and the

more we spoke about Ellie's experience at the Peabody, the more I began to see what Harvard was protecting. A year after Ellie's piece was published, the museum made it impossible for her to continue working there. "The director wanted her to do clerical work," Dr. Reichlin said. She wound up leaving the museum in 1978.

When I asked Dr. Reichlin what drove her, to risk her job, to tell this story, his response was: "Ellie was so troubled whenever Harvard allowed those pictures to be published. She knew it was important that people knew that this had happened—but she also worried. She'd say to me, 'Seymour, someday the descendants of these people will recognize the degrading ways in which they were photographed—and treated.'"

Ellie recognized back then that Harvard needed to be a better custodian of these artifacts, and that one day, a family member, like me, would come forward and voice their outrage at Harvard's unethical stewardship. All I could think was, What a visionary.

12

The Making of a Dream Team

That same fall, Attorney Crump called.

"I think I've found our Connecticut attorney," he said. "Have you heard of Mike Koskoff?"

I certainly had. His firm was one of Connecticut's largest practices, known as the "giant slayers" for going up against huge corporations. At the time, Koskoff, Koskoff & Bieder had been in the news for representing nine of the families who lost loved ones in the Sandy Hook Elementary School massacre in Newtown, Connecticut, in 2012. They took an unprecedented approach of suing Remington, the gun manufacturer that made the AR-15 rifles used in the murders of twenty children and four adults. This was the first time a gun manufacturer was being held accountable for the damage caused by their product. This was precisely the kind of out-of-the-box thinking my case needed.

Ben was not licensed to practice law in Connecticut, so we needed to find a lawyer who, like him, would not be intimidated by

Harvard. I could not have dreamed up a better co-counsel than Mike Koskoff.

Ben told me that he had met Mike on the set of *Marshall*, the Hollywood biopic about Thurgood Marshall, who became the first Black Supreme Court justice in 1967. Mike cowrote the film with his son Jacob Koskoff—and Ben had a cameo role. At the end of the movie, Ben, playing a lawyer, approaches Marshall, beautifully acted by Chadwick Boseman, and says, "We need you for another case."

Sybrina Fulton and Tracy Martin, Trayvon's parents, were cast as Ben's clients in this very symbolic moment, illustrating how Marshall paved the way for lawyers like Ben Crump to continue fighting for civil rights.

"I have a good feeling about this," Ben said.

I did too.

Mike Koskoff was also a renowned civil rights attorney who had worked with his father, Theodore Koskoff, to represent Lonnie McLucas, a New Haven member of the Black Panthers accused of murder in the late 1960s. That led to Mike representing Black police officers in Bridgeport, Connecticut, who were fighting to integrate its force, which prompted a similar campaign for fire departments in New Haven and Stratford.

Ben introduced me to Mike via email and that was the start of another deeply meaningful relationship. What stood out most to me was Mike's excitement about the case. He understood from our first conversation that this was a landmark. He also saw it as an opportunity to tell the history of slavery in a new way.

"To prevail in court, you have to capture the hearts and minds of the jurors," was one of the first things Mike said to me. He came from a family of entertainers and his first love was theater. He even went to school for drama, but realized that he was not the best actor, so he went back to law school. The combination—supreme storyteller and brilliant legal mind—was Mike's superstrength.

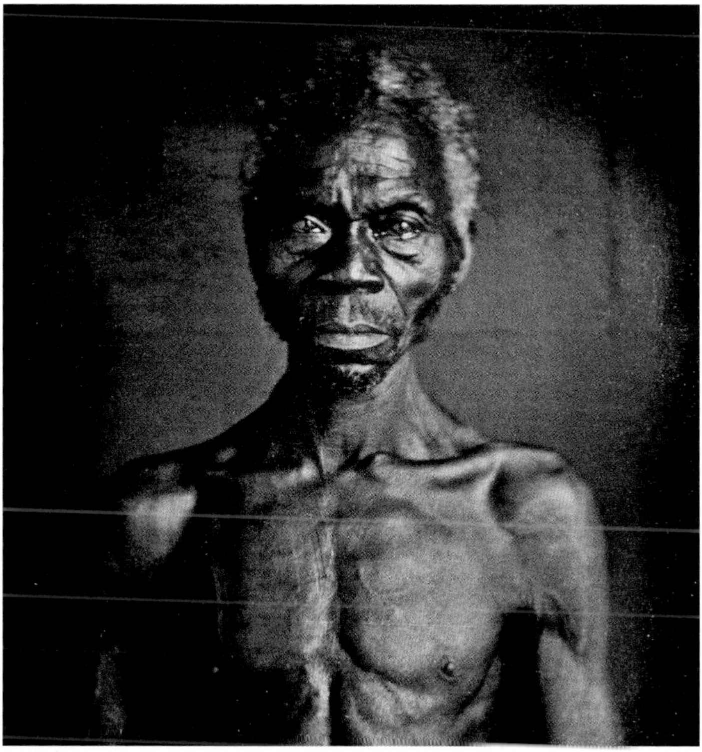

Renty Taylor,
Congo Renty,
Papa Renty.
*Eraza Collection/
Alamy Stock Photo*

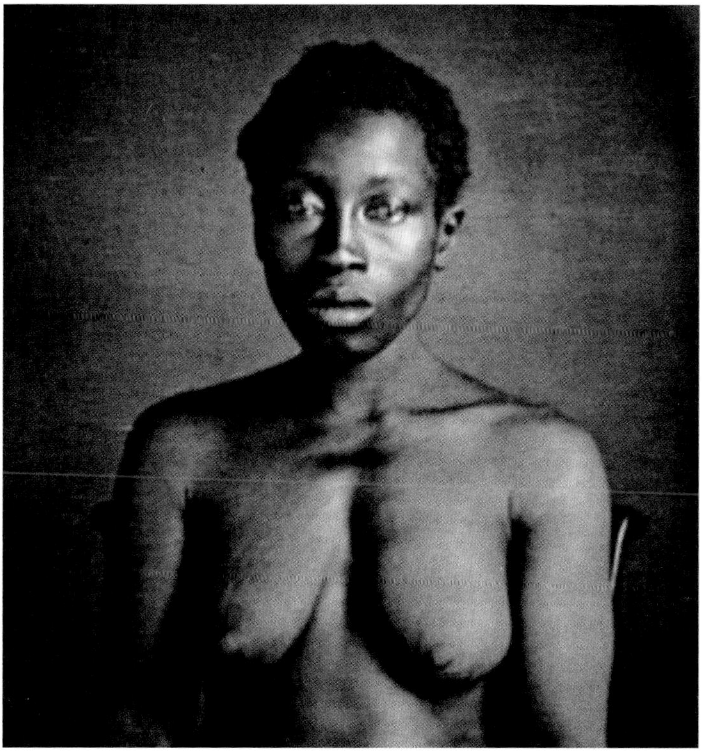

Delia Taylor,
Renty Taylor's
Daughter.
*The Picture
Art Collection/
Alamy Stock*

My mom,
Mattye Pearl Thompson Lanier,
the keeper of our family story.
Courtesy of the author.

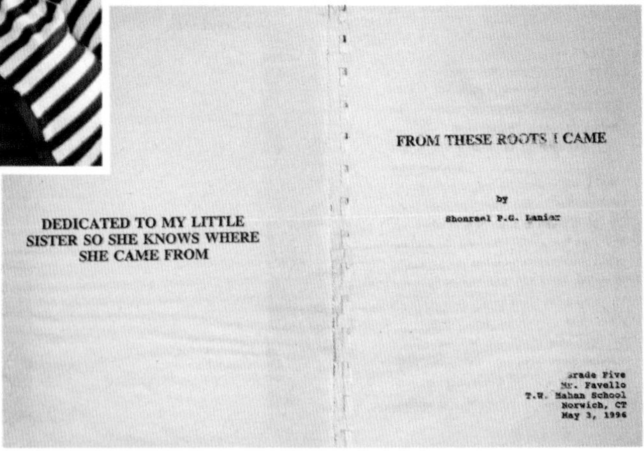

FROM THESE ROOTS I CAME

by

Shonrael P.G. Lanier

DEDICATED TO MY LITTLE SISTER SO SHE KNOWS WHERE SHE CAME FROM

Grade Five
Mr. Favello
T.W. Mahan School
Norwich, CT
May 3, 1996

Shonrael Lanier's fifth grade research report written in 1996 about her Papa Renty.
Courtesy of the author.

Research for this book.
Courtesy of the author.

Image of the documents collected as research over the years, including a reissued Blue Back Speller by Noah Webster and an image of Papa Renty as depicted by the artist Sasha Huber. *Courtesy of the author.*

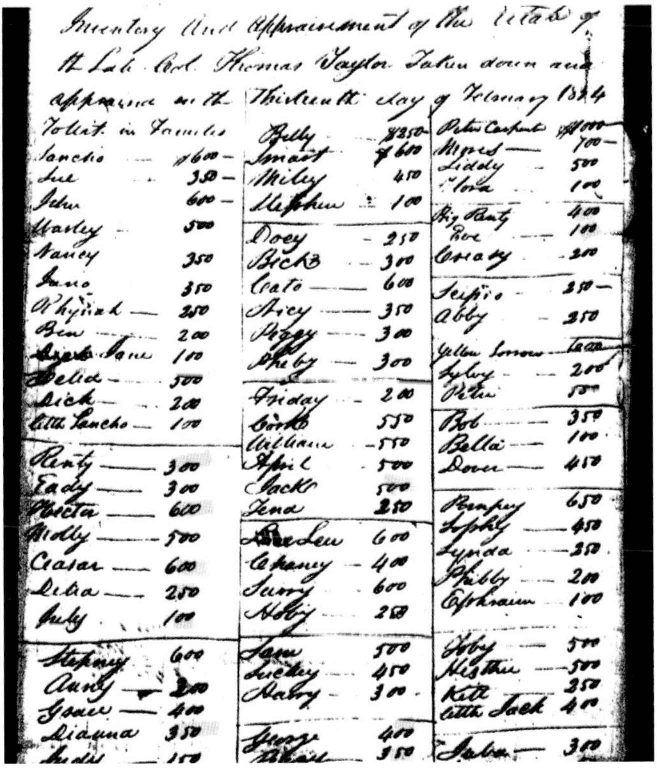

Inventory And Appraisement of the Estate of the Late Col. Thomas Taylor Taken down and appraised on the Thirteenth day of February 1834

Toliver in Families		Belly	$250	Peter Carpenter	$1000
Sancho	$600	Smart	$600	Moses	700
Sue	350	Miley	450	Liddy	500
John	600	Matthew	100	Flora	100
Harley	500	Doey	250	Big Renty	400
Nancy	350	Beck	300	Eve	100
Juno	350	Cato	600	Creasy	200
Rhyiah	250	Aicey	350	Scipio	350
Ben	200	Peggy	300	Abby	250
Sarah Jane	100	Sheby	300	Yellow Simon	[illegible]
Delia	500	Friday	200	July	200
Dick	200	Cork	550	Peter	50
Little Sancho	100	William	550	Bob	350
Renty	300	April	500	Bella	100
Eady	300	Jack	500	Dove	450
Hector	600	Jena	250	Pompey	650
Molly	500	Reuben	600	Sophy	450
Caesar	600	Chaney	400	Lynda	350
Delia	250	Sunny	600	Phebby	200
July	100	Holly	250	Ephraim	100
Stepney	600	Sam	500	Toby	500
Aunty	200	Luckey	450	Hesther	500
Grace	400	Harry	300	Kett	250
Dianna	350			Little Jack	400
[illegible]	150	[illegible]	400 / 350	[illegible]	300

The Colonel Thomas Taylor's South Carolina 1834 slave index, which groups the people he enslaved by family members: Renty, Eddy, Hector, Molly, Caesar, Delia, and July are in one group; Big Renty, Eve, and Creasy are in another. *Courtesy of the author.*

Item 8th. To my son Benjamin Walter Taylor I give and be-
queath the following slaves and their increase vis: Carpenter
Prince, Hannah his wife, and their children(Except Jenney)
also Eve and William James Phoebe and John Children of
Hannah Thompson.
Item 9th. To my daughter Nannie W. Mazyck I give and be-
queath the following slaves and their increase vis: July
(brother of Eve) and Jenney and her two children.
Item 11th. In making the division of my negroes among my
children under the Sixth Clause of this my last will and
testament, I desire that the negroes herin specifically
bequeathed to my said children, and also any negroes here-

Transcriptions for Items 8 and 9:
To my son Benjamin Walter Taylor I give and bequeath the following slaves and their increase vis: Carpenter Prince, Hannah his wife, and their children (Except Jenney) also Eve and William James Phoebe and John Children of Hannah Thompson.
Item 9th. To my daughter Nannie W. Mazyck I give and bequeath the following slaves and their increase vis: July (brother of Eve) and Jenney and her two children.
In Benjamin Franklin Taylor's typed will from Alabama, he refers to July as the brother of Eve, thus connecting the two families as one.
Courtesy of the author.

Image of the many yucca plants that fill the Childs cemetery, a historic slave burial ground in Columbia, South Carolina. There, plants were used to mark the final resting place of the enslaved buried there.
Courtesy of the author.

Tamara Lanier in front of the Peabody after the interview with the *Crimson* on April 6, 2018.
Courtesy of the author.

Sasha Huber placing a plaque at the apex of the Swiss mountain she renamed Rentyhorn as part of her art intervention. Photo: Siro Micheroli. *Courtesy of Sasha Huber.*

Tamara Lanier at the De-mounting Agassiz event in Grindelwald, Switzerland. In photo: (right to left) Hans Fässler; the Swiss-Haitian artist Sasha Huber; Roger Busngi Puati, Congolese minister of the Swiss Reformed Church and historian; Kanyana Mutombo, Congolese journalist; Tamara Lanier; the German historian Hans Fassler; and Christian Anderegg, mayor of Grindelwald, Switzerland. *Courtesy of the author.*

Rich Morrison and Tamara Lanier being interviewed by David Grubin in Lanier's living room on December 15, 2018.
Courtesy of the author.

Tamara Lanier with Attorney Michael Koskoff at Quinnipiac University on March 29, 2018, where Mike was presented the Thurgood Marshall Award by the Quinnipiac Black Law Students Association.
Courtesy of the author.

The Reichlins and the Laniers: The Reichlin and the Lanier families meet for the first time, at Tamara Lanier's home, holding images of the storytellers in their respective families: Ellie Reichlin and Mattye Thompson Lanier, as well as Delia, who brought them all together.
Courtesy of the author.

Tamara Lanier and Gabrielle Foreman, the Paterno Family Professor of American Literature and Professor of African American Studies and History at Penn State University, pray over the remains of Fortune, an enslaved man who died in 1798, at a memorial event at the Connecticut State Capitol Rotunda in Hartford. This photo led to the 2014 *Hartford Courant* article "In Search of a Truer Picture of Papa Renty."

Associated Press

Attorney Benjamin Crump, Tamara Lanier, and attorney Josh Koskoff at Harvard University on June 20, 2019, when they delivered the letter signed by Agassiz descendants who asked that the Renty and Delia daguerreotypes be returned to the Lanier family.

Courtesy David Grubin Productions, Inc.

Shonrael Lanier, Tamara Lanier, and Megan Lanier-Gomez at the Connecticut Legislative Office Building in Hartford, Connecticut, on May 15, 2015, for the Women of the Year Ceremony. *Courtesy of the author.*

A photo collage of Tamara Lanier, Papa Renty, and Mattye Pearl Thompson Lanier created by Shonrael Lanier. *Courtesy of the author.*

"We must be the best storyteller. If we tell your story in the most compelling way, not only will we prevail in the court of public opinion but in the court of law as well," he said.

Mike also believed that my oral history, combined with the genealogical proof I had unearthed, established beyond any reasonable doubt that Renty was my ancestor. Mike knew from our first meeting this was about reparations. It was about repairing the harm that Harvard inflicted on my enslaved ancestors. He also understood that the word could be a distraction from the important legal questions this case raised. Yet he believed that our case would test the legal system in a way that had never been done before.

"There is no legal precedent," he explained. "And until now, no complaint has challenged the courts to look at the harms caused by slavery and offer a just remedy. With this case, we will force the courts to do so."

Every conversation with Mike was an exploration of complex legal strategies, which was intertwined with his profound understanding and acknowledgment of the historical struggles caused by chattel slavery. He also understood the irony of the role Harvard played in this evil institution and the racism that has marred this country ever since. In one of our many meetings, he said, "Historical amnesia, particularly where racism is concerned, is an American tradition. But Harvard's transgressions run much deeper." He went on to summarize precisely what Harvard has done to protect the role they have played in that history:

"In 1976, Harvard discovered that the daguerreotypes were stored on its campus, realized their incalculable value as the earliest known photographs of American slaves, and commenced a decades-long campaign to sanitize the history of the images and exploit them for prestige and profit."

I sat there, nodding my head, in awe of how clearly he understood what had happened and the impact.

"That as a direct descendant of Renty and Delia, you have asked Harvard to recognize your lineage and relinquish the daguerreotypes to the family," he said, growing even more animated. "By turns dismissive and arrogant, Harvard has refused to do either."

"Precisely," I said, so relieved to have someone so studied and brilliant distilling the issues that had plagued me since I first approached Harvard. And I had written a subsequent letter to Drew Gilpin Faust on October 27, 2017, asking Harvard to relinquish the daguerreotypes of Congo Renty and Delia to me following the Universities and Slavery: Bound by History conference.

On November 13, 2017, I received a nonresponsive response from Harvard, another failure to address my request.

"Harvard has asserted an exclusive right to possess, restrict access to, and profit from the daguerreotypes—without ever explaining the basis for that purported entitlement," he continued. "Harvard has also denigrated the legitimacy of your heritage, which is established based on a rich and detailed family history passed down through generations."

This was where I got emotional and had to acknowledge the generational trauma caused by slavery. Every rebuttal, every refusal to acknowledge me and my story was an insult to my mother, and her grandfather before her—and ultimately Papa Renty. The keepers of our family stories and legacy.

"Every day that Harvard maintains those positions compounds the injustices inflicted on Renty and Delia in its name, and further harms you as their descendant and the rightful owner of images taken without their consent," Mike said. "By denying your superior claim to the daguerreotypes, Harvard is perpetuating the systematic subversion of Black property rights that began during slavery and continued for a century thereafter."

He was on a roll, and I was not about to stop him. Every point he was making articulated my own feelings.

"And by contesting your claim of lineage, Harvard is shamelessly capitalizing on the intentional damage done to Black Americans' genealogy by a century's worth of policies that forcibly separated families, erased enslaved family names, withheld birth and death records, and criminalized literacy," he said, with emphasis on *forcibly*, *erased*, and *criminalized*, as I nodded along. He understood. He got it.

To help tell this complex story, Mike reached out to his cousin David Grubin, a world-renowned director, documentarian, and cinematographer responsible for countless historical films, including one on Abraham Lincoln. David was also the recipient of three George Foster Peabody Awards, five Writers Guild prizes, and ten Emmys.

I met David that summer in Mike's office. He wanted to focus on the genealogy—proving my connection to the world makes my claim on the artifacts obvious. Then, once we established that I am the lineal descendant of Congo Renty in the Zealy daguerreotypes, whom I know to be my Papa Renty, he would cover the legal case since we all knew it would be historic.

This was 2018 and I had spent the past eight years since my mother's death trying to get the media to tell my story. Now I had Ben Crump, Mike Koskoff, and David Grubin all together. It was the making of a dream team. And this team wanted to help me tell my story on a large platform, one Harvard could not shut down. I was thrilled.

David started filming that fall. I introduced him to Rich, whom he interviewed, and then we traveled to South Carolina, where David interviewed Toni Carrier, a renowned genealogist who was responsible for piecing together the amazing genealogical journey of First Lady Michelle Obama. Toni had been instrumental in unearthing the historical ties that bind my family with the Taylors as they traveled the South. During a subsequent interview with a reporter, and after reviewing my documentation, Toni stated, "Tammy is who she says she is."

Toni also offered an alternative understanding as to the enslaved woman known as "Drana": "It is very likely that she has been misidentified and that her true name is not 'Drana' but 'Diana,'" she explained. In a book published by the Peabody, *To Make Their Own Way in the World: The Enduring Legacy of the Zealy Daguerreotypes*, a Harvard researcher ponders the following:

"Drana, it should be noted, is not listed in the 1852 slave inventory of Benjamin F. Taylor's estate, nor have I discovered her name in the many related inventories for local planters and their relatives that I have reviewed; this suggests that either she was sold before 1852 and a record of the sale has not been found, or that she perished at one of Taylor's slave labor camps sometime between May 1850 and August 1852. She may have been buried in an unmarked grave in the slave section of the old Taylor family graveyard near the corner of Richland and Barnwell Streets in present-day Columbia."

But if we consider the profound insight as offered by Toni Carrier, that "Drana," like many of my other enslaved ancestors, has been misidentified, and that her true name is "Diana," then she doesn't die or disappear, as Harvard surmises above. In fact, "Diana" is in both the Colonel Thomas Taylor and Benjamin Franklin Taylor slave indexes, grouped with Jack and/or in proximity with Papa Renty's children. This was yet another example of the hubris of Harvard and the notion that only they can speculate about the daguerreotypes—only they can tell my enslaved ancestor's story. They were wrong.

The filming wrapped up with a visit to the construction site of the International African American Museum in Charleston and a trip back to the Child's Cemetery, which was this time narrated by the two Koskoff attorneys and historians Preston Tisdale and Craig Smith. Our attention was directed to the thick, unruly, and invasive brush that appeared to grow in a wild and unkempt manner. Among the neglect was a sea of yucca plants. What I learned broke my heart.

"The wave of yucca plants that filled this cemetery were used as markers," Craig explained. "These resilient plants were planted in African American and enslaved burial grounds to mark the graves of loved ones."

There were so many yucca plants! So many unnamed souls who toiled their entire lives to build wealth for others. Yet in death they were thrown away, as if they never existed. Overcome by loss and sadness, I had to walk away.

Simultaneously, Mike had begun introducing me to all the attorneys who would help build our case: the goal was to force the legal question, Who has the legal right to the violence of the past? He assembled a brilliant legal team, which included Mark Marderosian, a lawyer who had successfully petitioned foreign governments on behalf of victims of the Holocaust and secured reparations for them. One of his tasks was to do a deep dive on Harvard's historical ties to slavery. Carey Reilly, another lawyer in Mike's firm, focused on backing up all my already credible genealogy. Craig Smith and Preston Tisdale were also hard at work. Craig was originally from Charleston, South Carolina, and would focus on the history of that key state. Tisdale, a Brown graduate and past Brown alumni president who played an intricate role in that university's early study of its ties to slavery, would focus on African American history and how it related to my case. Each one brought their own unique talent to the table.

Mike was most excited about telling the history of slavery in a way that proved its relevance today: how it did not end but it evolved to sharecropping, then convict leasing, debt peonage laws, vagrancy laws, Jim Crow, mass incarceration, and racial profiling today. He wanted to shine a light on the fact that Harvard was responsible for the propaganda that enslaved people were subhuman. Harvard's leadership supported Agassiz when he commissioned the images—so they were complicit. Mike also wanted to give a fuller picture of history that included the North's direct involvement.

"Cotton was the thread that held the North and South together," he explained. The plantations in the South supplied the factories in the North—the biggest, we'd soon learn, was the Boston Manufacturing Company, owned and operated by Harvard graduate Francis Cabot Lowell in eastern Massachusetts.

Mike's office had a big conference room where all the attorneys would gather to discuss the case. Ben Crump would Zoom in, and I'd usually show up in person, or every so often on Zoom. These discussions happened several times a week as we compared notes and mapped out our strategy. Mike sat at the head of the table like a beloved professor and laid out the legal framework of the complaint.

"Slavery was abolished one hundred and fifty-six years ago, but Renty and Delia remain enslaved in Cambridge, Massachusetts. Their images, like their bodies before, remain subject to control and appropriation by the powerful, and their familial identities denied to them," Mike said at one of many meetings. "It was an act of both love and resistance that Renty and Delia's kin kept their memories and stories alive for well over a century. It is unconscionable that Harvard will not allow Ms. Lanier to, at long last, bring Renty and Delia home."

Everyone around that table would be nodding in agreement. His ability to comprehend, integrate, and articulate what this case was about was stunning to us all.

"The story of this case spans one hundred and seventy-five years. It is a story about opportunism, greed, and profound moral abdication by one of the country's most revered educational institutions," Mike said. "It is a story about the extent to which history is told and appropriated by the powerful—and denied to the powerless."

In addition to assembling top-notch lawyers, Mike had also hired investigators in Columbia and Charleston to unearth more evidence connecting me to the Taylor family, trying to figure out how my ancestors went from South Carolina to Mount Meigs, Montgomery County, Alabama. Carey worked with them to research the Taylor family and discovered through a patchwork quilt of official documentation that included the probate will, cemetery records, and census information that the Taylors had plantations all throughout the South—from Virginia to the Carolinas, Georgia, Alabama, and Louisiana too. This correlated with Denise Hardin's research, as well as with Dr. Edmund Taylor's stories of how his family had built churches throughout the South. Carey's research once again proved that they were also proliferating plantations.

Within a few months, she also unearthed Benjamin Franklin Taylor's will in Mount Meigs and then, upon further research, we learned that he and other Taylor family members owned property on Pike Road—the same address as my mother's family home. I cannot tell you how many times I have been asked, How did your great-grandfather Renty Taylor Thompson get to Alabama from South Carolina? This was the proof we were looking for. With that document I can place my family in the small rural community of Mount Meigs on Taylor-owned land and with Benjamin Franklin Taylor's family. Carey found a cemetery record for Jesse Peter Taylor, who was born in South Carolina and migrated to Mount Meigs, where he died and was buried. I knew from Denise Hardin that Jesse was Benjamin Franklin Taylor's brother—and Carey placed him in Mount Meigs. Denise had mentioned Jesse Taylor four years earlier when we spoke, but he did not fit into the puzzle that was my family—until now. One of the things I learned with genealogy is that you will come across clues that might not make sense in the moment of discovery—but will one day. Suddenly, four years later, they did.

As the lawyers were piecing together my case against Harvard, David was interviewing all the key people who helped me along the way, including Rich, Rose, Dr. Reichlin, Shonrael, Megan, and Sonya Hodges-Grantham, the woman I met through Rose who was engaged in a campaign to restore the Child's Cemetery in Columbia. Sonya is the linear descendant of Sancho Thompson, the enslaved person Dr. Edmund Taylor spoke of so lovingly. His name showed up in the Taylor slave indexes with my family members, so I feel certain that he knew or was related to my ancestors.

As I was sharing all my research with Carey and David, I came across an article Rich had sent me right after he discovered the "Black Bodies, White Science" story, which put me on this path. That was when I first saw the image of Congo Renty and knew in my bones and blood that he was my ancestor. My Papa Renty. A week later, on May 24, 2010, Rich sent me another email that read, "Here is some more Renty information.... The Louis Agassiz daguerreotype photography of Renty Taylor that was taken in 1850 could be a picture of the Renty discussed in the below record."

He included a link to an academic paper from Louisiana State University that was translated from French and included a letter from Charles Norwood, the executor of the Turnbull and Joyce estate in Baton Rouge, to a widow named Catherine Turnbull.

"According to this record, Renty was 13 years old in 1800," Rich wrote. "That would make the Renty in the daguerreotype 63 years old. It also states that he was from the coast of New Guinea, which, I believe, is part of the Congo, or at the very least abuts it. This Renty's mother was Rose and his father was Hector."

When I first received this email from Rich, it did not make any sense—much like Denise mentioning Jesse Peter Taylor. Sure, the names were familiar, but I was unable to make the connections.

Now, with all of the genealogical research I had done, I knew that Hector and Rose were in the same family groupings as Congo Renty from the slave indexes. Connecting these dots was electrifying. This was proof that he arrived in the United States prior to the slave embargo of 1808, and that he traveled here with his family. This document also described my Papa Renty as a child who demanded a checkered shirt, and Rose, his mother, as insisting he come home for lunch between running errands. It may seem insignificant to most, but for me it was describing a defiant, confident child, even in times of enslavement—which correlated with my oral history. This statement is in Renty's voice. This was a documented incident when Renty stubbornly insisted on that shirt. That resonated deeply, as did the demanding mother who did her best to care for him under the horrific circumstances. I saw in those moments my own mother. She would move heaven and earth to do whatever needed to be done for her family.

These were needle-in-haystack clues that I was able to find due to all the extraordinary people who wanted to help me prove my kinship. When I shared this paper, which I called the "Little Boy Renty" document, with the lawyers, I noticed that Caesar and Sancho are both mentioned as well. Again, I thought, That's familiar! Caesar and Sancho both show up in the Taylor slave indexes. They did know one another.

I spent hours on the phone with Carey, talking her through the dead ends and helping her put the puzzle pieces together with my oral history. My family traveled with the Taylor children throughout the South, which was how they were able to stay connected and reconnect after slavery ended.

Learning that Benjamin Franklin Taylor's brother Jesse Peter Taylor lived in Mount Meigs explained how Tena, Renty Taylor Thompson's mother, arrived in Mount Meigs as well. It was ultimately discovered that his plantation was on Pike Road—the same road in

Mount Meigs where my mother and many other of my family members lived. And where the Antioch Church is. I felt then that I had answered every question about my genealogy. This reminded me that my story was purpose-driven and ordained by a divine power who set in place all these series of events.

Mike always said the burden of proof was not on me to prove these relations, because of the violence of slavery—which makes this story all that much more unique and powerful. I *can* prove it. I can put my ancestors on Taylor-owned land in South Carolina and Alabama.

The fact that Harvard had said, from the beginning, "She can never prove it," was demeaning and offensive, and each time they repeated this publicly it only amplified that pain. But it was also a source of inspiration. It drove me to prove Harvard wrong.

As Carey and I pieced together and backed up my genealogy, Mark Marderosian was doing extensive research into Harvard's history with enslavement, which he compiled into a thirty-four-page report with the title "Harvard's Cotton White Heart."

This was a whole new education for me, not just about the history of slavery in the United States but of northern complicity and how they perpetuated the racism that allowed it to flourish. Mark made it clear in his impeccable research that Harvard, during the time of the great slavery debate that ultimately led to the Civil War and emancipation, was supporting enslavement through Agassiz's theories. In the mid-nineteenth century, cotton was the equivalent of cash in the South, which fed and funded the manufacturing factories up north.

In his report, Mark wrote: "Harvard was literally giving aid and comfort to a belligerent enemy, the nascent Confederacy and those Southern slave-owners whose: (1) primitive, pre-industrial plantation economy would have collapsed in short order without African-American slave labor; and (2) whose primary crop, the World's finest and most sought-after cotton fiber, fed the voracious Massachusetts cotton mills whose owners launched our First Industrial Revolution, while building and sustaining their alma mater, Harvard."

I was stunned—but not surprised. This document was revelatory and helped me understand just how complicit Harvard was, and still is, in perpetuating white supremacy. Francis Cabot Lowell was a Harvard graduate who founded the Boston Manufacturing Company. His father, John Lowell, married into the slave-trading business and is credited with "creating the now-universal stock company corporate model," as well as "converting Massachusetts from an agriculture-dependent region into a mechanized industrial one—whose principal cultural institution—Harvard—spawned graduates and professors who would help America emerge as a world superpower in the twentieth century."

I also learned from Mark's research that Agassiz was first brought to the United States in 1846 by the cotton milling and textile magnate John Amory Lowell, who sponsored the Swiss "scientist" to give twenty-four lectures over a two-year period in which he begins to spread his theories of his "white supremacist, unapologetically slavery-friendly hypothesis based on ostensibly innate intellectual and capacitive differences between 'the races.'"

Mark's research was groundbreaking: I did not realize just how pervasive Agassiz's theories were—and still are. As a professor, he had many students who espoused his theories, including Nathaniel Southgate Shaler, who went on to become Harvard's dean of sciences and continued to "advocate extensively on polygenist principles" well after Charles Darwin debunked the ridiculous theory. He also published an article in the *Atlantic Monthly* in November 1884 titled "The Negro Problem," where he described Black children as "lost in the woods, needing the old protection of a strong mastering hand." I was constantly amazed and sickened by just how pernicious Agassiz's racist theories were, and how they proliferated hate.

I met regularly with Mike throughout this research and compilation process as he built my case against Harvard. He loved the impossibility of this story—and the insurmountable odds we were able to overcome. Mike's strategy sessions reminded me of the legendary Knights of the Round Table. I was simply in awe of the brilliance in the room. Through these sessions, I learned that Louis Agassiz had also met with President Abraham Lincoln and that his racist theories had a profound effect on Lincoln's point of view. This was evident in the debate he had with Stephen A. Douglas, the Illinois senator he was challenging for his seat, on September 18, 1858—just three years before Lincoln was elected president of the United States.

"I am not, nor ever have been, in favor of bringing about in any way the social and political equality of the white and black races, I am not nor ever have been in favor of making voters or jurors of negroes, nor of qualifying them to hold office, nor to intermarry with white people; and I will say in addition to this that there is a physical difference between the white and black races which I believe will forever forbid the two races living together on terms of social and political equality," Lincoln stated. "And inasmuch as they cannot so live, while they do remain together there must be the position of superior and inferior, and I as much as any other man am in favor of having the superior position assigned to the white race."

I was floored. This was a side of Lincoln I had not studied. I had majored in history in college, and had never learned about Louis Agassiz, or how his theories had influenced so many of our nation's leaders.

Mike was excited for the opportunity to share the full story of how intertwined the North and South were during this time when Agassiz commissioned the daguerreotypes. He was also thrilled to use replevin, a law that was created in the 1800s to return fugitive slaves to their owners, to our advantage. The law argues that property must be returned to its rightful owner, and in this case, Mike argued, I was more a rightful owner of the artifacts than Harvard. He was excited because it was a law created out of the Fugitive Slave Act, which white slaveholders used to recover their slave property. As descendants, we were embracing replevin to recover the property of our enslaved ancestors.

From the moment I met Mike, I had a new assignment every day—something to send or research or respond to. In the fall of 2018, I noticed that Mike's daily deluge of emails were fewer and far between. That struck me as odd. We had plans to meet David in New York, and Mike wrote to say he could not go.

"I am not feeling well," he explained.

I was disappointed.

Then, on November 19, 2018, Mike wrote me another email: "Tammy, I have very good news about Ta-Nehisi Coates. He is very excited about the project and wants to meet you."

He had been in touch with Coates about the unfortunate Harvard symposium. No one at Harvard had mentioned me to the acclaimed writer. Mike was arranging a meeting so I could share my story with him.

One week later, I got another email.

> Tammy, I know you have been concerned about my health, so I wanted to update you.
>
> Recently, I was diagnosed with pancreatic cancer. It had already spread beyond the pancreas when I was diagnosed so it cannot be treated with surgery. Last week, I started a course of chemotherapy that I will continue every other week for the foreseeable future. Though the chemo makes me sick some days, for the most part, I am handling it well. I try to be positive at all times, and that attitude will continue.
>
> Meanwhile, I consider your case of great historical

importance, and we are treating it as such. We have assembled a very talented team of lawyers to work on it and great things happen when great minds get together. We have put together a complaint that should rock Harvard back on its heels. We are fortunate to have one of the nation's outstanding documentary filmmakers on your side. There are new developments daily and when Ta-Nehisi Coates surfaces on our side, it could be a game changer.

The case has what many see as overwhelming legal obstacles, but, as recent news stories show, history is on our side. I want you to know that I am with you 100% and will continue to dedicate my personal efforts to bring your case to a favorable conclusion with all of the energy I have. If the time ever comes where I need to step back, our team will be there to carry it on.

Mike

I have been dealt many blows in this journey—beginning with losing my mom. I felt a deep sadness when I learned that Ellie had died before I got to meet her. This was different. I felt, in my heart, that God would not put Mike in my life for such an important historical milestone only to take him away. That could not be.

On November 26, 2018, I responded:

My Dear Attorney Koskoff, it is with such a heavy heart that I say that I am so very sorry to hear this; but I am encouraged, and I pray that you stay encouraged as well, because God has joined us together for a Divine purpose!

I often think about what we are doing, the historical significance and its relevance to current events. I marvel at how a story, almost 200-years-old, can today be

> substantiated with official records; I am at a loss to understand how somebody like me could garner the attention of mega-stars such as yourself, Attorney Crump and David Grubin?
>
> I say this all to say that we are a chosen people and God has brought us together to make a claim that will ask this country and the world to search its soul. Please never forget that God has chosen you to lead this very important assignment and no matter how long it takes you will see it through! In everything there is a season and a time for every purpose; that in every great test there is a greater testimony! Know I will be praying for your health and strength!! Tammy

A week or so later, I had to go to New York City to film something for the documentary, and Mike sent his daughter Sarah to be on the film set with me because he was not well enough to join me. He knew that I did not like being in the city on my own.

Sarah was worried about him. We all were. Mike did not have time to be sick. He worked on this case every waking moment—through chemo and hospital stays. He made calls from his hospital bed, determined not only to finish the complaint but to be there to file it.

He told his son Josh, who was a senior partner at the law firm, that he wanted this case to be filed in his lifetime—he was known for Sandy Hook and for his work with the Black Panther Party. Yet, he often said, this case was the one he was most proud of.

March 18, 2019, was Mike's seventy-fourth birthday—and on March 19, 2019, we filed the lawsuit.

We all met in New York City, across the street from the Harvard Club, for the press conference. Mike came. He was thinner than I remembered him but still had such a feisty attitude. I felt his strength. The lawyers had already been in touch with various press outlets and gave the *New York Times* an exclusive. They ran a front-page story on our historic case that same morning: "Who Should Own Photos of Slaves? The Descendants, Not Harvard, a Lawsuit Says."

Beneath a photo of me, holding one of the "Free Renty" tote bags Shonrael made, Ben is quoted: "It is unprecedented in terms of legal theory and reclaiming property that was wrongfully taken.... Renty's descendants may be the first descendants of slave ancestors to be able to get their property rights."

I flashed back to the moment I posed for a selfie with him two years earlier and said, "I have a case for you. It is about reparations."

When I set out on this journey, to write down our family story, I had no idea that it would lead to this historic moment.

On that same morning of Wednesday, March 19, 2019, the landmark *Lanier v. Harvard* legal complaint was filed with Middlesex Superior Court in Massachusetts. The complaint marks the first time in modern history that an enslaved man and woman would petition the court for their freedom. It opens with a quote from Maya Angelou's poem "On the Pulse of Morning": "History, despite its wrenching pain, cannot be unlived, but if faced with courage, need not be lived again."

The five basic elements of the complaint were:

1. That we brought this action against Harvard for its wrongful seizure, possession, and expropriation of the cultural property of my Enslaved ancestors.
2. That the daguerreotypes were illegally commissioned in 1850 by Harvard's leading scientist, Louis Agassiz, as part of his quest to "prove" Black people's inherent bio-

logical inferiority and thereby justify their subjugation, exploitation, and segregation.

3. That, at Agassiz's behest, Renty and Delia were stripped naked and forced to pose for the daguerreotypes without consent, dignity, or compensation.
4. That Harvard legitimized Agassiz's poisonous myth of white superiority.
5. That Harvard has never reckoned with this grotesque chapter in its history, let alone atoned for it.

When Harvard commissioned the daguerreotypes, slavery was an illegal act, abolished by the commonwealth of Massachusetts in 1783. In a suit brought by Quock Walker, Chief Justice William Cushing of the Massachusetts Supreme Judicial Court explained that slavery was abolished by the new state constitution, which had rendered slavery illegal because "all men are born free and equal." He concluded that slavery was "inconsistent with our own conduct and constitution." Thus, when Harvard commissioned the daguerreotypes via Agassiz, their employee, later in 1850, it was illegal to do so.

Our attorneys argued that it was a basic tenet of common law that the wrongdoer is never rewarded with the fruit of their tort, that another basic precept of common law is the protection of one from the wrongful acts of another. And finally, that Harvard was a tortfeasor, responsible for irreparable harm.

This all happened less than two years after the Harvard conference on slavery and universities. Prior to this historic moment, members of "Team Renty" were sworn to secrecy. The attorneys were adamant that neither I, my family, nor any member of the "dream team" could speak publicly about our intent to sue. The element of surprise was an important part of the legal strategy, making it imperative that the details of the complaint were not leaked publicly. It was said over and over: "This case will be tried in two courts—the Court of Law and the Court of Public Opinion—and we must prevail in both."

Now that the news was out, I was inundated with media requests—*Democracy Now!*, TV shows with Ben, news stories with Mike and some of his attorneys. This went on for weeks, during which time I was in daily contact with all the attorneys—so it struck me when I had not heard from Mike for a few days.

I texted Sarah to ask, "How is he doing?"

She responded, "Not so well."

On April 25, 2019, five weeks after we filed the lawsuit, Mike Koskoff died.

The *New York Times* ran a lengthy obituary that heralded him as a "Fierce Litigator in Momentous Fights" who "won record malpractice awards, mounted racial job-discrimination battles, and sued gunmakers whose weapons were used in the Sandy Hook school massacre." I knew all of that, and yet there was no way an article could capture what he meant to me.

When I received the text from Sarah confirming what I already suspected, I was driving. I pulled over to respond to both her and Josh:

> I knew your dad for only a year, and I feel such a loss! I can only imagine the difficult goodbye having spent a lifetime with such an amazing person. He was the best at everything he did and each and every time we talked; I learned something new. He was a kind and giving soul who didn't just give of himself, but he always gave the very best of himself! I'm going to miss his energy and excitement and I'm going to miss the fondness I felt when I knew he approved. Somewhere I read that, "We will all one day lose someone

we love, that the true test of character is what we do once they are gone." It's good to know that your dad's interest will live on in his children.

Tammy

When I spoke with his son Josh, who would take on my case, he told me, "Tammy, my dad said this was the most important case he had ever taken on."

I also knew that, in my heart and bones, like I knew Congo Renty was my ancestor. Mike believed me, from the moment we first met. He also understood how my story was in so many ways the American story of slavery and the harm it has caused. He knew that in my story we could prove to the world that Renty and Delia and every single person stolen from Africa and enslaved in this country deserve to be recognized and celebrated, to be reconnected and rewarded. And more than anything, to be loved.

He knew what I knew.

Losing him, at this moment: what a bond to break.

13

The Agassiz Descendants—"Shame Makes You Not Curious"

In the flurry of messages I received after we filed, one came in the form of a Facebook message—from Marian Moore, Louis Agassiz's great-great-great-granddaughter. I opened it apprehensively: "Hi Tamara. I read about your important lawsuit in the Times. I applaud you. You are 'a direct descendent of Renty' and I am a direct descendent of Louis Agassiz—who wants to see justice and liberation made real. I was trying to see how I might be of service to y/our cause. If you are interested in being in touch, my email address is.... At your service, warmly and in solidarity, Marian Moore."

While blown away by this message, I was not sure how to respond. Louis Agassiz had such negative feelings about Black people, and so I assumed that feeling had been passed down through the generations. This note came as a surprise on so many levels. I was still reeling from the media interest in the case, and while the majority of the responses were overwhelmingly positive, I was still dismayed by any negative comments about my story in the press. While there were very few, I didn't want to open myself up to the possibility of another attack. What if this was a troll? Yet something inside me said, Don't hold her ancestor's beliefs against her. See what she has to say.

I responded to her message, thanking her for reaching out: "You sound sincere. I'm open to speaking with you."

Her message back to me was immediate:

> Oh Tamara, I have chills. Thank you for responding. Since I wrote to you, my son, sister and nephew have been working on an open letter to Harvard in support of your case. We provided siblings, nephews, nieces, etc. with background information while a small group of us have been working on the letter. We want to share it with the family to get as many signatures as possible. We will have another draft ready soon and would love to share it with you before we share it with the family to get signatures—and then our plan is to share it more broadly. When would you like to talk? Would be great to do it by Zoom or FaceTime or something. I am available right now . . . or can make a date for whenever. Please let me know some available times. Hearing from you is bringing me to tears.
>
> Thank you.
>
> Warmly, Marian

Her note moved me as well. I wrote back to say as much and sent my phone number, which she called that same day. That was the beginning of a unique sisterhood, one I believe can provide an example of how we can all begin to heal from the wounds of enslavement that this country has ignored for far too long. The conversation I had with Marian was the beginning of that between us, two women on opposite sides of a deeply painful moment in history.

"I'd heard so many stories growing up about how my famous ancestor had discovered how glaciers moved," Marian explained. "It wasn't until my thirties that I learned from a sibling that he had problematic views about race. I'm ashamed to say that I did not pursue learning anything more—until I read about your lawsuit."

That, she said, was a call to action.

"My son Eamon is a journalist, and my nephew Eli is a social justice activist. It was Eli's idea to write an open letter to Harvard, which Eamon and my sister Susanna worked on together."

Marian invited me to join the next family Zoom to meet everyone and learn more about their written response to Harvard. I was so intrigued—and just like my anticipation of speaking with Dr. Reichlin after receiving his letter, I could not wait for the following Saturday morning, when the Zoom had been scheduled. When I clicked the link from my kitchen table, I saw Marian's face for the first time. It was so open and warm. I immediately knew that I was in safe hands. She was sitting with her son Eamon in their kitchen in Minnesota, and I could tell they were both as excited as I was. Then she connected Eli and her sister Susanna, both of whom were in California. I saw the resemblance in the sisters' sparkling blue eyes, silver-gray hair, and soft smiles.

"Thank you for allowing us to be part of this," Susanna said. "We want to apologize for the acts our ancestor committed and know that would never be enough to repair the harm done to you and your family—or to Renty and Delia."

I had to hold back my tears.

"That makes me very emotional," was all I could say.

"Me as well," Susanna replied. "I always knew that there was something controversial about our ancestor. There were rumblings.

But everyone focused on his great naturalist accomplishments—not the shameful racist theories. When we read about your lawsuit, it made me realize that shame makes you not curious."

I was so struck by that—and by this family's willingness to confront that shame. To move past it to action. I was also deeply moved that Marian's son Eamon was on the call, as was his cousin Eli, the son of Paul, Marian and Susanna's brother.

"I was shocked and deeply troubled by the fact that this was an ancestor of mine," Eli said. "I've been an activist since I was a teenager. I knew I had racist ancestors—but I did not know anything about my connection to Louis Agassiz or how dangerous his views were."

As I was listening to these family members speak, I felt a wave of relief. They were unafraid to face their own racist history. They understood that this was an opportunity to move forward, and to begin addressing the immense pain and destruction caused by Agassiz's views. I found it so brave. I also learned that Eli's activism was focused on formerly incarcerated people in the San Francisco Bay area, and that Marian worked with an organization called Jubilee Justice. She helped organize gatherings of people who were descendants of enslaved people and enslavers.

"I just did not know I had my own dark connection to this work," she said.

I was not surprised to learn that Susanna, Marian, and Paul's father was a progressive priest who had worked with both Thurgood Marshall and Martin Luther King Jr. during the civil rights movement. Marian shared a passage that King wrote about her father in his book *Where Do We Go from Here: Chaos or Community?* In it, King discusses the importance of white people working in the civil rights movement: "During the Meredith March in Mississippi, when some of the young activists were saying, 'We don't want whites,' Bishop Moore of the Episcopal Church said to Walter Fauntroy of the

Washington Southern Christian Leadership Conference . . . 'That march is protesting a moral evil, an evil detrimental to me and every American. I'm going down there.'"

Marian, Susanna, and Paul were raised understanding that enslavement was wrong for all parties, white and Black, and that both were impacted by the violent institution. This further proved Papa Renty's power to move people. His gaze in that daguerreotype was not just compelling me to do the right thing—to free him and Delia once and for all from all the racist assumptions that had held them, and all Black people, back for centuries. It compelled white people strong enough to get past the shame of enslavement and confront the racism it has spawned, and work actively to undo it. These Agassiz descendants understood that legacy—how their ancestor's theories fed white supremacy and systemic racism. They also were able to admit to me that my story emboldened them to look critically at their own histories.

It was Eli's idea to take this a step further, into the public realm, by writing a letter to Harvard—and to make a poster of both our families' genealogical trees, presented side by side to make clear that slavery was designed to break Black families apart. When he sent it to me, I was again blown away. He called it *Family Photos*, and whereas the Agassiz descendants were populated with dozens of easily obtained photographs of his ancestors, beginning with Louis Agassiz on one side and Papa Renty on the other, my family tree was sparse.

"What we as white people take for granted, knowing who our ancestors are, is a privilege," Eli said.

That poster made it so painfully clear.

The Agassiz descendants wanted to confront the past, say what they knew to be true, and begin addressing all the harm that had happened as a result. The Taylors, on the other hand, were reluctant. I firmly believe that the evil institution of American chattel slavery persisted for over four hundred years because good people chose to remain silent or turn a blind eye. Silence is violence; silence is complicity. Dr. King knew this; so did Bishop Moore. I knew it; so did Susanna and Marian. In the six weeks between writing me that first message on Facebook and being on this Zoom call, the Moores had mobilized more than forty other relatives to sign a letter they had written collaboratively, supporting my claim as Renty's descendant and wanting to do whatever they could to repair the damage their ancestor had inflicted on my family, as well as the world, vis-à-vis his racist theories.

Meeting them at this moment was another meant-to-be miracle.

As soon as I got off that Zoom, I was so energized, I couldn't wait to tell the attorneys about this development. I wrote a group email to my team, which elicited an array of "Wows!" and "This is amazing!"

I connected Josh with the Moore sisters, who wanted him to review their letter before they sent it to Harvard. They shared the draft with me, and Ben Crump as well. It was May 2019. Drew Faust had retired in June 2018, so their "Open Letter to Harvard University" was addressed to the newly instated "President Lawrence S. Bacow and Members of the Harvard Corporation and Board of Overseers."

> As direct descendants of Louis Agassiz, we celebrate many of his groundbreaking contributions to natural science. We also lament the widespread damage he wrought with the theory of polygenism, which he used to promulgate the supposed inferiority of African people. For too many years we have ignored his role in promoting a pseudoscientific justification for white supremacy. We see this as a collective failure to live up to our values of anti-racism and compassion. Now is the time to name, acknowledge and redress the harm done by Louis Agassiz.

In 1850, to support his theory that Africans descended from a different "zone of creation" than Europeans, and thus were essentially inferior, Agassiz commissioned daguerreotypes of [seven] enslaved people living in South Carolina, [two of whom were] Renty and Delia.

We ask Harvard University to relinquish the daguerreotypes of Renty and Delia to their descendants, including Tamara Lanier, who has filed a lawsuit for their release. As enslaved people, Renty and Delia could not consent to be photographed. They were regarded as property, not human beings.

For Harvard to give the daguerreotypes to Ms. Lanier and her family would begin to make amends for its use of the photos as exhibits for the white supremacist theory Agassiz espoused. It is time for Harvard to recognize Renty and Delia as people. The daguerreotypes are, as Ms. Lanier has said, family photos.

At a time when racism is ascendant, from the streets of Charlottesville to the White House, we believe that both individuals and institutions need to take a stand and acknowledge our part in it, past and present.

To claim that Agassiz was merely reflecting the popular ideas of his era would be selling his legacy short. He was a respected public intellectual and an active, influential advocate of racist ideas and policies. As an elite university, Harvard provided Agassiz intellectual legitimacy, and together, Harvard and Agassiz strengthened the myth that what we call "race" is a biological, not social, category. More than any other, this falsehood lays the groundwork for the ongoing subjugation, dehumanization, and extraction of wealth from people of African descent.

In 2016, Harvard's then-president Drew Gilpin Faust said, "Harvard was directly complicit in America's system of racial bondage from the college's earliest days. . . . This is our history and our legacy." Yet as recently as 2017, Harvard again used Renty's likeness on the cover of a textbook [*From Site to Sight: Anthropology, Photography, and the Power of Imagery*, published by Harvard University Press]. Does the University want to continue to gain from an image stolen from enslaved people? Until Harvard commits to redress the harm it wrought, complicity will continue to define and mar its legacy. It is our hope that releasing the daguerreotypes will be a first step in a long overdue movement of reckoning and repair.

We stand in solidarity with Ms. Lanier and urge Harvard to join us.

Signed,
Eamon Moore Whalen, Minneapolis, Minnesota
Eli Moore, MA, Cali, Colombia
Marian Shaw Moore, Minneapolis, Minnesota
Susanna McKean Moore, PhD, Berkeley, California
Leo Christov-Moore, PhD, Los Angeles, California
Violet Shneider, New York City, New York
Jay Coogan, Providence, Rhode Island
Miranda Warburton, PhD, Sedona, Arizona
Rosemary Moore, MFA, Brooklyn, New York
Patience Moore, LCSW, Montclair, New Jersey
Maeve Sargent Moore Whalen, Bozeman, Montana
James McKean Whalen, Oakland, California
Paul Moore, PhD, Berkeley, California
Avery Busta Moore, Oakland, California

Quincy Moore, MD, Chicago, Illinois
Arlo Moore-Bloom, Medford, Massachusetts
Ruby Moore-Bloom, Amman, Jordan
George Mead Moore, Oaxaca, México
Rowan Moore Gerety, New York City, New York
Amias Agassiz Moore Gerety, AB, Harvard, 2002, Washington, DC
Carrick Moore Gerety, AB, Harvard, 1998, Los Angeles, California
Quentin Moore, MFA, Queens, New York
Thomas Sargent Moore, Pittsburgh, Pennsylvania
Indiana Francesca Christov Moore, Xalapa, Mexico
Faye Shneider, New York City, New York
Honor Moore, Harvard, 1967, New York City, New York
Cressida McKean, Arlington, Virginia
Jenny Reed, Seattle, Washington
Hans Hardisty, Minneapolis, Minnesota
Nicolas Hardisty, Newport, Rhode Island
Rosemary Warburton, Tiverton, Rhode Island
Lee McKean Marshall Strang, Edina, Minnesota
Theo Moore-Manakas, Washington, DC
August Moore-Manakas, Montclair, New Jersey
James Madden, Bozeman, Montana
Henri J. Bourneuf, Harvard, 1969, Ipswich, Massachusetts
Thomas Agassiz McKean, Bath, New Hampshire, and Aberdeen, Scotland
Kate McKean, Oakland, California
Elizabeth Lee McKean, Bath, New Hampshire
Jessie Bourneuf, MBA, Harvard University, 1975, Milton, Massachusetts
Jennie Dougherty, Milton, Massachusetts
Paul McKean Madden, Middletown, Rhode Island

Every single person who signed this letter was a descendant of Louis Agassiz.

I could not have drafted a more succinct summary of my own feelings. To have Agassiz's descendants do this for me was beyond my wildest dreams. After Josh reviewed it, he called me to say, "This is perfect. I cannot imagine a better response."

"Me either," I said, elated.

Ben called as well, equally excited. "This is how we win in the court of public opinion," he said. "Let's have a press conference, let's present the letter to Harvard together, a united front. And let's invite Susanna and Marian to come with us—two families forged together by history."

His enthusiasm was infectious.

"And we will do it on Juneteenth, which is also the day after the congressional hearing on reparations," he added.

Representative John Conyers Jr. was a big proponent of reparations. He first introduced legislation to create a commission to develop proposals for reparations in 1989—and had pushed it every year in office, until he retired in 2017. The bill, called the Commission to Study and Develop Reparations Proposals for African Americans Act, was finally being discussed by Congress on June 19, 2019—thirty years after Conyers had introduced it. Representative Sheila Jackson Lee, of Texas, was the new sponsor now that Conyers had retired, and Ta-Nehisi Coates was the keynote speaker. I loved the kismet of this moment.

I'd met Conyers many years earlier, at an NAACP event shortly after the passing of my mother. He was there to garner support for HR 676, a bill he first proposed in 2003 that would establish universal health care for all through a strike (now called Obamacare). This was a raw and sensitive subject for me after the battles waged in fighting for my mother's care. I introduced myself and he asked, "Are you familiar with HR 676?"

"Oh boy am I!" I responded.

The conversation started with health care grievances but quickly turned to Papa Renty and reparations since I had just discovered the daguerreotypes. He told me about a conference he held every year in DC on reparations—and invited me to come back in 2013. The conversation about family, legacy, and generational love seemed to touch him. Congressman Conyers was emotional. He put his hand over his heart and said, "Here in my breast pocket, I carry with me the two things I value the most."

He pulled out a copy of the US Constitution and a picture of his sons.

"I never leave home without them."

He believed in the Constitution and its promise—that we should all be treated equally under the law, which was why he continued to fight for reparations.

We met well before I had been able to prove that Renty was my ancestor, yet I went to his reparations conference because I knew, even then, that Renty was owed so much. I am convinced that those experiences gave me the confidence to approach Ben Crump that day. When he agreed to work with me, I sent a message to Conyers on Twitter that said, "I finally found someone to take on my case!"

John Conyers and his long, drawn-out push to get reparations on the national radar was part of my story, and so delivering the letter to Harvard the day after Congress would finally hear about his proposal to consider reparations felt prescient.

When I shared Ben's idea with Marian and Susanna, that they meet us at Harvard to deliver the letter directly to President Bacow, they both said immediately, "We'll be there."

They flew in, and I drove up to Harvard, this time with Shonrael.

The day before, on June 19, 2019, I watched the congressional hearing on television. Ta-Nehisi Coates opened his remarks by responding to Senator Mitch McConnell's comment on reparations, that "no one should be held accountable for something that happened one hundred and fifty years ago."

"It was one hundred and fifty years ago, and it is right now," Coates said in his stunning speech. He went on to explain all the ways that's true. "The matter of reparations is one of making amends and direct redress. But it is also a question of citizenship. . . . That if Thomas Jefferson matters, so does Sally Hemings. That if D-Day matters, so does Black Wall Street. That if Valley Forge matters, so does Fort Pillow. Because the question is not whether we will be tied to the somethings of our past, but whether or not we will be courageous enough to be connected to the whole of them."

David Grubin was filming all of this for the documentary—the congressional hearing, the Zoom with the Moore sisters, and had even arranged individual interviews with both. In one clip, Susanna said, "Tammy's great-great-great-grandfather was Papa Renty, who was made to strip nude and pose for a photographer. My great-great-great-grandfather was Louis Agassiz, who ordered that that photograph be taken. I didn't look it straight in the face until . . . Tammy's lawsuit. There was this vague feeling that you did not want to look too hard at his legacy because you would find things that were uncomfortable."

She also said, "It is important for white people who enjoy white privilege whether we are consciously aware of it or not, it is important for us to interrogate where did white supremacy come from and what are the continued impacts? We started realizing that our ancestor in a very specific way caused harm. We have a part in it, and we can work as hard as we can to make some kind of reparations for the harm that was done."

We all met up in Boston on June 20, feeling buoyed by the conversation that had happened in Washington, DC, the day before. Like Mike, Ben was also a master of using a good story, and the press, to win in the court of public opinion. He knew that the descendants of Agassiz coming together in solidarity with the descendants of Renty would have a ripple effect. It was pouring rain that morning, but our spirits were bright. We gathered near Agassiz Hall, a red-brick building with his name chiseled into the façade. Shonrael was recording live on Facebook, David Grubin was filming for the documentary, and there were dozens of reporters there to cover the story, since Crump had set up a press conference. There were also campus security police, which was odd, because we were not doing anything illegal. Marian and Susanna had brought the letter as well as the poster of our family's trees that Eli had made.

Just prior to the press conference, Ben gathered us all together to pray.

"Heavenly Father, we thank you for this moment in history," he said. "When brothers and sisters come together united."

How surreal, I thought, to have the lineal descendants of Louis Agassiz and Renty come together on Harvard's campus in this moment. It felt historic and reminded me of Martin Luther King's "I Have a Dream" speech, where he says, "I have a dream that one day on the red hills of Georgia, the sons of former slaves and the sons of former slave owners will be able to sit together at the table of brotherhood."

Then Ben addressed the crowd: "Yesterday, a congressional hearing took place that discussed reparations for the linear descendants of African slaves. One day later, we are gathered here at Harvard University not far from a building bearing Louis Agassiz's name, where the lineal descendants and the family of Louis Agassiz, the celebrated Harvard professor, as well as the lineal descendants and the family of the African slave known as Renty, come together to make a proclamation and to speak truth to power."

I was standing next to Marian, our arms linked in solidarity. Then she took the microphone. "I am here today with my family to deliver a letter to Harvard University that is signed by forty-three direct descendants of Louis Agassiz. To begin, we would like to apologize to Tamara Lanier for what our ancestor did to her family. And we want to thank you for bringing your family story to light."

Her sister Susanna then took the mic: "Do we think Renty and Delia consented to be part of a project to justify their own enslavement? Of course not. Their images were stolen from them. He may have been good on ice and fish, but Agassiz's ideas were deadly when it came to Black people. And today, one hundred and sixty-nine years later, Agassiz's legacy and Harvard's complicity are very much of this historical moment, our historical moment. It is time for reparations. A time for reckoning and repair."

I was so swept up in the moment that I was caught off-guard when Ben next announced that I would say a few words. I had not prepared anything, and was still reeling from the fact that Susanna, the descendant of Louis Agassiz, was insisting on reparations—a term that was still considered radioactive. Yet this was an example of her speaking her truth, and not hiding behind shame. It was the past and the present colliding, where the descendants of two men, one who had greatly harmed the other, decided to stand in solidarity together to model and force a conversation about reparations and what that means—to us, to this nation. The day after Ta-Nehisi Coates spoke, we were a shining example of what he was trying to say. I was thinking all of these things as I approached the microphone. But rather than try to articulate them, I decided to speak from my heart.

"I want to start by saying there are two people who are missing who are the real MVPs of this story: my mother, Mattye Lanier, and my attorney Michael Koskoff. But for them, we would not be here today, and I want to take a moment to share my gratitude. I know they are watching from heaven. I also want to say that I am extremely excited to partner with the Agassiz children on the endeavor that we push Harvard to do the right thing, to restore dignity to Renty and Delia."

From there, we all linked arms once again and walked across the campus to deliver the letter to President Bacow's office, where we were met by a Harvard police officer blocking the door. Susanna and Marian pushed past, explaining that they had a letter for the president. I was astonished by their confidence—white privilege used for good.

When I tried to follow them, the officer told me I could not enter.

"She's with us," Susanna said. I knew I would never have been let in without her insistence. Shonrael tried to come with me, but the officer was aggressively blocking the door.

"No one else may enter."

"That's my mother," I heard Shonrael say amid the clicking of the reporters' cameras as the door closed behind me. Inside, Susanna explained why we were there to a very stunned-looking assistant who said, "President Bacow is not available at the moment."

"Please make sure he receives this," Marian said, placing the envelope in the assistant's hand.

I was in awe of their unapologetic insistence. Ben later told me that he thought they might get arrested. They did not care—nor were they intimidated. I thought of their father, and his work. As well as something Susanna shared with me earlier that day.

"Eli often says, in his work, that white people lose out when we are isolated and informed by racist assumptions. I want to thank you for trusting us and sharing your story with us. We are two families that have been wronged by Agassiz's racism—yours far more potently."

That helped me understand that we can, together, rewrite the past.

We were in the office for only a few minutes—enough time to leave the letter and walk outside, where Shonrael was anxiously waiting for me.

"I'm so proud of you, Mom," she said, smiling and relieved. "Grandma would be too."

As we made our way back across the campus, Ben started to chant "Free Renty!" and others joined in. Our small, powerful protest. Then someone started singing "We Shall Overcome" and we all sang together, arms linked. As we sang, I thought to myself, We shall, we must. Renty and Delia had been held captive at this institution for too long. It was time to let them come home. By then I was imagining a repatriation that included a ceremonial process, a homegoing that would restore their dignity and offer them an appropriate final resting place.

14

The Harvard Students Mobilize

President Bacow never responded to the Agassiz letter, which was not surprising. Instead, a few months later, a Harvard student named Meredith McKinney reached out to Josh because she was doing a research project inspired by Renty. Meredith was a public health researcher who was pursuing her second graduate degree at the Harvard international relations program. That fall 2019 semester, she was taking a social justice course—and for one assignment had to come up with an artistic expression that illustrated her relationship to the Black Lives Matter movement.

"I'm German Irish," she explained when we finally connected that December. "I kept thinking, How can I, as a white person of European descent, respond to something so painful as slavery? I did not have a direct connection to it that I knew of and felt a tremendous pressure."

In class she had watched the James Baldwin documentary *I Am Not Your Negro* and read Ralph Ellison's novel *Juneteenth* and felt even more conflicted. As she was googling around, looking for ideas, she happened upon an image of Congo Renty.

"It was so powerful that it stopped me from scrolling," she said. "I began researching the image and learned that Harvard owned the copyright. I was like, Why does Harvard have the oldest images of enslaved people? It did not make sense to me!"

Meredith found this both confusing and disturbing. Just like Ellie Reichlin, she began her own research to try to understand how an elite university—one where she was pursuing an advanced degree—could own and license these images. That was how she eventually discovered my lawsuit—and felt compelled to reach out.

"Tammy, no one is talking about this on campus," she explained. "None of the students even know what's going on. I'd really like to help change that."

For her BLM artistic expression, she wrote a letter to Bacow expressing her deep concern over Harvard's relationship to the daguerreotypes, questioning the institution's right to ownership, and requesting that they return the artifacts to the lineal descendants of Renty, Delia, Fassena, Jack, Jem, Alfred, and Drana, whom she calls the "Harvard Seven." She also created a petition as part of that project in direct response to my lawsuit. On the day she presented her letter to her class, in a packed auditorium, she used that opportunity to gather signatures.

"I was swarmed afterwards," she said. "I got eighty signatures in one afternoon. As I anticipated, students were outraged that this was happening on our campus."

Meredith shared the petition with me, which noted my lawsuit and described Harvard's actions as "wrongful seizure, possession, and expropriation of photographic images of the patriarch of [Lanier's] family and his daughter (named Renty and Delia, respectively)" and then gathered signatures from "Harvard degree candidates, students, and faculty members" who "respectfully request our President and Fellows of Harvard College AKA Harvard University and affiliates named in the aforementioned suit to immediately transfer ownership of and all respective rights to the images detailed in the case filed in the Commonwealth of Massachusetts Superior Court, to the named Plaintiff, Tamara Lanier."

I'd been looking for someone at Harvard to align with for almost a decade by then and kept hitting brick walls, beginning with the staff at the Peabody in 2010, then the long list of professors whom I was sure would take an interest in my story. I was still bewildered by Professor Gates's nonresponsiveness. He was viewed by many as a leading authority on African American history, yet he remained silent when it came to my connection to Renty. President Faust had retired, and Bacow adopted her same stance—standoffish and disinterested. To finally connect with someone like Meredith, whose empathy buoyed me and whose energy propelled me, was very gratifying. I never understood how Harvard, one of the world's most widely respected academic institutions, could be so steadfast in denying my familial connection to these infamous artifacts. But Meredith understood the power of the student body and she firmly believed that once they knew what was going on, they would condemn Harvard's actions. And she was right.

"No one could believe Harvard was doing this," she said. "It went against everything I thought the school stood for—after being so proud of getting to study there, I suddenly felt ashamed."

Meredith then asked how I felt about her forming a student-run group on campus that she wanted to call the Harvard Coalition to Free Renty. I told her that I loved the idea—and I knew in my heart that it would be a game changer. For years I had tried to make a connection on campus, but the students always seemed to be in a state of transition. I would contact an organization; the leadership would change; the semester would end, and I'd lose touch. But there was something about Meredith's proposal that felt different. The students are the lifeblood of any academic institution; their collective voices have something Harvard can't ignore—power.

The coalition was created in January 2020, and since it was not a formally recognized university club, which would need a university sponsor, Meredith reached out to other formal clubs on campus for their support, starting with the Generational African American Students Association (GAASA). Their response was immediate: "What can we do to help?"

That same month, Meredith launched the Harvard Coalition to Free Renty website as a way to spread awareness about my lawsuit—and to demand that Harvard do the right thing regarding the way they would treat the daguerreotypes moving forward. As a public health researcher, she was most disturbed by the fact that Renty and Delia, and the other five human beings captured in those daguerreotypes, were being treated as medical specimens. This had not dawned on me until Meredith explained that Agassiz was using their bodies to prove his theory of polygenism, and that the daguerreotypes were therefore one of the first documented examples of Black bodies being used as medical data.

"Agassiz collected data from the seven human beings that were photographed against their will," Meredith explained. "This was human data that Agassiz and others were studying. And Harvard continues to use them today—people, as data points. It's sickening."

This was revelatory to both me and my lawyers, since we had always thought of the daguerreotypes as personal property—but Meredith helped us understand that Renty, Delia, and the other enslaved men and women were a part of an evil scientific experiment to prove white supremacy and there were now protocols in place to protect people from such human experimentation.

Renty and Delia were also being used to justify medical apartheid, I thought, and remembered my conversation with Harriet

Washington, the author of the book of the same name. Now I understood why Harriet was so determined to use the Papa Renty image in that book. Everything seemed to be connected. I had given Mike Koskoff a copy of it for his birthday, with highlighted passages that Harriet had written about Renty and Delia; she had included both in her research. I thought of James Marion Sims—the so-called father of gynecology, who had performed fistula surgeries on enslaved women without anesthesia from 1845 to 1849, just before Agassiz's trip to South Carolina to create the daguerreotypes. Both men believed that Black people did not feel pain in the same way that white people did—and that ideology has permeated ever since. This new understanding of the daguerreotypes added another layer of pain to the humiliation of Renty and Delia being forcibly stripped and photographed: they were also the first human guinea pigs who were documented.

I also understood my mother's and other relatives' distrust of medical science in a new light now. My mother had always preferred natural remedies as her first line of defense against any illness, whether ginger tea and asafetida bags to ward off colds or chrysanthemum tea to treat asthma. These were African and indigenous traditions that had been passed down through the generations. She only sought medical treatment when it was absolutely necessary—and cited the Tuskegee syphilis experiment, which took place at the Tuskegee Institute, a school in Alabama that she once attended, as one of her many reasons for suspicion. Meredith had a background in researching human data for medical experimentation. During one of our many discussions, she compared the six hundred Black men used in that study to Renty, Delia, and the others in the daguerreotypes from a right-to-privacy angle. None of the men in that experiment were treated for the disease—and seventy-four died as a result. It disturbed her that these men were still identifiable.

"If you google that experiment, you can see photographs of the men who were used as human guinea pigs," she said. "I thought of them as I started looking at Renty and Delia from the perspective of the protections that human victims have today."

She was referring to the Belmont Report, which was written by the National Commission for the Protection of Human Subjects of Biomedical and Behavioral Research in 1974 to set ethical guidelines for research of human subjects.

"Renty and Delia are human subjects, who are still being used today by Harvard as well—an institution that continues to profit over their abusive treatment," she exclaimed. "Equally infuriating is that Harvard is not following the Belmont Report guidelines!"

I appreciated Meredith's outrage. For so long, I had encountered academics who took a more disconnected stance. Like Ellie, Meredith understood that these were not subjects to be studied—they were human beings. Mothers, fathers, daughters, and sons. She asked my permission to further explore this connection in a research paper, which I readily agreed to. I was so eager to learn what else she might discover. I also appreciated how thoughtful she was being about the treatment of my ancestors—and of me.

Shortly after the Free Renty Coalition officially launched, the *Harvard Crimson* ran a story about the student-led group that quoted Meredith: "For Harvard to take a position where they're fighting against families to maintain ownership of that family's image and their history was deeply concerning to me as a student. It bruised my pride in my affiliation with this University in a big way, big enough to make me start asking a lot of questions around campus and engaging with student associations."

By the end of January, more than 250 people had signed Meredith's petition, 35 students had joined the coalition, and several Harvard student groups, including the Harvard Democrats and the Harvard Society for Mind, Brain and Behavior (HSMBB), signed on as supporters. The momentum was exciting. Then Meredith invited me to participate on a panel discussion for an event cohosted by GAASA called "Social Reparations, Beyond the 40 Acres." My girls were both busy that evening, so my friend Jean Jordan accompanied me. It was my first time back to the campus since we delivered the letter to President Bacow, and I was looking forward to returning to engage with students who were eager to hear my story. I was finally going to have the opportunity to give Renty and Delia a voice on campus.

The event was held on February 4. That day, as I was driving to Cambridge, Meredith called to say that someone had leaked the event to the press.

"Tammy, just a heads-up, there are a bunch of reporters here," she said.

I thought that was great—the students had also invited James DeWolf Perry, a descendant from the Bristol, Rhode Island, DeWolf family, who, he learned later in his life, earned its vast fortune through the slave trade. James, a Harvard graduate, participated in the Emmy-nominated PBS documentary that his cousin Katrina DeWolf Browne directed, *Traces of the Trade: A Story from the Deep North,* to confront and investigate that dark history. David Harris, a leading civil rights advocate and managing director of the Charles Hamilton Houston Institute for Race and Justice at Harvard Law School, would also be joining. I'd been in touch with both men over the years and looked forward to reconnecting. Harris was a friend of Charles Ogletree and I'd met Katrina DeWolf Browne at John Conyers's annual reparations conference in Washington, DC. I was certain the discussion would be illuminating.

As I neared the campus entrance, I saw clusters of media people standing outside the gates and realized that they were not being let in. That made me nervous and uncomfortable. Then I spotted Meredith, who looked overwhelmed, standing with David Grubin, who had brought his camera crew to interview students and their reactions to my story.

"The administration has made it clear that no press is allowed to cover the event," Meredith said, clearly disappointed—as was I.

"Not even David?" I asked.

"No press—or media," she said.

Once again, Harvard was trying to suppress my story. They were relentless. So I was glad when a young Black reporter with a local TV station approached and asked, "Do you mind if I interview you here?"

"I do not," I said, and then pulled Jean by the hand and added, "but I'm not doing this alone."

She stood next to me as I answered his questions.

"The station requested permission to cover the event and we received an email that said that under no uncertain terms are we allowed to come onto the premises, or even enter through the gates," the reporter said. "Now it's funny, because a week ago we were here to cover Hasty Pudding, Harvard's big parade. That was something they wanted us to cover. This isn't—so we're outside."

I was impressed by his diligence. He was clearly outraged by the way Harvard was conducting themselves—and was willing to tell the story even if it meant filming outside of the campus. Harvard was trying to silence me—and this reporter saw through it.

"So please explain to me what it is that you want Harvard to do," he continued.

"Surrender the images," I said as calmly as I could. "Return the images to the descendants of the enslaved."

"So, release the property that was taken unjustly and return it back to the family," he said. "And that is your simple request."

"Correct," I said.

After he finished filming, he said to me off camera, "Your story is my story. Your Papa Renty is my Papa Renty. That's why it is so important to tell it."

His words stayed with me as Meredith escorted me to Boylston Hall, a stone building on the outskirts of the campus. Just as we were about to enter, her cell phone rang. I could hear a woman's voice through the speaker.

"If any press is allowed in that room, we will shut the whole thing down."

Meredith looked at me, exasperated.

"Understood," was all she said before hanging up.

Inside the auditorium, Samantha O'Sullivan introduced herself. She was the then president of GAASA. We'd been speaking on the phone prior to the event, and she made it clear that despite Harvard's opposition, the students insisted I come to speak.

"Thank you for being here," she said.

"Thank you for having me," I responded. I commended these students for being Harvard's moral compass.

Inside the auditorium, there were one hundred or more people in attendance. I created a PowerPoint presentation for the event—starting with a photo of my mom, describing her as the keeper of our family story and the daughter of sharecropper parents who insisted that I write the Papa Renty story down. I used that image to begin the discussion of my journey that started a decade earlier, when Rich sent me the "Black Bodies, White Science" scholarly article in the spring of 2010, the very first moment I saw Papa Renty.

James DeWolf Perry spoke next. Similar to the Moore sisters, he'd heard stories of his ancestors that focused more on their celebrated accolades—they'd come to America on the *Mayflower*, some were Revolutionary War heroes, and his namesake, James DeWolf, became a United States senator for Rhode Island. But when he and other family members began to dig deeper, they learned that he was also the largest slave trader in American history. This was the subject of the documentary that Katrina directed, and that James participated in with nine other DeWolf descendants.

James was making the point that any white person who had ancestors in the United States prior to 1865 directly benefited from enslavement—even if their relatives did not own or trade slaves. "I can't celebrate my ancestors' contributions to the Revolutionary War without also acknowledging that they participated in a monstrous series of crimes," he said. "It's absolutely essential that we reveal both stories."

It was powerful to hear him lay this out so clearly.

While filming, James and his relatives visited Ghana, tracing his ancestors' slave-trading routes, which brought them to the dungeon of the Cape Coast Castle slave fort, where kidnapped Africans were held in chains before being forcibly boarded onto ships for the Caribbean and America.

"Your first instinct is to desperately wish your ancestor had not done this," he said. Then he heard children playing, beyond the stone walls, in the nearby fishing village, and he thought that he could at least begin to acknowledge the harm caused by his ancestors, and how it still resonates today. "There's no way to undo that family history, which is why we must acknowledge our connection to it," he said.

As a result of making the film, James and his relatives are now active in a variety of racial healing and restorative justice practices. James and Katrina started the Tracing Center in 2009. Its mission is to "educate the public about the history and legacy of race and other forms of discrimination, in order to change hearts and minds, foster dialogue, and encourage healing and justice." Their cousin Tom DeWolf is the codirector of a national organization called Coming to the Table, whose mission is similar: "Working together to create a just and truthful society that acknowledges and seeks to heal from the racial wounds of the past, from slavery and the many forms of racism it spawned."

The DeWolf descendants reminded me of the Agassiz descendants, since none of them knew the extent of their ancestors' involvement with enslavement until they were adults.

"There's a powerful lesson in helping other white people see what might be in their backgrounds," James said. "Part of this is coming to understand that while we're not responsible for what our ancestors did, we do have a responsibility to address injustice in our society today, and that includes being very honest about the injustices that persist from what our own ancestors have done. Not to atone for what they did, but to address how it shows up via racism today."

David Harris spoke next—and directly to me.

"When I look at your family, I see my heritage," he said. "I'm thrilled for you that there's a personal connection [to Renty and Delia] but there is a connection for all of us. There is a history of exclusion. We the people is our founding lie. We the people did not include us."

This may sound strange, but I feel so lucky that I have Renty and Delia to fight for. David was speaking to the fact that so many African American descendants of slaves feel the pain of Renty and Delia—but it's abstract. I can, at the very least, ground it in the daguerreotypes. I have proof: my ancestors were treated inhumanely. I wanted Harvard to restore their dignity once and for all.

After the panel ended, I was swarmed by students who wanted to apologize to me personally for the way Harvard treated Renty and Delia.

"What can I do to support you?" was something I heard often that evening.

Many of the students also agreed to speak with David Grubin for the film, and others were so moved by the discussion that they filmed a series for the Free Renty website, directly addressing President Bacow.

"I've seen the daguerreotypes twice in person and I cried both times," a senior says directly into the camera. "It's an absolute shame that the daguerreotypes are still in the Peabody for display and for students to study. They should be in the hands of the families. Those are heirlooms. That is the first step you can do to deal with Harvard's very complicated relationship to slavery. It would be courageous and simply the right thing to do."

The students' frustration and support made me hopeful at a time when Harvard was clamping down on their claims of ownership. Bacow was quoted in the press stating that Harvard's possession of the daguerreotypes was not illegal, and that the Peabody Museum's treatment of the artifacts was to "draw attention to the fact these people were not chattel. These were real people."

He spoke to the press about Renty and Delia, but never to me.

Earlier that November, Bacow had launched a "university-wide initiative to address and further research the school's ties to slavery" and designated $5 million for the program. But both Meredith and the Free Renty Coalition thought that was not nearly enough. They did not let up. On February 20, 2020, several weeks after the panel discussion, Meredith sent another letter to Harvard administrators, including President Bacow and Jane Pickering, who had replaced Ilisa Barbash at the Peabody. The title of the four-page missive was "Harvard Human Subject Complaint: The Gross Mishandlings of the Harvard 7 Dataset." She then meticulously outlined all the ways in which she believed Harvard's insistence on "ownership" of the images was wrong, stating: "Their images and information, commissioned by Harvard's Louis Agassiz, have been repeatedly published in newspapers, were released online by Harvard for public access, and remain on display at the Peabody Museum of Archaeology and

Ethnology. Additionally, the personal information of these subjects and their images continue to be sold and circulated in a variety of publications and forthcoming books authored by Peabody affiliates, for profit."

The daguerreotypes were on display at one point but have since been stored away; replicas have been made for public viewing. This was the research paper that Meredith had asked me about earlier—and in it, she argued that since the "Harvard Seven" images were taken against their will to prove a quickly debunked scientific theory that Harvard's employee Louis Agassiz developed during his tenure at the university, they were liable for the mistreatment of the "dataset," in this case the daguerreotypes themselves, since they each represent a human being used as a data point. She believed, as I do, that every time Harvard uses those images—which are not anonymous—it violates the Belmont Report's guidelines to protect an individual's identity. She also asks for "an immediate withdrawal of and/or voiding of all contracts granting permissions for the publication, reproduction, purchase or further dissemination of subjects' data and images (until possession of consent is obtained from subjects and/or their legal descendants or representatives)."

Meredith's point—to use the images without consent and/or approval from the family—was a violation of the Belmont Report and it continued to strip Renty and Delia of their humanity. She was among a growing number of writers and academics who had reached out to me to ask my permission to use the images and discuss my case. It made me wonder, why did Meredith and those other academics see the value in reaching out to me, whereas Harvard did not?

This was the beginning of my receiving an outpouring of support from Harvard students. Inspired, I reached out to Noah Harris, the first African American student to be elected president of Harvard's Undergraduate Council. We connected in the fall of 2020. He explained that the members of the Undergraduate Council felt strongly that an action was warranted. Their first order of business was to pass a statement condemning the university for its possession of the daguerreotypes. The vote was unanimous!

I thought of the mantra that had kept me going all these years: "It's not might that makes right—it's right that makes might."

15

An Opportunity for Harvard

Shortly after we filed our legal complaint, Josh was interviewed by Attorney Lloyd Bell of Georgia for his podcast, *Face the Jury*. Bell explained that the complaint had forever changed the way he views these legal documents. "You impressed me with the storytelling in the suit," he said to Josh. "It was probably the first time that Renty and Delia received the respect that was due to them as human beings. It brought home that our complaints are not mere pleading outlines. . . . [They are] opportunities to tell compelling, meaningful stories. We've adopted a similar approach with all our lawsuits because of you."

The lines from Maya Angelou's poem at the start of our complaint set the tone: twenty-four pages long, it succinctly and eloquently summed up my grievances against Harvard and exposed the university's complicated relationship with slavery and scientific racism in such a powerful way. Building on Harvard's complicit history, the complaint in part reads:

8. In 1976, Harvard discovered that the daguerreotypes were stored on its campus, realized their incalculable value as the earliest known photographs of American slaves and commenced a decades long campaign to sanitize the history of the images and exploit them for prestige and profit.
9. The plaintiff, Tamara Lanier, is a direct descendant of Renty and Delia. She has asked Harvard to recognize her lineage and relinquish the daguerreotypes to her family.
10. By turns dismissive and arrogant, Harvard has refused to do either.
11. Harvard has asserted an exclusive right to possess, restrict access to, and profit from the daguerreotypes—without ever explaining the basis for that purported entitlement.
12. Harvard has also denigrated the legitimacy of Ms. Lanier's heritage, which she has established based on a rich and detailed family history passed down through generations.
13. Every day that Harvard maintains those positions compounds the injustices inflicted on Renty and Delia in its name, and further harms Ms. Lanier as their descendant and the rightful owner of images taken without their consent.
14. By denying Ms. Lanier's superior claim to the daguerreotypes, Harvard is perpetuating the systematic subversion of black property rights that began during slavery and continued for a century thereafter.
15. And by contesting Ms. Lanier's claim of lineage, Harvard is shamelessly capitalizing on an intentional damage done to Black Americans' genealogy by a century's

> worth of policies that forcefully separated families, erased slaves' family names, withheld birth and death records, and criminalized literacy.

I was stunned by this legal analysis and what it revealed. Harvard's refusal to recognize my rightful claim over the daguerreotypes was a blatant continuation of the systemic disenfranchisement of Black property rights, a legacy deeply rooted in slavery and aggressively enforced for more than a century. This lawsuit meant so much to me, as we were finally telling the world that Harvard's actions were emblematic of the ruthless policies that have historically devastated Black life, dismantled families, and erased enslaved identities by stripping away their family names, deliberately withholding essential birth and death records, and criminalizing literacy. I thought of my mom and many other family members who lived most of their lives without a birth certificate—and all the more appreciated the importance of this lawsuit, as I was beginning to understand that it stood for so much more than these artifacts. It was evidence of all the ways in which enslavement robbed African Americans—of their dignity, their humanity.

Following the introduction, which laid out why I was suing Harvard, the complaint was split into five parts:

"The Making of a Harvard Man" was the first. It detailed Agassiz's relationship with the university, beginning in 1846, when he first arrived in the United States at Harvard's invitation, and included Agassiz's first encounter with a Black person. That fueled his support for polygenism and his relationship with the Philadelphia-based anthropologist Samuel George Morton, an ardent believer. The complaint details this meeting of like minds:

> 45. Agassiz crossed paths with Samuel George Morton, an anthropologist living in Philadelphia who was known for his collection of some 600 human skulls.

46. Morton was devoted to the classification and ranking of human beings based on race. He was an ardent believer in polygenism, the theory that racial groups do not share a common origin and are thus fundamentally and categorically distinct.
47. Morton claimed he could place racial groups in a descending order of intelligence by measuring the interior capacity of human skulls. His methodology was a sham, but it conveniently "confirmed" Agassiz's newfound prejudices by placing black people at the very bottom of the racial hierarchy.
48. Agassiz embraced polygenism with a convert's zeal.

It continued to connect the historical dots from Agassiz to Harvard. It also revealed the South's and North's shared interest in keeping slavery legal at a critical time in history.

49. At his first lecture in Boston, delivered just months after he arrived in America, Agassiz announced for the first time in his career that white and black people had separate origins.
50. Several months later, Agassiz was invited to South Carolina to repeat his lecture, and his view that black people were a distinct species, at a meeting attended by local scientists, theologians, and politicians.
51. "The brain of a negro," Agassiz announced to the men gathered in the Charleston Literary Club, "is that of the imperfect brain of a 7-month's infant in the womb of White."
52. His audience was thrilled. At a time when South Carolina's slave population outnumbered whites and the abolitionist movement was gaining traction, Agassiz's

message—wrapped in the trappings of science—was a gift.

53. But it wasn't just the South that was listening. Agassiz's newfound passion made him an unlikely, but important, asset to Harvard.
54. The same year that Agassiz committed to the polygenism crusade, Harvard procured $50,000 to establish its scientific school. At the time, it was the largest single gift ever donated by an individual to an American institution of learning.
55. Notably, the donation guaranteed the salary for a new academic appointment intended specifically for Agassiz.
56. The deal was struck between Harvard's president, Edward Everett, and Abbott Lawrence, a textile magnate and prominent Bostonian.
57. Lawrence had originally intended to underwrite a school of applied science, which would pay dividends in the form of better engineers for his textile mills.
58. Lawrence's plans appear to have changed when Agassiz entered the picture, a shift that was likely propelled as much by self-interest as philanthropic vision.
59. Most of the textiles Lawrence's business sold, a business that had made him extraordinarily wealthy, were made from cotton that was planted, picked, ginned, baled, and shipped by enslaved men, women, and children. In other words, his livelihood depended on slavery's preservation—or, at a minimum, on access to cheap, black labor.
60. The Lawrence family professed to be anti-slavery. But business came first. As Ralph Waldo Emerson once observed, "Cotton thread holds the Union together; unites John C. Calhoun and Abbott Lawrence."

61. Fifty thousand dollars bought Lawrence a school named in his honor—it was dubbed the Lawrence Scientific School—and something even more valuable: a field of "science" sanctioned by Harvard that would help keep supplies of cheap cotton flowing north.
62. Agassiz's views on race also appear to have been consistent with those of Harvard's president, Everett. While serving as a US representative years earlier, Everett had given a three-hour speech during congressional debate where he noted that "the New Testament says, 'Slaves obey your masters.'"
63. In 1847, Everett offered Agassiz the newly created Lawrence Scientific School on a silver platter. Naturally, Agassiz accepted. Almost overnight, Agassiz was catapulted to the highest echelons of Boston high society. Agassiz married Elizabeth Cabot Cary, a daughter of a Boston Brahmin family, who would later cofound Radcliffe College. His standing in the famous Boston "Saturday Club," a literary dining and conversation society that included Hawthorne and Emerson among its ranks, was such that the gathering was popularly referred to as "Agassiz's Club."

. . .

65. From this gilded perch, Agassiz spent the next fifteen years lending celebrity status and "scientific" legitimacy to the poisonous myth of white racial superiority and championing the vital importance of separation of the races.
66. Harvard steadfastly supported Agassiz every step of the way.
67. [The year] 1850 was a pivotal moment for polygenists and the political implications of their theory. The

Fugitive Slave Act, widely seen as a barometer of the relative strength of the pro-slavery and abolitionist camps, was being hotly debated in Congress.

68. Not coincidentally, Agassiz was invited that year to return to Charleston for a meeting of the American Association for the Advancement of Science. He delivered a paper at the meeting in which he explained that racial groups, "viewed zoologically," could not be considered part of the same species.
69. After hearing Agassiz's lecture, a fellow polygenist wrote excitedly to Samuel Morton in Philadelphia: "With Agassiz in the war, the battle is ours."
70. For Agassiz, the final frontier in the battle to establish the legitimacy of polygenism was the collection of empirical data.
71. Agassiz was singularly focused on perceived physical differences between whites and blacks. He had written, with a frightening lack of humanity, about being repulsed by Black people's "thick lips and grimacing teeth, the wool on their head, their bent knees, their elongated hands, their large, curved nails, and especially the livid color of their palms."

This section made it crystal clear to me that, at this precise moment in history, both the North and South needed Harvard and Agassiz to create and circulate proslavery propaganda that would disenfranchise Black life and simultaneously, and most importantly, protect the financial interest of those benefiting from free labor. Agassiz's pseudoscience supported false narratives that vilified and dehumanized African people to justify the institution of enslavement. While reading, I also remembered the excruciatingly painful moment when I first saw my ancestors listed among livestock in the Taylor family wills. How inhumane. And I was able to understand, thanks to my attorneys' thorough research so stunningly distilled in this document, that Harvard's support of Agassiz further contributed to that dehumanization as well as the disinheritance of Black people by manipulating public perception with false information. The daguerreotypes were among the first images of Black enslaved people, and the complaint illuminated that Agassiz's false narratives planted the seeds of the racist framing of both public opinion and public policies ever since.

As a result, I had a greater awareness of the dangers of misinformation—and a greater awareness of Elizabeth Cabot Cary Agassiz and the role she played in supporting her husband's work. I always wondered why Harvard was so protective of the Agassiz family. Elizabeth not only cofounded Radcliffe; she was also the women's college's first president and a naturalist who collaborated on several books with her husband. She wrote his biography and edited *Louis Agassiz: His Life and Correspondence* after he died in 1873. She was never publicly critical of polygenism, which leads me to believe that she likewise supported that theory. Yet she believed deeply in white women's rights—and was one of the founding members of the Harvard Annex, incorporated as the "Society for the Collegiate Instruction of Women," which promoted women pursuing advanced degrees.

The rest of "The Making of a Harvard Man" described how Agassiz came to select my ancestors for this racist experiment.

That section ends with the following statements:

76. At the Taylor Plantation, Agassiz selected several enslaved men and women to be photographed.
77. One was an older man named Renty. Another was his daughter, Delia.

78. To Agassiz, Renty and Delia were nothing more than research specimens. The violence of compelling them to participate in a degrading exercise designed to prove their own subhuman status would not have occurred to him, let alone mattered.
79. Agassiz would never know that he had selected a man whose life and accomplishments, even within the crushing constraints of slavery, made a profound mockery of his theories.
80. We know that today, nearly 170 years later, because of the resilience of Renty and his descendants, and the power of oral history in preserving their family in the face of a system designed to obliterate it.

Part 2 of the complaint is called "Papa Renty" and details that oral history, beginning with my mother's mandate: *Always remember, we're Taylors, not Thompsons.*

It ends with the following lines.

107. Mattye's brother, Renty "Willie," walked to his job as a plumber throughout the Montgomery Bus Boycott. He never got rid of the shoes from that time, which were worn all the way through. He called them his "civil rights shoes."

I first learned about my uncle's civil rights shoes as a young child. Sunday evenings were usually reserved for family time and often that would include long-distance calls to loved ones. My mom would wait until off-peak hours to reconnect with her family in Alabama. She would sit and talk for hours and was often heard to say, "I am sitting with my little pitcher with the big ears."

I would later learn that this was her way of alerting the person on the other end of the call that I was in the room, listening intently to their conversation.

One afternoon, my mom and I were watching the news coverage of the attempted assassination of Alabama governor George Wallace. I was about eight or nine years old and confused by my mom's reaction—it seemed so out of character. There was no remorse or concern for what appeared to be a tragic event. It wasn't Sunday but she called her brother Renty "Willie" in Mount Meigs and asked, "Have you seen the news?"

"He shall reap what he sows."

After she hung up, I asked, "Who was this man?" and "Why were you so upset?"

My mom replied that George Wallace was an evil man who did terrible things to hurt the Black people of Alabama. This led to a conversation about segregation and the Montgomery Bus Boycott. She explained that her brother Renty "Willie" was a master carpenter and plumber, and that just before the boycott, he had purchased a new pair of work boots. But before the boycott could end, she said, "he had walked a hole clean through. Those were his civil rights shoes, proof of them many miles walked for justice."

I also learned something not taught about the boycott. According to my mom and uncle Renty "Willie," the Black people of Montgomery had grown weary, and walking had become overly burdensome. Fights were erupting as people were threatening to get back on the buses. Renty "Willie" described a scene where mayhem broke out and no one could separate the two opposing sides. My uncle said that from out of nowhere, Martin Luther King Jr. stepped out and shouted, "Y'all go home! Go home."

The chaos turned to calm.

"And just like that," Renty "Willie" explained, "the folks parted like the Red Sea."

Both my mom and uncle were certain that had the bus boycott

gone on for much longer, the Black people would have abandoned the campaign and returned to riding the bus. Fortunately, the Montgomery officials folded first.

Part 3, "Agassiz's Legacy," illustrates the influence his theory of polygenism had long after Darwin debunked it.

> 125. In 1859, when Charles Darwin's "On the Origin of Species" was published and provided a stunning rebuke to polygenism, Harvard continued to celebrate Agassiz while he derided Darwin's impeccably researched work as a "scientific mistake" that was "mischievous in its tendency."
> 126. Indeed, the very next year Harvard dedicated the Museum of Comparative Zoology to Agassiz. The museum was founded with specimens from Agassiz's personal collection and funded through his extensive connections. It was unofficially called "Agassiz Museum," a name that retained its relevance when Agassiz's son, Alexander, was made curator and then director after his father's death.
>
> . . .
>
> 134. Agassiz retained his professorship and served as director of the Harvard Museum of Comparative Zoology until his death in 1873.
> 135. After his death, Harvard chose Nathaniel Shaler, an Agassiz protégé, to lead the Lawrence Scientific School.
> 136. Under Harvard's banner, Shaler inveighed against black people's "animal nature," "very low morality," and "feeble nature" of their family ties.

Part 4 of the complaint lists all the ways in which Harvard could have seized on this historic opportunity and worked with me, a descendant of Renty and Delia, to tell the real story of these extraordinary people. It includes Ellie's discovery in 1976, a moment the university could have embraced. Instead Ellie's work was discouraged and she was relegated to being referred to as "the Harvard associate," while the Peabody began to control the narrative of how and when the daguerreotypes were viewed and interpreted. When I approached them in 2010, they could have invited me to be part of the storytelling of these historic images, but instead they doubled down, claiming that I could not prove my relationship.

This section of the complaint also developed the legal dispute between Harvard and the artist Carrie Mae Weems. Harvard had previously threatened to sue Weems for using the images without their permission.

I loved that Weems did not cower in her response: "I think your suing me would be a really good thing. You should. And we should have this conversation in court."

When I first learned about Weems, I was inspired. Her artistic act was, in my opinion, an act of civil disobedience. She took a stand—and used the images without Harvard's permission to recover Black voices. It was artivism, or activism through art. It reminded me of Sasha Huber's work. Art as a form of protest.

In July 2018, I was connected to Carrie Mae Weems via Dr. Reichlin and wrote, "Good afternoon, Ms. Weems, I am writing to share that the Renty in the Slave Daguerreotypes is my grandfather, several generations removed! I found a very interesting article about you and Harvard and was compelled to find you."

I was elated when Weems wrote back that same day.

Dear Tamara:

I've just received your extraordinary email!!! What fate.

I would love to speak with you directly about this, and

> I'm also forwarding your email to Professor Barbash at Harvard University, who is in the process of finishing a book focused on the important set of remarkable photographs of your grandfather. How extraordinary.

As soon as I saw Ilisa Barbash's name, I felt a pinprick in the balloon of hopeful air that had buoyed me since she first wrote. I let her know via email that I'd been in touch with the university, to which she responded, "It occurred to me that given the nature of this, that Skip Gates might be interested in pursuing this. Have you sent him your materials?"

Further deflated, I wrote, "I reached out to him several years ago, on multiple occasions, but no response."

This also tempered her initial enthusiasm: "So sorry to hear this. I think it's fascinating and a wonderful case study. Is there something that you want from me?"

It was a fair question. There was so much I wanted from her. She saw the inhumanity and injustice in the way Renty and Delia were captured in those images. She wanted to give them a voice to tell their own story. I expected an enthusiastic response—for her to be interested in the stories I knew about my ancestors. I ultimately had a brief phone conversation with her in which I did most of the talking. By then I had learned that instead of suing Weems, Harvard bought her art piece—thereby remaining in control of the narrative. I found that disappointing. We never spoke again.

The final section of the complaint is called "History Repeats Itself":

> 161. In 1976, the year Harvard appropriated the daguerreotypes for the second time in its history, Tamara Lanier was a teenager who had already heard the story of Papa Renty dozens of times from her mother, Mattye.

162. As Mattye got older, she told the story more frequently and with greater urgency. Eventually even her grandchildren knew it by heart.
163. In 1996, Tamara's daughter wrote a book for her fifth-grade class about Renty called *From These Roots I Came.* The first page reads: "Dedicated to my little sister so she knows where she came from."
164. At the very end of her life, in 2010, Mattye Thompson-Lanier implored her children to document the 150-year-old oral history of their family. "Write it down," she would say, "write it down."
165. Tamara recorded her mother telling the story of Renty and his lineage one last time from her hospital bed.
166. When Mattye died, Tamara was compelled to learn the rest of Renty's story so that she could fulfill her mother's wish and commit the family's history to paper. Though her mother was gone, she knew where to start: "Always remember we're Taylors . . ."
167. Tamara scoured libraries and archives in South Carolina for information about the Taylors, plumbed the depths of genealogy sources online, and spoke to anyone who might have a sliver of information.
168. The project became a years-long journey that led Tamara, finally, to the daguerreotypes and Harvard.
169. In May of 2011, Tamara Lanier wrote a letter to Drew Faust, Harvard University's then president. In it she relayed the history of the daguerreotypes as she understood it and explained that she believed she was a direct descendant of Renty and Delia.
170. Her requests to Dr. Faust were modest: "to learn more about the slave daguerreotypes and how they have or

will be used," and "a formal review of my documentation to reaffirm that Renty and Delia Taylor are indeed my ancestors."

171. This was yet another moment for Harvard to face its history with courage. This was yet another moment for Harvard to refuse to perpetuate the wrenching pain of its past. This was yet another moment for Harvard to make amends.
172. Again, Harvard chose not to.
173. Dr. Faust's response to the letter was evasive and vague, making no mention of Ms. Lanier's invitation to discuss her heritage. She wrote that the Peabody Museum was "involved in projects regarding those daguerreotypes" and that Peabody employees "have agreed to be in touch with you if they discover any new information."
174. Harvard never contacted Ms. Lanier about ongoing projects, new information, or interest in verifying her lineage and connection to the daguerreotypes.
175. In fact, despite making no effort to meet with Ms. Lanier or conduct any investigation of her relation to Renty and Delia, Harvard demeaned Ms. Lanier in her own community by publicly casting doubt on the legitimacy of her claim.
176. In a 2014 article in the *Norwich Bulletin* about Ms. Lanier's story, the Director of External Relations for the Peabody Museum, Pamela Gerardi, was quoted as saying of Ms. Lanier: "She's given us nothing that directly connects her ancestor or the person in our photograph."
177. Throughout this time, Ms. Lanier continued to conduct research and consult experts in an effort to confirm that Renty and Delia were her ancestors.

178. In March 2016, Ms. Lanier was interviewed by the *Crimson*, Harvard's student newspaper, about her investigation into her family history and the connection to the daguerreotypes.
179. Soon thereafter, Ms. Lanier received an email from an editor at the *Crimson* informing her that the story was being killed due to "concerns the Peabody Museum has raised."
180. In a rich twist, the *Crimson* instead ran an op-ed by then-president Dr. Faust. In it, Dr. Faust acknowledges Harvard's complicity in slavery. "This is our history and our legacy," she wrote, "one we must fully acknowledge and understand in order to truly move beyond the painful injustices at its core."
181. The purpose of that reckoning, according to Dr. Faust, is to "better equip ourselves to combat our own shortcomings and to advance justice and equality in our own time."
182. This public display of soul-searching was a charade. In the two years since, Harvard has demonstrated a complete unwillingness to either acknowledge its history or advance justice today. It has continued to sanitize Agassiz's legacy, profit from the fruits of his crimes, and treat Ms. Lanier as little more than a pest.
183. In 2017, Harvard used Renty's image to sell its 30th Anniversary edition of *From Site to Sight: Anthropology, Photography, and the Power of Imagery*.
184. Here the complaint includes an image of the book, using Renty's image.
185. Harvard describes the book as an exploration of "the historic and contemporary uses of photography in

anthropology"—even though Harvard knows Agassiz's purpose in photographing Renty and Delia cannot fairly be described as anthropologic in nature.

186. Perhaps Harvard believed that Renty's arresting face and semi-nude body would sell more copies. *From Site to Sight* costs $40.00.
187. But the most egregious example of Harvard's ongoing exploitation of Renty and subversion of the truth occurred in March 2017, when Harvard hosted a national academic conference that Ms. Lanier attended. The conference was called Universities and Slavery: Bound by History.
188. As writers and scholars discussed educational institutions' complicity in slavery and Harvard congratulated itself for this ostensible public reckoning with the past, Renty's image was emblazoned onto a massive screen onstage.
189. The conference program, which was also adorned with Renty's image, contained a description of the photograph that took Ms. Lanier's breath away: The man you see on the program's front cover, Renty, lived and worked as a slave in South Carolina in 1850, when his photograph was taken for the Harvard professor Louis Agassiz as a part of Agassiz's scientific research. While Agassiz earned acclaim, Renty returned to invisibility.
190. These words, no doubt carefully chosen, are as dishonest as they are manipulative.
191. Harvard conspicuously omits the nature of Agassiz's work—even having the gall to characterize the photograph as a part of "scientific research" rather than a racist and dehumanizing crusade—and implies that Agassiz had rightfully "earned acclaim" for his work.

192. Even more insidiously, Harvard relegates Renty to "invisibility," in flagrant disregard for Ms. Lanier's repeated attempts to share Renty's story and restore a measure of the humanity that Agassiz stripped from him.
193. At this moment, Tamara Lanier realized—sitting in the audience with her daughter—that Harvard would never face its history with courage. It would never stop perpetuating the wrenching pain of its past. And it would never willingly make amends.
194. As Frederick Douglass once reminded us, "power concedes nothing without a demand. It never did and it never will."
195. On October 27, 2017, Ms. Lanier made her demand.
196. By letter addressed to Dr. Faust, Ms. Lanier explained that in the absence of any action by Harvard she had completed her own research and confirmed that she is a lineal descendant of Renty.
197. The letter concluded with a formal request to have the daguerreotypes of her family members "immediately relinquished" to her.
198. Harvard's response, from Ms. Gerardi of the Peabody Museum, was straight from its playbook: it was nonresponsive and deceptive.
199. It made no mention whatsoever of Ms. Lanier's demand to have the daguerreotypes returned to her.
200. And it offered a new version of history that conveniently distanced Harvard from the daguerreotypes: "As you know the photographs were commissioned by Dr. Robert W. Gibbs [*sic*] of Columbia, South Carolina, in 1850."
201. It is well-established that Agassiz was behind the daguerreotypes and there is no chance that Harvard is confused on that point; this is a blatant lie.

202. It is long past time for Harvard to live up to the word that adorns its seal and shield: *Veritas*. Truth.

As I read through this blow-by-blow recount, I was struck by the historical nature of our complaint and its novel legal implications. The statement that "power concedes nothing without a demand," as first used by Frederick Douglass, was symbolic of the crisis all educational institutions and museums now face. Harvard's unwillingness to return plundered property underscored the notion that those in positions of authority are unlikely to surrender contested artifacts or objects of cultural significance voluntarily. The demand for repatriation, or in this case reparations, serves as a necessary measure for addressing historical injustices and restoring cultural heritage and/or plundered property to its rightful owners.

I firmly believe that Harvard's "white-knuckled" retention of my ancestors' pillaged property is deeply rooted in historical practices of cultural appropriation, colonization, and unethical stewardship. I also believe that my demand for redress challenges the status quo by prompting these institutions to confront the ethical implications of possessing cultural property acquired through violence and/or plunder. But more importantly, I believe that the power dynamic between Harvard and myself is not merely about institutional resistance or legal complexities, but more so about the precedent it may set. The demand for reparations and/or repatriation will open doors historically closed to the descendants of American chattel slavery.

This is why I fight!

It was not lost on me that I had two powerhouse attorneys fighting with me, using all of their resources and every available tool to maximize the visibility of our landmark complaint. It was working. Legal scholars took note and there were many articles written about the historic and unprecedented nature of our case in the *Harvard Law Review*, *Justice Law*, *Verdict Justia*, the *Hyperallergic*, and many more.

Douglas Kysar, a professor of torts at Yale Law School, reached out to my attorneys and to me personally. In an email, he wrote: "The complaint in Lanier v. President and Fellows of Harvard College should be taught in every law school in America. In just two introductory pages, the wrenching facts of Harvard's past treatment of Renty and Delia, and present misconduct toward Ms. Lanier, are conveyed in a way that connects those facts and Harvard as an institution to the country's larger history of slavery, oppression, and racism. After reading those two pages, any judge presiding over the case will already be looking for a way to grant relief to Ms. Lanier. The remainder of the complaint goes on to tell in gripping detail the story of Harvard's past abuse and present indifference toward Ms. Lanier's family. It is bone-rattling and leaves the reader with an undeniable awareness that America's legacy of racial exploitation continues to reverberate in the actions and choices of centers of power like Harvard today. To tell these stories and to call for accountability so powerfully within the confines of a twenty-four-page legal complaint is a remarkable achievement of writing and advocacy."

He saw what I saw.

16

Facts Are Stubborn Things—Summary of My Genealogy

That was the legal case my lawyers were putting forward, and I felt confident that my claim was sound because I had done the work. I had spent more than a decade tracing my family's history and to me that research was irrefutable. The facts of my lineage are static and stubborn things, indifferent to skepticism and based on a rich oral history and official government records.

Truth be told, this work would not be possible were it not for the road map gifted to me by my mother. Unlike the scholarly work that many fight so hard to defend, my narrative is not a collection of suppositions, theories, or speculations. It's a compilation of generational love and legacy.

The elders knew that they could not trust history or history books to tell their family stories. So, for safekeeping, they embedded these stories in the hearts and minds of their young. It was both a privilege and a responsibility to be entrusted with the family stories: "Always remember," "Never forget," and "Write it down." And because of the obedience and perseverance of his children, I am able to prove that I'm a direct descendant of Renty Taylor, the subject of the Harvard slave daguerreotypes.

Facts not in dispute are that Papa Renty or Renty Taylor, my great-great-great-grandfather, was born in the Congo, purchased by Colonel Thomas Taylor in the early 1800s, and enslaved on the Taylor Plantation in Columbia, South Carolina. Also not in dispute is the fact that my great-grandfather was born Renty Taylor and through the transfer of property assumed the name Renty Taylor Thompson. His mother was Tena Taylor, his father was Papa Renty's son Renty Taylor, and his parents were both enslaved on the Taylor Plantation.

It should be noted that Renty Taylor Thompson's oral history was that he descended from an African-born slave affectionately called Papa Renty, the Black African. It should be further noted that prior to any awareness of the daguerreotypes, I was assisted by independent researchers who were asked to search for an African-born slave named Renty Taylor.

Probate records reveal that at the death of Colonel Thomas Taylor, the slaves were indexed in a February 20, 1834, document and divided among the Taylor children. Death records confirm the residences of the Taylor children at that time as Columbia and Charleston, South Carolina, and Mount Meigs, Alabama. Identified as slaves owned by Colonel Taylor were Delia, Renty, Tena, George, Eve, Fed, Prince, Hannah, and "Big Renty." All of them are my ancestors. Slave index records group these families together in the "Little Boy Renty" document, later in the probate record of Colonel Thomas Taylor of 1834, and finally in the will of Benjamin Franklin Taylor after his death in or about 1851.

Under item 8 of the probate record, B. F. Taylor writes, "To my son Benjamin Walter Taylor, I give and bequeath the following slaves and their increase: Carpenter Prince, Hannah his wife and their two children except Jimmy, also Eve, William, James, Phoebe and the children of Hannah Thompson." Records reflect that Benjamin Walter Taylor was born, lived, and died in Columbia and thus this part of my family may have settled in that area.

Through these probate records, we learn that several of the men and women enslaved by Benjamin Franklin Taylor had a surname that was not Taylor. While it is not explained, it is documented by Benjamin Franklin himself that he did own enslaved men and women with the surname Thompson.

Under item 9 of the probate record B. F. Taylor writes, "To my daughter Annie W. Mazyck, I give and bequeath the following slaves and their increase: Marian, Tena, Betsy, and Nora." Records reflect that Annie was born in Columbia but lived and died in Charleston, where my great-grandfather Renty Taylor Thompson was born in or about 1851. Therein lies the answer to the elusive question raised by Renty Taylor Thompson's death record, which indicated a Charleston place of birth, not Columbia. Renty's birth coincided with the death of Benjamin Franklin Taylor, whereas Tena's increase was also bequeathed to Annie Mazyck of Charleston.

My mom spoke of Renty Taylor Thompson's brother George. In a miraculous discovery, George Thompson's death certificate reveals that he lived and died in Columbia, that his mother was Tena, and his father was Renty. But most remarkably, the certificate determines the domicile of the decedent as "Arthurtown," which, prior to 1871, was land owned by Benjamin Franklin Taylor. George Thompson's death record offers a very compelling argument. It points to a kinship between the Taylors and Thompsons; even more incredibly, this record places my ancestors not only in Columbia but on land owned by the slave owner Benjamin Franklin Taylor.

By 1880, the US Census confirmed that my great-grandfather had migrated from Charleston to Mount Meigs. In the household at the time was Renty Taylor Thompson; his wife, Ophelia Murdock Thompson; and his two children, William and Tena.

By 1900, the US Census confirms that Renty and his wife, Ophelia, now had nine children: William, Tena, Emma, Annie, Jim, Renty, Scin, John, and my grandfather Fred. It should also be noted that, in keeping with the Taylor family tradition, Renty's daughter Annie was named after the woman he was bequeathed to, Annie W. Taylor Mazyck, the daughter of B. F. Taylor. In the 1930 census, Fred, also known as Fed Thompson, and his wife, Pearl Jackson Thompson, had the following children: William (Renty), Bernice, John, Mattye (my mom), Simon Benjamin, and Sarah.

Benjamin Franklin Taylor, his brother Jessie Peter Taylor, and his nephew Thomas Burge Taylor owned land in the small rural community of Mount Meigs. At his death, wills were filed in both Columbia, South Carolina, and Montgomery, Alabama. The Taylors owned the Chantilly Plantation on Pike Road in Mount Meigs. Also on Pike Road were the Antioch Baptist Church, the Antioch Cemetery, and the homes of many of my family members.

In his probate will filed in Montgomery, Benjamin Franklin Taylor decrees:

> Item 8: To my son, Benjamin Walter Taylor I give, and bequeath the following slaves and their increase, Carpenter Prince, Hannah his wife, and their children, except Jimmy, also Eve and William, James, Phoebe and John, children of Hannah Thompson.
>
> Item 9: To my daughter Annie W. Mazyck I give, and bequeath the following slaves and their increase, July, brother of Eve, and Jenney and her two children.

It is important to note that Eve was listed in the "Little Boy Renty" document with her twin brother, Adam. It is also important to note that in the slaveholder's own words, Eve and a man named July are brother and sister. With this piece of factual information, I am able to definitively point to a kinship between the two Renty family groupings in the Colonel Thomas Taylor slave index of 1834. This confirms that the "Big Renty" is Papa Renty and the second Renty is his son and the father of Renty Taylor Thompson.

Professor Warren Perry was right: the truth is in the ground. If we seek insight, or a cultural understanding of the lived experiences of our enslaved ancestors, we have to look to dark and desolate places. The truth is in the ground; the answers lie in the neglected land we now call slave or African American cemeteries. After many years of research, I now possess indisputable proof that my family members lived, died, and are buried on land owned by the slave-holder Benjamin Franklin Taylor. This is confirmation that Papa Renty, who also lived, died, and is buried on this same land, is my ancestor.

17

Reparations Flow from the Tortfeasor to the Victim, Not the Other Way Around

I was so looking forward to the trial. I wanted both Renty and Delia to finally be seen and heard. To be apologized to for their horrific treatment. I also wanted Harvard to apologize to *me* for insisting that I could not prove a lineal relationship that enslavement made almost impossible to prove. I marveled, as I still do, that I was able to prove a connection that I always knew to be true. I wanted to do all of this, for Renty and Delia, and for my mother, Mattye Pearl Thompson-Lanier.

And so I was deeply disappointed, but not surprised, when Harvard filed a motion to dismiss on November 25, 2019. The reason was stated in a succinct paragraph in their motion: "All but one of Ms. Lanier's claims rests on the legal assertion that Ms. Lanier has a property interest in the daguerreotypes of Delia and Renty at the Peabody Museum because (i) the enslaved individuals depicted in these daguerreotypes are the rightful owners of the daguerreotypes due to the horrific circumstances in which they were created; and

(ii) Ms. Lanier, as a descendant of those individuals, now possesses their property interest."

They also stated, that for the purpose of this pleading, they would not dispute my claim of ancestry, but added "there is no support for the proposition that a person, in any circumstance, derives a property interest in a physical photograph (or painting or sculpture) because that photograph contains his or her image."

The second issue they raised was that my claim had exceeded a three-year statute of limitations. My lawyers were using replevin, a law that states that you must recognize that someone has something that lawfully belongs to you, and then make a demand for its return. There is a three-year window, from the date of the demand, during which you must file a cause of action.

Harvard argued that I first told them about my relationship to Renty and Delia in a letter to Drew Faust in May 2011—and that my three-year window began then. According to their reasoning, I should have made my claim by May 2014, and since I did not file my lawsuit until March 2019, I exceeded the statute of limitations.

Back in 2014, I was still in conversation with Drew Gilpin Faust, the Peabody Museum, and other professors at Harvard, including Charles Ogletree. At that time I was still anticipating that the university would keep me informed on how they intended to use Renty's and Delia's images—as Faust had indicated in all of her correspondence. It was not until the Universities and Slavery: Bound by History conference in 2017 that I realized that Harvard was knowingly misrepresenting the truth about my relationship to Renty. That was when I wrote to Faust to make my request that the university surrender the daguerreotypes to me and my family. And so according to the law of replevin, I had three years from *that moment* to file my complaint.

On February 19, 2020, my attorneys responded to Harvard's motion with my Opposition to the Defendants' Motion to Dismiss. In it

Josh wrote: "The simple fact is that Harvard engaged in tortious activity in kidnapping, invasion, assault, battery, and false imprisonment of Renty and Delia and this conduct resulted in the fabrication of tangible property. That property was used by Harvard for profit, for prestige, and for promotion of racism masquerading as science. To this day, Harvard continues to benefit from its unlawful dominion, control and use of these images. Under the common law and equity, tortfeasors like Harvard are not rewarded by bestowing upon them the fruit of their torts. Reparations flow from the tortfeasor to the victim, not the other way around."

He included another simple fact, and to me the most important: there was no precedent for this case. The Harvard attorneys were looking to established law to make their case. My attorneys had a radically different point of view: "To the plaintiff's knowledge, this case presents the first civil dispute in our country's history wherein a direct descendant of an African-born slave has asserted property rights to historical and cultural artifacts, created under brutal conditions, depicting her ancestors during enslavement."

Unprecedented. Reparations.

Harvard claimed that I did not have the right to claim a property interest, but they had never once stated why their right was superior to mine—either in their motion to dismiss, before that, or even to date. Another argument Harvard had consistently made was about "ethical stewardship." Their claim was that they were better equipped to decide how the daguerreotypes should be used than I was. As my lawyers stated in our response, "taking care of property that has been compelled by your own wrongdoing can never be ethical."

Less than a month after we filed our opposition to Harvard's motions to dismiss, Covid shut down the world. This meant all matters before the court would take place via Zoom. I was, truthfully, devastated. As a probation officer, I knew the impact of being in a courtroom—and I wanted my day *in court*. I wanted to face the judge.

I had testified on the stand many times before and worried that a virtual hearing might present certain disadvantages: How would I communicate or pass messages with my attorneys? Would I be able to see the other players on Harvard's team and gauge their reactions? A virtual hearing felt unnatural and disconnected. In a strange way, I felt cheated.

The date was finally set for October 20, 2020—almost two years after the filing of our complaint and a decade after my mother's death. In between our filing in February and that scheduled court date, George Floyd was murdered, and the world erupted in support of the Black Lives Matter movement. Confederate monuments came down and white supremacist names were removed from public spaces, including Louis Agassiz. In February 2020, prior to the Black Lives Matter reckoning that Floyd's murder inspired, the Cambridge City Council voted to remove Agassiz's name from its neighborhoods and cited the *Lanier v. Harvard* lawsuit as their inspiration. To have a reparations lawsuit being heard in this very moment felt prescient. I was cautiously optimistic that the judge would be open to new interpretations of the law—and would motion to move forward with our case.

As I drove to the Koskoff law firm the morning of October 20, I thought, Finally! This was Renty's date with destiny.

The matter of *Lanier v. Harvard* would be heard by the Honorable Judge Camille F. Sarrouf Jr., who was ruling on Harvard's motion to dismiss. I got to the office early and was set up in a conference room all by myself, so I could be on camera without a mask. Josh was in his office and two other lawyers were in a separate office with a big whiteboard visible to Josh. Ben was in his office in Florida. When it was time to log in to the courtroom Zoom, I took a deep breath. I had no idea what to expect. I was excited about moving forward, but anxious about what might happen.

As we were each invited into the virtual courtroom, I saw my computer screen populate with faces I recognized: Ben, Josh, and other lawyers I'd been working closely with as well as Shonrael and Megan, Seymour Reichlin, Meredith McKinney, Sasha Huber, Marian Moore, and Susanna Moore. There were an equal number of familiar faces and new faces whom I did not recognize—all there to support me.

The judge welcomed everyone and noted that the one good thing about a virtual court case was how many people were able to attend as a result.

"We have one hundred twenty-six participants, and it is highly unlikely that so many would fit in the courtroom," he said.

I was trying to read the judge—to see if I could get a sense of where he stood—so that comment was encouraging. But then he added, in a very dispassionate way: "I've read the full file, I understand the claims, I understand the relief requested."

That made me nervous—he seemed to only be interested in the relief, not the entirety of the complaint itself. He next asked for introductions, and Josh took the opportunity to say, "Your honor, it could be argued that Renty and Delia have waited one hundred and seventy years for their day in court."

May it be so, I thought, and wished my mother were alive to witness this first hearing, as it would establish whether or not I had the right to a trial by jury. The judge would rule on Harvard's motion to dismiss my claim. I felt that we had an excellent chance of moving forward to trial, but I also thought about *Open Season: The Legalized Genocide of Colored People*, the book Benjamin Crump had written about his experience as a Black lawyer in America who had witnessed firsthand the two systems of justice. I could not make any assumptions.

Following the introductions, each side stated their case. Anton Metlitsky, Harvard's lawyer, went first as the defendant and explained that Harvard's biggest issue with our complaint was that photographs were always owned by the photographer. He argued that was the law, and our complaint was therefore without merit. I was dumbfounded, as were my attorneys, because Harvard was not the photographer. What was their property interest? They have still, to date, not answered this question. During Josh's response, he countered, "But our claim is that [Harvard doesn't] own them because [Renty and Delia] were the *victims* of criminal acts that created these daguerreotypes. . . . There's no question that Harvard's agent, Agassiz, and his accomplices committed crimes against Renty and Delia. As a matter of rock-solid tort principle law, they are not entitled to ownership of those daguerreotypes. . . . The only owner that would be entitled to those would be Renty and Delia, as victims. The only question Harvard won't answer is, why don't they just give them back?"

The judge then allowed Ben to speak, and he began by evoking the promise I made to my mother: to write down my family story. The prompt that led me to this very moment. Ben reiterated what Josh had said about Renty and Delia being victims, but he took it a step further by asking the judge to consider what might have happened if my ancestors had refused to be photographed.

"They would have been beaten. They would have been starved. They would have been tortured to death. Put simply, it is clear beyond any doubt that Renty and Delia would never have been given any option to refuse. These pictures were created at Harvard's direction and at Renty's expense, at Delia's expense, at the expense of Renty's lineal descendants and at the expense of every lineal descendant of African slavery in America."

As he spoke, I was beginning to recognize just how historic this moment was. This was bigger than me. It was not just about me, Renty, or Delia. This was about the redress of all American descendants of chattel slavery. This was about reparations.

The judge then allowed Harvard to respond, in rebuttal. Metlitsky agreed that enslavement was horrible, as was Agassiz's pseudo-science and racism, and the conditions under which the daguerreotypes were taken. But, he added, "the Peabody is a museum with an educational mission. And these images are crucial for not only trying to understand the lives of the people captured in the daguerreotypes but trying to understand the institution of slavery itself."

We had agreed beforehand that I would not speak that day, so I had to hold my tongue. That was hard. I so badly wanted to ask, "Do you even understand what you are saying? You are making an argument for plunder. That your right to spin and tell Renty's story is superior to mine and that my legacy and my Black ancestry do not matter. This is miseducation, colonization, and cultural appropriation at its worst! This is unethical stewardship!"

Thankfully, Ben had the last word and ended with a powerful summary: "Judge, I implore you to let Renty finally make his case in court and to the world, even if it's a hundred and seventy years later. Your honor, this court has the power to make the law an instrument for good, not to be used as a weapon to oppress by the enemies of equality. This was a landmark case. If Ms. Lanier is granted an opportunity, this could be the first time in history that an American institution has been required to make a lineal descendant of an African slave whole according to the American system of justice."

Ben compared my fight to Free Renty to the Black Lives Matter movement. He said, in closing, "She made a promise on her mama's deathbed, that her Papa Renty's life mattered. That Black lives matter."

As the hearing ended, the judge indicated, in an emotionless way, that he had heard our arguments and would make his ruling. After his closing remarks, people were allowed to turn on their microphones. Suddenly I heard a symphony of familiar and unfamiliar voices shouting, "Free Renty!" and "Black Lives Matter!" in an almost choral effect. It made my heart swell knowing how many people had shown up to support me—as well as Renty and Delia. I knew many of the participants, and realized, just as I was about to sign off, that everyone on the Zoom had shown up for me. No one was there to defend Harvard—because they were indefensible.

Afterward, during our debrief, Josh said, "It's that argument of institutional entitlement."

He was frustrated.

"That got me," Ben said. "They were saying, Okay, Black people, we are going to tell you about your Black experience. Why can't [Tammy] decide where her family photos are going to be?"

—

Several months later, we were still in Covid lockdown. It was a brisk March afternoon and I was out for my daily walk when I received an incoming call from France. By then I was used to getting calls from reporters from all over the world, so I assumed this was someone who wanted to talk to me about my case. I was right. He introduced himself as a Harvard graduate who had written about me for the *Crimson* and was now working in France for a newspaper.

"I just wanted to get your comments," he said.

"On what?" I asked.

"On the court's decision to throw out your case," he responded.

That stopped me midstride.

"I don't know what you are talking about!"

My heart began to race. Was this a joke?

"I'm looking at the judge's decision right now," he said.

Within a matter of moments, he'd texted it to me.

"I'm sorry but I can't comment until I speak with my attorneys," was all I could muster. I hung up and immediately texted Josh and Ben at the same time. Neither had heard the ruling either, so I forwarded the document to them. Then I opened it up on my phone and read the first paragraph: "After hearing and careful review, for the following reasons, the motion to dismiss is **ALLOWED**."

I felt so beaten up.

As I read through his fifteen-page decision, all I could see was a reiteration of Harvard's argument. The judge did not consider anything my attorneys had said, nor did he seem to be moved by any part of the complaint. Instead he embraced Harvard's argument and did not give our pleading any consideration. He took every single one of their arguments and summarized why they were, in his opinion, legally defensible. He then ended each point that Harvard motioned to dismissed with the word **ALLOWED**. All caps and bolded.

Each time I read that word, repeated throughout the document, it felt like a slap in the face. I believed that I had a right to a trial by jury, and that our arguments were sound and deserved to be argued in court. With this decision, the judge pulled the rug out from underneath me. I was halfway through the verdict when my phone rang. It was Ben.

"Don't worry, Ms. Lanier," he said. "We're going to appeal this."

My phone beeped, and I saw that it was Josh.

"Take it, Tammy," Ben said, his voice always a salve, even in a moment like this. "We're with you."

I clicked over to Josh, who was equally disappointed in the verdict.

"Tammy, in Massachusetts the normal process would be to appeal to Mass. Appellate Court," he said. "We'll go straight to the Massachusetts Supreme Judicial Court. You will have your day in court, I promise you that!"

This was a devastating blow, but then I heard the inspirational words of my mom: "Be encouraged. Life is about turning setbacks into comebacks."

18

Documents of Dubious Origin

As the news spread about the devastating ruling, people began reaching out, offering their support. My lawyers immediately began the process of filing our motion for direct appellate review by the Massachusetts Supreme Judicial Court, and fielding requests from various people who offered to submit amicus, or friend-of-the-court, briefs. One was from Ariella Aïsha Azoulay, a professor of modern culture and media and comparative literature at Brown University whose scholarship focuses on photography and the political theory of reparations, plunder, and restitution. She'd written several scholarly pieces on our case. David Grubin had interviewed her for the documentary, and her book *Potential History: Unlearning Imperialism* had a section on Papa Renty and Delia.

Her amicus brief was a stinging indictment of Harvard's claim to the daguerreotypes. As she wrote, "If Harvard 'possesses' these daguerreotypes it can only be because of the cultural logic of its wealth, property, and ownership flows directly from slavery and preserves its lingering presence in our own era."

Her thesis was stunning in its simplicity: "Harvard's dismissal of Lanier brings to mind Jewish German philosopher Walter Benjamin's observation that when history is written by the victorious and at the expense of the victims and survivors, the spoils become 'cultural treasures.' Only the victorious are permitted to claim as legally theirs what was seized from others. The latter were deprived of their freedom and rights and continue to live under the institutional condition dictating that their grievances go unheard."

Azoulay was able to articulate the feeling I had since the moment I saw Renty and Delia imprisoned in those images. She pointed out that since the daguerreotypes were created the same year as the Fugitive Slave Act of 1850, Renty and Delia were used to "train" white Americans to see Black people as "enslavable." Also, by "holding these images as part of its archival and museal capital, Harvard continues to train millions to view Renty and Delia not as ancestors or relatives, but as enslaved people."

It confirmed my feeling that Harvard wanted Renty and Delia to be seen as symbols of enslavement. They refused to see them for who they were, and only would see them as who they want them to be. Not as people—and certainly not as my ancestors. The appropriation of their identity, their humanity, and their likenesses was a furtherance of Agassiz's racist propaganda.

Azoulay is an expert in restitution, the practice of giving back something that was lost or stolen to its original owner. In her amicus brief she points to the return of art objects "plundered from the Jews of Europe by the Nazis and the Vichy regime" as an example of why this act of repatriation is both possible and necessary. Two laws—one in France, the other in Germany—allowed victims and their heirs to lay claim to such property. As recently as 2017, an American couple was ordered to return a Camille Pissarro painting to the heirs of the original Jewish owner. The couple did not know, when they purchased the art piece, that it had been stolen as the result of "a crime against humanity"—the persecution of Jews during World War II—and that the act of restitution, or returning the artwork to the person originally harmed as a result, was necessary to begin repairing that harm.

Reading this made me lament that there are two systems of justice. There are laws that protect the cultural relics and property of Holocaust survivors and their descendants, and other laws that protect the same for Native Americans and their descendants. But they don't exist for the descendants of chattel slavery—nor is there even a willingness to entertain that they should. That's what I wanted to change with my case.

Beyond restitution, Azoulay also delves into the politics of photography—and the question, both legal and moral, of who owns the rights to the image itself. Judge Sarrouf states in his decision, "It is a basic tenet of common law that the subject of a photograph has no interest in the negative or any photographs printed from the negative. . . . Rather, the negative and any photographs are the property of the photographer." In sum, the photograph always belongs to the photographer.

It's not so simple with the daguerreotypes. Harvard was not the photographer. Agassiz commissioned Zealy to make the daguerreotypes, which is a separate and distinct process from photography. Instead of addressing any of these issues, Sarrouf adds: "This principle is even held true when an image is taken without the subject's consent."

Azoulay focuses on this point in her brief. While Sarrouf acknowledged the "horrific circumstances" under which Renty and Delia were photographed, and "the continuing impact of slavery in the United States," he still concluded that "the law, as it currently stands, does not confer a property interest to the subject of a photograph regardless of how objectionable the photograph's origin may be." Azoulay sums up why this interpretation of the law needs to be revisited: "Photographs taken under circumstances of violence are not reducible to what is recorded in them, since the violence that enable their creation does not disappear after the camera's shutter clicks. Photographs taken to support violent regimes or acts retain the original violence in the image; they *continue to sustain the original act of violence* well after the image was produced."

Her interpretation helped me understand the physical pain I experienced every time I saw Renty's or Delia's image being used, whether as a backdrop to a lecture or on the cover of a pamphlet or book. Each time, I felt the violence Renty and Delia experienced in that Charleston studio in 1850. It was as if the act of forcing them to strip naked and be photographed as "human data" for a scientific experiment to prove their inhumanity was directly transferred to me. The violence lives in those images—it happened not only to Renty and Delia, but was passed down to their loved ones, their families, their descendants.

Azoulay's argument works on both a personal level and a global one. Returning the daguerreotypes to the descendant of the person forcibly photographed is an act of restitution that begins the process of repair. It is also an example of how we can begin to respond to enslavement—in the United States and beyond—as a "crime against humanity." I know, from my years as a probation officer, that the role of the court is to make crime victims whole. Restitution, the return of property that was plundered, is a way of repairing this harm. "Slavery in the United States was ended without any kind of proceeding akin to the Nuremberg trials, in which perpetrators of crimes against humanity were indicted and punished, while reparations and restitution followed," Azoulay writes. Agassiz created the daguerreotypes to justify the enslavement of Black people—and as Azoulay summarizes, "As long as spectators possess the right to view the photographed persons in scenes of captivity—with the photographs handled as if they are the museum's property—Black [people] will forever be presented as 'slaves.'"

She compared the return of Renty and Delia's daguerreotypes to me and my family to the other infamous objects that have been restituted. One macabre example: "The University of Pennsylvania announced plans to repatriate human skulls from Morton's collection, including several skulls of enslaved people." She ends her brilliant report with a section on "Restitution as Family Reunion." After arguing that as long as the daguerreotypes are handled as Harvard's property, Black people will "forever be presented as slaves," she sees a way for the world to see Renty and Delia as human beings. "We have the opportunity now, amid the wealth of activism and scholarship on the entanglement of photography and museums with slavery, and in parallel to an increasing number of restitution cases, to redress what Renty and his relatives were deprived of in the 1850s. We have the opportunity for the unique imprint of Renty's presence on a silver plate to finally find its place where it belongs—with his family."

Amen.

Azoulay was just one of several brilliant scholars who reached out and offered support. Jarrett Martin Drake was working on his PhD in anthropology at Harvard when he came across my story. Intrigued, he reached out to Ben Crump, who sent me a text to say that he had been contacted by a very gifted young man who was interested in our case. Jarrett and I arranged to meet one Sunday morning—he came early as I always leave for church at 11 a.m. sharp. We talked over coffee, and I was blown away by his academic résumé.

Prior to his arrival at Harvard, he had received his BA in history from Yale; his MA in science of information, with a focus on archives and record management, from the University of Michigan, and had worked as Princeton University's first-ever digital archivist. He had already attained his MA in anthropology at Harvard and had authored more than two dozen articles about archives, memory, and justice.

That morning, Jarrett shared that he had been doing research on the daguerreotypes for a school project and had concerns about Harvard's ownership claim. In a follow-up letter to me and the attorneys, he wrote, "Neither the [Peabody] Museum nor the University has produced any documentary evidence to substantiate a clear chain of custody for the principle of provenance." He found this troubling, since when he worked at Princeton's department of archives, he said, "provenance guided everything from how we stored materials to how we described them in online publications for researchers to find them. Practically, this entailed maintenance of any and all documentation pertaining to how the materials came into our custody."

Harvard had never supplied any of that documentation to me, or my lawyers. Why did they feel they had the right to own the artifacts? Jarrett was asking the same questions as I was: "Who precisely gifted the daguerreotypes to the museum and the university? When precisely did such a gift take place? And were such persons authorized to make such a gift?"

Jarrett was trained as an archivist and in this same letter he cited the International Council on Archives (ICA) Code of Ethics, published in 1995, which states, "Archives and archivists should observe faithfully and apply impartially all agreements made at the time of acquisition, but, in the interest of liberalization of access, should renegotiate conditions in accordance with changes of circumstances." He added that "no such agreements" had been provided by Harvard that would "more than meet the criteria of documents of dubious origins" for which the ICA provides a "clear, unambiguous ethical mandate."

He ends his letter with his professional assessment: "Given that Ms. Lanier has demonstrated her descendancy from Delia and Renty, it would follow that she—not the Museum or University—is the rightful custodian of their images."

That letter became an early draft of his brief, which he circulated among colleagues and peers in the world of archivists, anthropologists, and doctoral candidates. Jarrett also wanted to include the issue of privacy in his brief, which was something Meredith McKinney had also explored from a public health background as well. In her amicus brief, she cited the Belmont Report, whereas Jarrett referenced the Society of American Archivists (SAA), whose code of ethics, revised as of 2020, states that archivists must "establish procedures and policies to protect the interests of the donors, individuals, groups, and organizations whose public and private lives and activities are documented in archival holdings" and "promote the respectful use of culturally sensitive materials and their care."

Both briefs made me realize how the daguerreotypes are historic for many reasons: When the images were taken, slavery was legal in South Carolina. Yet we now have protocols across disciplines—regarding privacy and provenance—to protect the rights of vulnerable people, and to ensure that the violence that happened specifically to Renty and Delia will never happen again. Harvard was not adhering to any of this.

Jarrett turned his letter into an even more researched brief, which was formalized in October 2021. In it he states his two concerns clearly:

1. First, neither the Museum nor the University has produced any documentary evidence to substantiate a clear chain of custody for the daguerreotypes in question. This absence of custodial information is in direct conflict with the core archival principle of provenance.

2. Second, by widely publishing and distributing copies of Renty's and Delia's images of nearly naked bodies, the Museum and University have flagrantly violated Renty's and Delia's rights to privacy, which was certainly an anathema to antebellum law, but is an essential ingredient for archival practice.

He ends his brief just as powerfully, stating: "SAA has published guidelines for how and when an institution ought to re-evaluate and return materials in custody. These practices, known as 're-appraisal' and 'deaccessioning,' provide archival repositories with an important framework for offering correctives to past wrongs. The professional and ethical guidance from national and international archival bodies hold that the daguerreotypes of Delia and Renty belong to Ms. Lanier. By allowing the defendants to retain these materials, the Court would encourage other institutions to acquire materials in such a dubious and illicit manner."

As moving as his argument was the fact that more than fifty people in his profession signed in support of his brief—including many archivists, librarians, and researchers from Harvard, Yale, the University of California, Los Angeles, and more.

Renty's army of angels was growing. Cornelia Bewersdorf, a German attorney based in Connecticut who specializes in human rights issues, wrote an amicus brief that focused on the fact that slavery was illegal in Massachusetts, where Harvard is based and where Agassiz was employed in 1850. She cites the lawsuit of Quock Walker in 1783, when Chief Justice William Cushing declared, "And upon this ground our Constitution of Government, by which the people of this Commonwealth have solemnly bound themselves, sets out with declaring that all men are born free and equal—and every subject is entitled to liberty, and to have it guarded by the laws, as well as life and property—and in short is totally repugnant to the idea of being born slaves." If we brought this case in any other state, it would not have the same legal impact.

Harvard funded Agassiz and supported his research at a time when slavery was illegal in the Bay State—and Renty's and Delia's images were taken without their consent. Bewersdorf uses the Peabody publication *To Make Their Own Way in the World: The Enduring Legacy of the Zealy Daguerreotypes* to prove that Harvard continues to use their images in the same dehumanizing way. "Renty's image is published as one among many. Harvard refused to publish his story as known by the plaintiff through historical knowledge of his person handed down from generation to generation. Conversely, Harvard uses Renty's daguerreotype to fill the book to primarily give editors and scholars a place to publish their work. The photographer Zealy is mentioned more times than the enslaved persons that were violated."

This was the book that Manisha Sinha told me about the day I went to hear her speak. It was also the "project" Ilisa Barbash said she was working on—so I was not surprised to see that both she and Molly Rogers were listed on the cover as editors, along with Deborah Willis. For me, the fact that Zealy was mentioned more than those he photographed against their will that day was another example of how Harvard celebrates the wrongdoer and marginalizes my enslaved ancestors and the others.

When that book came out, in September 2020, the book critic Parul Sehgal wrote a review in the *New York Times*—and dedicated several paragraphs to my story. She was amazed, as was I, that my relationship to Renty and Delia is only mentioned once in the nearly five-hundred-page tome. Henry Louis Gates Jr. wrote the foreword, titled "Who Are These People?" In it he states, "We know their names: Delia, Jack, Renty, Drana, Jem, Alfred, and Fassena. Details of their lives are scarce, but the scholars in this volume have filled in some of the gaps."

Toward the end of his essay, he writes, "[The daguerreotypes] have also raised searching questions of provenance and ownership. In 2019, for instance, Tamara Lanier filed a lawsuit to gain ownership of the daguerreotypes of Renty and Delia, claiming that she is a descendant of Renty and charging Harvard used the images for advertising and commercial purposes."

To boil down my relationship to one sentence, this sentence summarizes Harvard's treatment of me: Marginalized. Erased.

Sehgal too finds it "odd," writing, "In his introduction, Gates downplays Lanier's connection to Renty. . . . Why would Lanier's claim threaten the 'pondering' and protection of the pictures? What does he imagine Lanier has in mind for them?"

Harvard has never asked me—they have only dismissed me. And yet, so many others have rallied behind me. Sehgal also notes, "Lanier's revelation arrives in the midst of decolonial movements around the world, calls for museums to repatriate stolen relics and universities examining their ties to slavery. She has found popular support."

To that point, the amicus brief filed jointly by Dan Hicks, a professor of contemporary archaeology at Oxford University, and Nicholas Mirzoeff, a professor of media, culture, and communication at New York University, echoed Drake's and Azoulay's questions around repatriation and restitution, emphasizing that "it is a normal, mainstream museum process for human skulls and sacred ancestral cultural items to be returned to descendant individuals and communities on a case-by-case basis."

With each argument, I felt a growing momentum. Meredith McKinney continued her advocacy on Renty and Delia's behalf, and by the time she had submitted her brief, the Coalition to Free Renty had partnered with over ten recognized Harvard student associations and had collected nearly 58,000 signatures, "all calling for the surrender of the daguerreotypes and associated data to descendants as well as the surrender of Harvard's claimed ownership over the Lanier family legacy."

Harvard was fighting to hold on to these ancestral artifacts while academics from all these other prestigious institutions—Brown, Oxford, NYU, and even Harvard itself—were urging them to do the right thing and let them go. Harvard had an opportunity to take a leadership position on restitution and they refused.

It was a titan against titans.

And more of the titans were siding with me.

19

Renty Finally Has His Day in Court

In our motion for direct appellate review by the Massachusetts Supreme Judicial Court, the attorneys argued that it was a basic tenet of common law that the "wrongdoer" is never rewarded with the fruit of their tort; that another basic precept of common law is the protection of one from the wrongful acts of another. And finally, that Harvard was a tortfeasor, responsible for irreparable harm.

In defense of the university, Harvard's attorneys filed a motion to dismiss, arguing that a photo, irrespective of the violent or criminal nature in which it was acquired, *always* belongs to the photographer—there are no exceptions, this is settled law.

Thankfully, Massachusetts's highest court agreed to hear our case.

Oral arguments were scheduled for the morning of November 1, 2021. As Megan and I approached the historic John Adams Courthouse in Boston, I kept thinking, This is our date with destiny. From 1850 to November 1, 2021, I had to acknowledge the many extraordinary events that led me to the place where I now stood. To begin, the courthouse was named for John Adams, our second president, who was born in Massachusetts. His son, John Quincy Adams, petitioned the US Supreme Court for the freedom of Cinque and thirty-four other Mende men from the slave ship *Amistad*. He argued that case in 1841, which led to the men being returned to Africa in what has been considered the first civil rights case in the United States. Decades earlier, in 1783, this was also where the Massachusetts Supreme Judicial Court made the courageous decision to abolish slavery in Massachusetts and free Elizabeth "Mum Bett" Freeman, one of the first enslaved people to sue for her freedom after hearing her owner and his friends discussing the newly ratified Massachusetts Constitution.

There was so much history in this one building—I desperately wanted Renty and Delia to contribute to that pathway of freedom for all that Mum Bett had begun nearly two centuries earlier. It made me think of the famous line from *Hamlet,* "There is a special providence in the fall of a sparrow," which I interpret to mean that nothing in our past, present, or future happens without God's knowledge or consent. I knew that there was a greater purpose for everything that we had been through. And I believed that the answers lay within this courthouse.

As I walked through the marble halls with their stately columns and into the courtroom, I was distracted by the majesty of the building and the history contained within its walls. I could not help but wonder, Why does the courtroom look like a museum? It made me remember that the Peabody, also a museum, was where my journey began. I had come full circle. My thoughts were of the layered histories of this moment: we were there petitioning for Renty's and Delia's freedom—would these justices have the courage to grant that? Like those who did for Mum Bett back in 1783?

In his opening remarks, Attorney Crump echoed that sentiment: "The fact that I stand before you as a free man, and not a slave, is a testament to someone's decision to change the course of human history. It's a testament of our legal system—a testament that was led by the courts here in Massachusetts when Chief Justice William Cushing in 1783 judicially abolished slavery in the Quock Walker case. And it is the reason why he's so often quoted even 250 years later, with the holding that the idea of slavery is inconsistent with our conduct and our constitution. The second historical reference is from the great Negro abolitionist Frederick Douglass, who once said, 'genealogical trees do not flourish among slaves.' In essence, what Frederick Douglass was saying is that slavery destroyed the African American family connection to their ancestral lineage."

His point moved me: The fact that I even had to prove my lineage, considering that Renty had been stolen from the Congo and his family repeatedly broken up and violated since that first heinous act, was a testament to my own resilience and defiance. And to my mother's before me.

During the proceedings, the justices had many questions for the Harvard attorney:

"What is your property interest in the daguerreotypes?"

"Isn't your argument that the photo always belongs to the photographer too broad?"

"Aren't there exceptions to that rule?"

"Does a child pornographer have a property interest in his photos?"

The court, on several occasions, referred to Harvard as the employer of the wrongdoer, the joint tortfeasor. The justices each took turns rigorously interrogating the Harvard attorney, Metlitsky. He was peppered with deeply probing and complex legal questions. It was interesting to watch the crafty way in which he danced around and dodged the direct line of questioning.

Justice Scott Kafker asked: "In these awful circumstances where you're performing, in the words of Mr. Crump, an illegitimate scientific racist experiment, should Harvard get to keep the pictures? I understand that they've got some difficult arguments to make to explain their property interest, but your simple point, just because you are the photographer you get to keep the pictures—there are exceptions to that rule. If you kidnap somebody and take half-naked pictures of them, you don't get to keep the pictures. You take pictures of a child naked, that's a crime—you don't get to keep the pictures. So, there are limits on your possessory interest if it arises out of criminal or tortious behavior, right?"

"Exactly!" I said out loud, prompting Megan to turn and shush me, motioning with her fingers that she was going to pinch me if I didn't keep quiet, as my mom would do when we were being too loud in church.

"It's hard," I whispered.

She smiled. We were both channeling my mother.

The rules of the courtroom were that everyone, except the judge and attorneys, would speak when directed. But I was imploding in my seat; I couldn't contain myself. I also understood the decorum expected during Supreme Judicial Court proceedings and prior to the hearing I had joked with Josh, promising that there would be no Perry Mason moment where I would interject from the aisles. But the line of questioning between Justice Elspeth Cypher and Metlitsky tested me.

Cypher asked: "All right, you are talking about it only as a photograph, and what we're actually dealing with are photographs of an object that can't be replicated. The object, I'm concerned about the object! Right now, for this argument, I don't want to talk about the photographs, just about the object. Are you disagreeing that human beings have an inherent property right in their body?"

Metlitsky responded, "No, of course not."

"All right," the judge continued. "So with that in mind, there's no question that this was done under circumstances, that at least in Massachusetts at the time were illegal, we don't even have to look to today, and say, Oh, today's different—then in Massachusetts it was not right. So why isn't this a fruit or an instrumentality of the crime?"

I felt like a jack-in-the-box who is unable to pop up. Under my breath, I was shouting, "Yes! Yes! Yes! She gets it—she understands!"

All nine judges spoke that day, and each pressed Harvard to answer the basic question, "What is your property interest in the daguerreotypes?"

Harvard was unable to answer it.

I left the court feeling cautiously optimistic.

That spring, another Harvard student reached out to me. Franco Paz was a third-year graduate student in the History Department, working on his PhD dissertation about capitalism and enslavement. That semester he was taking a class on investigative reporting with Jill Abramson, the journalist and former executive editor of the *New York Times*, and the first woman to hold that position. She had assigned my case to her students, and Franco asked me for an interview. I was happy to oblige. By then I knew to trust Harvard's students. Everyone I had encountered since my lawsuit was filed seemed passionate about Renty's story—and mine.

We spoke on the phone for several hours one evening in April and the next day Franco wrote me an email explaining that he now wanted to do a much larger story. It would not be just about me and the lawsuit, or Harvard's refusal to acknowledge me; he also wanted to focus on "the historical narrative of Renty's life and his significance to this nation's history," adding, "Here I want to stress the importance of oral histories—how we're reduced to thinking of people as 'invisible' when we refuse to take these seriously and instead favor only the most white-centric sorts of evidence."

I was floored. After one conversation with me, he understood precisely what I had been fighting for all these years. I was so relieved and grateful. His brilliant analytical insight reminded me of Meredith and Jarrett. It is because of them that I now often say, "The students get it!"

Franco also told me that he was one of the Harvard students asked to work on the *Harvard & the Legacy of Slavery* report, which was set to be released on April 26, 2022. I'd heard from other students that President Bacow was heading Harvard's initiative to attempt to address all the ways in which the university was involved in, and benefited from, enslavement. During our call, Franco said that Harvard did not include key findings he uncovered while researching Harvard's connections—which frustrated and disappointed him. He also said that the university was adamant that the daguerreotypes were not to be part of this project. He added that he was glad to have a place to use that reporting—not just for Jill's class, but he hoped to get this piece published in a national newspaper as well.

"People need to know that Harvard isn't just a university," he wrote. "It's literally the oldest corporation in the Western Hemisphere, and . . . they continue to behave as such. If Harvard has become the wealthiest university in the world, it has done so in no small part from profiting from the enslavement and exploitation of others."

Other students from Jill Abramson's class reached out for interviews as well, since she had assigned my case to her entire class of fifteen. Each and every one of them had thoughtful, insightful questions. Inspired, I emailed Jill directly to thank her for having what I described as "the courage to explore how racism intersects with ethical stewardship" and how, I believed, that was the "epitome of Veritas."

I also sent her a link to the *Free Renty* documentary, which had started to make the rounds at film festivals. Jill responded, "The thanks is all to you for helping my students. We watched the documentary and found it inspiring and excellent. . . . We are trying to find a location on campus to screen the film."

Her kind email ended with an invitation to meet at her home in Madison, Connecticut, that April. Jean came, my wing woman.

"Your story would make a good memoir," Jill said the afternoon of our visit. "Have you thought about publishing it?"

"Funny you should ask," I replied. "I've been working on one for the last ten years! I was thinking of self-publishing."

"I'd be happy to help you," she said.

When I left her house, I was amazed yet again at the power of Papa Renty's story to move people. He inspired the most formidable people to act in very specific ways on his behalf—whether it was Ellie Reichlin leaving her job at the Peabody in order to uncover the history of the daguerreotypes, or Sasha Huber renaming a mountain in honor of him. Or Charles Ogletree and David Harris, who were willing to speak up in support for Renty when so many other Harvard professors remained silent. Or John Lewis and John Conyers so clearly seeing the connections between Renty and reparations. Or Ben Crump and Mike Koskoff understanding that his case would be historic. These people were all legends in their fields, and now I had one of the most esteemed journalists and writers in the world offer to help me publish my story. The power of Papa Renty.

I marveled at how far I'd come since promising my mother to "write it down."

Back then, my goal was to document our family's oral history, like the one my mother's cousin had done for Big Mammy. Papa Renty's story, however, was inspiring not just to me and my immediate family, but to the whole world. I also thought, *Veritas*: telling the truth about Renty is what would ultimately make him free.

Jill understood this and helped me write a proposal, which she sent to her agent, Suzanne Gluck. It mapped my journey, beginning with my childhood stories, to this moment, waiting for the Massachusetts Supreme Judicial Court to share their decision.

Suzanne and I met via Zoom with two other agents. After we spoke, she shared with me that both agents told her that she had to represent me. She, like Jill Abramson, is a legend in her field.

"Tammy, all my colleagues agreed, this story is big," Suzanne said. "It could be the next *Roots*!"

At about 9:30 a.m. on June 23, 2022, I was waiting in my doctor's office for my Covid booster shot when my phone buzzed. It was a text alert and the subject line read, "Decision today in Lanier Case." The message indicated that the court's decision would be released at 10 a.m.

Ever since that reporter told me that the first decision was public, I had been stalking the Massachusetts Supreme Judicial Court website looking for updates on our case. I even signed up for an alert. This time around, I wanted to learn their decision before I was contacted by the media.

I knew that Josh was at the superior court in Waterbury, Connecticut, defending the Sandy Hook victims from libelous and slanderous accusations of Alex Jones that morning, and that Ben Crump was engaged with the family of a police brutality victim. Both lawyers were busy with very high-profile cases, and I was torn about contacting them. Yet, for almost eight months, I had been waiting for this decision. Now that it was on the verge of release, I was not ready.

I also needed my Covid booster! As I approached the counter to reschedule, the door opened and my name was called. I was in and out in less than five minutes and then raced to my car and called Josh, who asked that I forward him the link.

I next telephoned Attorney Crump, who said, "I'm on my way to Connecticut right now!"

As it turned out, he was heading to meet with the family of Randy Cox, who was paralyzed after being handcuffed and placed in a paddy wagon with no seat belt during his arrest. They had scheduled a press conference in New Haven for later that afternoon.

I sat in my car, waiting to access the link.

When it finally became public, I saw that the decision was ninety-one pages long. I don't know why but I scrolled to the last page and read the conclusion—it was a stinging indictment of Harvard.

I could not believe what I was reading.

"The result reached by the court underscores the need for the cause of action I have articulated in order to provide a full remedy for the harms alleged by the plaintiff. Failing to recognize that the plaintiff, as a descendant of Renty and Delia, may have a claim to the daguerreotypes superior to Harvard's is precisely the sort of miscarriage of justice that the late Chief Justice [Ralph] Gants warned us against perpetuating. We are faced with an aggrieved plaintiff who has pleaded facts that, if proved, demand a full remedy and nothing less. It is within this court's authority to provide such remedy by recognizing the cause of action I have articulated today."

The phrases "miscarriage of justice" and "demand a full remedy" stood out, almost as if the words were leaping from the page. In that moment I thought, This novel legal argument had never been tested in an American courtroom before and now the Massachusetts Supreme Judicial Court is looking for a way to fashion a remedy where there is no precedent. Wow.

Just then, Josh called back. He was in the clerk's office and was reading as fast as I was. I could hear the background on his end: the clerks were celebrating the news.

"We won! We are going to sue the pants off Harvard!" Josh was shouting into the phone.

Crump also called, equally excited. "Ms. Lanier, this is historic! We are going to make Harvard pay for what they've done to your ancestor."

Sitting in the front seat of my car, I was giddy. Every justice made a statement that aligned with our complaint. Once I got to the end, I drove home, thrilled.

That euphoria was quickly tempered by another call from Josh. By jumping to the end of the document, I had read one justice's concurring opinion—but not the court's decision, which was on the front page. What I missed was the court ruling to allow Harvard to keep the daguerreotypes.

"Josh! How could that be?"

Josh, in his best legalese, turned what felt like a setback into a potential comeback. He explained, "Harvard now knows, the Supreme Judicial Court made it very clear; they have a 'duty' to engage with you 'respectfully'—that anything other than that would lead to another cause of action, and trust me, they don't want that."

In other words, if Harvard does anything with the daguerreotypes from this moment on, or does not engage respectfully with me, I could bring another cause of action for emotional distress against the university.

Once I got home, Josh called again. "This is a landmark and historic decision!" he said. "Rarely do you see such language in a decision. Although Harvard gets to keep the daguerreotypes, this is the best-case scenario for you and the door is not necessarily closed on your recovering the images. Harvard has acted recklessly. Outrageously. The language is so convicting."

After I hung up with Josh, I went back and read the entire document.

Justice Kafker wrote the deciding opinion, which included:

> As we have already observed, Harvard's past complicity in the repugnant actions by which the daguerreotypes were produced informs its present responsibilities to the descendants of the individuals coerced into having their half-naked images captured in the daguerreotypes. Whether Harvard's response to Lanier's inquiries about the daguerreotypes resulted in a breach of basic community standards of decency cannot be evaluated without taking into account its historic responsibility for Agassiz's role in the horrific circumstances by which those very daguerreotypes were created. . . .
>
> As thoughtfully explained in the concurrence by the Chief Justice and in the amicus brief submitted by Jarrett Martin Drake, Harvard's actions in this regard starkly depart from standards of archival practices widely recognized today. . . . Because we conclude that the alleged facts, taken as true, plausibly support claims for negligent and indeed reckless infliction of emotional distress, we vacate the dismissal of the plaintiff's claim for negligent infliction of emotional distress and remand the case to the Superior Court to allow the plaintiff to amend her complaint to incorporate allegations of reckless infliction of emotional distress.
>
> The dismissal of Lanier's other claims, however, we affirm.

Chief Justice Kimberly Budd wrote a concurring opinion, which included:

> I agree with the court's holding that Harvard's exploitation of the enslavement of Lanier's ancestors forges a special relationship between Harvard and Lanier that obligates Harvard to exercise reasonable care in responding to Lanier's claim that the daguerreotypes in its possession depict her ancestors. As the court explains, because Lanier plausibly alleges facts that would support a finding that Harvard woefully failed to satisfy this duty of care, thereby causing Lanier emotional distress—an undoubtedly reasonable reaction in these circumstances, with physical manifestations—Lanier has stated a claim for Negligent Infliction of Emotional Distress against Harvard. . . .
>
> I write separately to emphasize that Harvard's alleged conduct here indeed transgresses contemporary standards and values adopted by museums and research institutions nationally and internationally, including by Harvard itself. These various ethical codes show that museums and research institutions across the United States and the world realize their special ethical obligations to the communities from whom their collections have too frequently been wrongfully extracted. They demonstrate a uniform commitment to proactive examination of the provenance of held artifacts and to respectful and transparent consideration of competing ownership claims to these artifacts. . . . For example, the Smithsonian Institution has created an ethical return working group that is in the process of developing an institution-wide policy for scrutinizing its collection practices and addressing any wrongs. The working group's focus is not on technical questions of legal title, but on "ethics." According to Kevin Gover,

the undersecretary for museums and culture at the Smithsonian, the institution "is going beyond legal title and asking, should we own this?, knowing the circumstances under which it came into our ownership?"

These examples show how archival institutions deal respectfully with individuals who are connected to pieces in their collections and prioritize those individuals' wishes for how the pieces should be used or displayed, particularly where the pieces were created or acquired under conditions of duress, violence, or non-consent. Such practices reflect a shared recognition on the part of these institutions that to disregard such individuals' concerns would be to signal that the inequitable power structures that enabled the archival institution to possess the contested pieces live on.

To send this signal is itself a form of violence. Harvard's alleged conduct here inflicted just this sort of violence on Lanier. It brushed her off, publicly dismissed her ancestral claim, and continued to display and profit from the daguerreotypes without Lanier's input or involvement. Harvard transgressed what it now upholds as its own values.

Harvard recently released a report detailing the university's historic ties to slavery and recommending reparative action. . . . The report declares that "[t]he damage caused by Harvard's entanglements with slavery and its legacies warrant action," even in "the absence of a legal requirement" to act. The report presents recommendations "that seek to remedy harms to descendants," in ways that are "visible, lasting, grounded in a sustained process of engagement, and linked to the nature of the damage done." One such recommendation is to "support direct descendants" of enslaved individuals who labored on Harvard's campus or were enslaved by Harvard staff through "dialogue" and "relationship building," with an aim of enabling these descendants to "recover their histories" and "tell their stories."

Lanier's ancestors did not labor on Harvard's campus or suffer from enslavement directly by Harvard staff, but it is without question—as detailed in the Harvard report, and described by the court, that Harvard, through its agent Agassiz, exploited Renty's and Delia's (and others') enslaved condition to extract from them value then used in furtherance of a white supremacist agenda. Thus, the spirit of the report would appear to encompass dialogue and relationship building with the descendants of those pictured in the Zealy daguerreotypes, as well as pursuit of a visible and lasting remedy to the harm worked by Agassiz and Harvard against them.

Lanier suggests such a remedy. Harvard's refusal even to discuss respectfully with Lanier her request to possess the daguerreotypes of Renty and Delia flies in the face of its aspirational report. Harvard's conduct thus belies its purported commitment to enable descendants to "recover their histories," to "tell their stories," or to repair meaningfully the harm it has done to them.

Justice Cypher's concurring opinion felt like a dissent:

Although it is easy to point to American chattel slavery as the direct instrument of Renty's and Delia's disenfranchisement, repressive legislation such as Black Codes and Jim Crow laws, and the indifference of many white Americans to the plight of Black Americans, systemically perpetuated the deprivation of rights of formerly enslaved individuals and their descendants and led to their continued exclusion from many

> legal protections, even after slavery was legally abolished. . . . As a result, the plaintiff now faces a legal system several generations later devoid of a sufficient remedy for the injuries and injustices she has faced as a descendant of enslaved Africans and African-Americans.

It was a two-part ruling that basically granted me a day in court to sue Harvard for extreme, outrageous, reckless, and negligent infliction of emotional distress for the treatment of Renty and Delia and for the treatment of me. But Harvard gets to keep the daguerreotypes.

All my attorneys were thrilled: "This is great. This is historic! This is major!"

As excited as everyone was about this news, I could not help but feel like I was leaving a family member behind. Yet I understood this was historical, and it was about reparations.

Once again, the press picked the story up and it spread like wildfire.

"Mass. Supreme Court Allows Emotional Distress Claim Against Harvard to Proceed in Suit Over Photos of Enslaved People" was the headline in the *Harvard Crimson.*

"The case has been remanded to the Superior Court, which will review Lanier's emotional distress claims in light of the decision by Massachusetts' highest court," the *Crimson* reported, and included a statement from the Supreme Judicial Court: "Harvard was put on notice that she would reasonably be greatly concerned about how the images—created through coercion and depicting her ancestors in a degrading, dehumanizing light—would be used, displayed, and disseminated . . . because, as alleged, Harvard did just the opposite, its actions plausibly rose to the level of extreme and outrageous conduct."

The *Crimson* noted that the decision came three weeks after the student-led newspaper published an article about a report that "Harvard holds the remains of 7,000 Native Americans and 19 individuals who were likely enslaved . . . held principally in the Peabody, [which] represent 'the University's engagement and complicity' with slavery and colonialism."

Renty and Delia are not alone, nor am I. This is a moment for universities and museums to do the right thing. While the ruling about "property interest" remained with Harvard, the justices made it clear how complicated this is—and why this particular law needs revisiting.

One judge said, "We're wrong for not giving this woman redress. And we're not giving a redress by allowing her to go back and file for this emotional distress and punitive staff that the laws were made by white men who have a purpose in the outcome of these decisions or an interest in these decisions."

Each judge made compelling arguments, but Justice Cypher's stood out to me because she was acknowledging the disinheritance of descendants of chattel slavery. "There should be legislative protections," she stated.

This is why I fight.

20

Fulfilling My Promise

Shortly after the decision, my phone began pinging repeatedly. People were tagging me and sharing news stories of the landmark decision. As I scrolled through the articles, one published by *Black Enterprise* captured my attention:

"Attorney Ben Crump Wins Historic Ruling: Black Woman Can Sue Harvard University for Displaying Photos of Enslaved Ancestors."

Attorney Crump's remarks gave me pause.

"As a free Black man, I am honored to have been at the forefront of this fight against the lasting remnants of slavery and the very institutions that benefited from the exploitation of Black ancestors. The high court recognized Harvard's complicity in the horrific actions surrounding the creation of the daguerreotypes," he said.

After reading the impassioned words of Attorney Crump, specifically, that he as a "free" Black man was honored to fight for my enslaved ancestors, I was reminded that freedom isn't free and should never be taken for granted, and that everything my family had endured was for a larger purpose. That purpose was to lay bare for all to see that slavery was an evil American institution, that the lingering effects of slavery persist even today, and that descendants of American chattel slavery deserve equal protection and proper redress.

This historic ruling marked the first time in the history of the United States that a descendant has been afforded the opportunity to seek accountability from an American institution for the atrocities caused by slavery.

While many wrote about this case as a historic milestone, others argued that the court failed to meet its judicial responsibilities. The *Harvard Law Review* has the dubious distinction of being the nation's most prestigious law journal, characterized by its intense and highly competitive admissions process—recruiting the best and brightest legal minds to find and research new material. In its 2023 publication, the *Harvard Law Review* offered a detailed legal analysis of the *Lanier v. President & Fellows of Harvard College* decision, explaining:

> The Lanier court's inability to conceive of "complete redress" for injustices it deemed "extreme and outrageous" raises the question—to whom is "the great principle . . . of natural justice extended"?

Ouch! This was not only a rebuke of Harvard by its own law journal, but of the "Lanier court" as well. The thorny and critical review continued:

> The court rightfully disparaged Harvard's mistreatment of Lanier, Renty, and Delia. And yet, by imprudently restricting itself to common law standards arising from fundamentally incompatible precedent, the court inhibited its ability to ac-

> cess the range of existing remedial interventions that would have made possible reparations in the form of granting property relationships or equitable interests to Lanier.

And there it was. This was validation. This was about reparations, as I had stated early on; as Attorney Crump had insisted, and both Attorneys Mike and Josh Koskoff as well. We all knew it. Now seeing it here in the *Harvard Law Review* felt strangely like a very small measure of justice.

The law review goes on to challenge what Harvard claimed to be settled law, that the photo always belongs to the photographer:

> The court's insistence that the photographer, and not the photographed, owns the right to a picture is anchored in inapposite precedent. In advancing this argument, the court cited three cases. First, in *Thayer v. Worcester Post Co.*, the plaintiff alleged that the defendant newspaper infringed on her right to privacy when it captured and published a photograph of her at an airport. . . . The Lanier court failed to acknowledge that these cases featured non-enslaved plaintiffs, rendering their legal status and circumstances so different as to be noncontrolling. As "chattel property," Renty and Delia were denied a right to privacy, including the right to refuse to take part in the making of the daguerreotypes—facts the court erroneously ignored. There is no indication from *Thayer*, *Ault*, or *Continental Optical Co.* that a photographer would retain a property right in images of people who could never consent to be photographed.

The *Harvard Law Review* closed with an analysis that seems to invoke Crump. In his book *Open Season* he explains:

> America is a great nation, because it was established upon a foundation of ideals—that all persons have inalienable rights endowed by their Creator and enforced through the rule of law. The Constitution and Bill of Rights provide the backbone of American greatness, but we still have to recognize and root out fundamentally racist beliefs and discriminatory laws that have contaminated and corrupted American greatness from our nation's birth.

In a much more personal and profound way, the *Harvard Law Review* appears to invoke *Open Season* as it acknowledges racial disparities in the judicial system.

> Put plainly, our judicial system—by appealing to "universal feelings" such as fairness and care for the deceased—has justified quasi-property interests for plaintiffs when it has deemed fit. Accordingly, it has the institutional capacity to grant descendant plaintiffs quasi-property interests in photographs of their ancestors that were coercively taken to advance racial eugenics. Granting such interests to descendant plaintiffs will require courts to "treat Black dead bodies" with the same respect as "white bodies," and "appreciate the unequal dishonor, destruction, and degradation" that the bodies of enslaved Black people "faced for centuries in life and in death." . . . While the court made room for descendant plaintiffs in future litigation to plausibly allege emotional distress, its mishandling of the most crucial parts of the plaintiff's complaint—her property-related claims—emphasizes an uncomfortable reality: until courts are willing to champion nuanced remedial approaches on behalf of descendant plaintiffs, they will be incapable of correcting injustices stemming from American chattel slavery.

This confirmed something I knew in my heart to be true: reparations for the descendants of American chattel slavery can and will be realized through the judicial process.

Amazed by this history, I had to acknowledge that this victory would not be possible if not for all the dedicated people who saw an incredible wrong and were willing to move heaven and earth to right it.

I thought of Papa Renty's steely resolve and soulful gaze, a reminder of his sweat and sorrow; I thought of Delia, looking so broken and profoundly sad, a reminder of her tearful despair; I thought of my mother telling me over and over again about our ancestor, the proud Black African, whose spirit lived in her, and within me.

Before my mother died, I promised her that I would "write our story down."

I have spent the last decade-plus fulfilling that promise. Along the way, I met legions of people who helped me understand that I was not just doing it for my mother and my daughters and future generations—I was doing this for everyone. This has always been bigger than me. My mother knew it. So did Renty. That was what I saw in his face when we first locked eyes. I saw it again when his image was displayed on the Harvard stage in 2017. I see it every time I look into his deep, wise, soulful eyes.

My relationship with Congo Renty is more than an emotional one. I do believe that there has been a divine intervention, ordering my footsteps, placing special people in my path to give me key information at critical junctures. Yes, I truly believe that this spiritual journey was ordained by God to test Harvard and the moral climate of this country. First, by placing the spirit of consciousness in my mom to hold on to this story, and then by instilling that spirit in me.

I thought of Ellie Reichlin, a kindred spirit who saw my ancestors as "survivors" of a painful epic and fought to restore their humanity; then there was the kindness of Rich Morrison and Rose Shiver, who gave so much of themselves to help me piece this complicated story together.

I also thought of the Agassiz descendants and the Harvard students who stepped out of their comfort zone to call out the university's unethical stewardship. Each and every one of them poured their hearts into helping me make my case.

Finally, there were the many attorneys of Ben Crump Law, Mark Marderosian, Talley Kaleko, and Koskoff, Koskoff & Beider, who all believed that there should be no harm without a remedy and who doggedly pursued justice for my enslaved ancestors.

When this book is published, the first thing I will do is lay it at my mother's grave. And I will say to her this: "Thank you for telling our story. Thank you for making sure I would write it down. Now both you and Papa Renty can finally rest in peace."

Acknowledgments

I would be remiss if I didn't first acknowledge and thank God for his favor and all the many miracles, signs, and wonders revealed to me throughout this decades-long journey. Proverbs 3:6 states that in all your ways acknowledge God, and He shall direct your path. Often, I have had to acknowledge that the battles won would not be possible were it not for the author and finisher of my faith ordering my steps. From the moment I first locked eyes with my Papa Renty, I knew that this was more than a chance encounter. It was both a gift and a test, and my endurance and perseverance were tested in ways that attacked my spirit. But my testimony was my inspiration. The race is not given to the swift, nor the battles to the strong, but to he who endures to the end.

To my Papa Renty, I want to acknowledge that I see your despair and feel your pain. The look in your eyes is a call to action, a plea for me to right a centuries-old wrong. I want you to know that for as long as I live, I vow to never stop naming, blaming, or shaming Harvard until they do right by you. Papa Renty, I am grateful for you and thankful for your tenacious and unwavering fight to safeguard our family legacy. Your message was not lost and because of you, generations will never forget.

To Mattye Pearl Thompson-Lanier, the woman whom I was blessed to call mother, there is not a dawn that rises nor a sun that sets where I don't think of you or miss you terribly. I will love you forever and you will always be with me. I want to thank you for being the keeper of our family story and acknowledge that it was your attention to detail and steadfast commitment to document our ancestry that have brought us to this moment in history. You are the epitome of selfless love, strength, and unfaltering determination. Thank you for being my constant source of inspiration. In our last moments together, I promised you something I believed to be impossible. I promised to document the life and legacy of the proud Black African. That promise is now fulfilled. This book is a testament to your enduring love and boundless spirit.

To my beloved children Shonrael and Megan, and to my sister, Cynthia, your tireless love, support, and unrelenting belief in me have been the source of my inspiration. Your presence by my side has been my greatest comfort and motivation. Thank you for being my confidantes, my constant companions, and my guiding lights. For all of this and for the love that sustains us, I thank you from the bottom of my heart.

To my grandson Elliot Nace Hardy IV, you are the light of my life and joy of my world. Though you are but an infant, you already embody the dreams and aspirations of our enslaved ancestors. As a beacon of hope for future generations, I am gifting you with a sacred responsibility. May you grow to understand the significance of our generational sacrifice. As guardian and custodian of our family story, I pray you safeguard and protect the legacy of Papa Renty with an unwavering sense of pride, dignity, and respect.

I have so many to thank for their efforts to make this book a reality, none more deserving than the former executive editor of the *New*

York Times and Harvard professor Jill Abramson. For years I struggled unsuccessfully to make inroads with the publishing industry. I had given up and decided to pursue self-publication. But once again, good fortune smiled on me, and I found myself the subject of a Harvard journalism class discussion where Jill was the professor. So moved by what she learned, Jill personally connected me to her amazing agent, Suzanne Gluck of William Morris Endeavor, who agreed this story must be shared with the world.

Suzanne introduced me to the award-winning journalist Liz Welch, who is also an acclaimed writer and collaborator. As luck would have it, Liz had been following my case via news coverage and had previously reached out to Attorney Ben Crump with an offer of assistance. Liz was able to hit the ground running, quickly absorbing the many complicated themes and legal complexities that made this story so compelling.

Thanks to Nina Iandolo and David Dumas for their help with the proposal. And I want to especially thank Madhulika Sikka, my editor at Crown, who helped shepherd these pages and chapters into the book you now hold. It was Madhulika's hands-on and unique editing style that moved the process along in record speed. Crown's publisher Gillian Blake was at our first meeting—and I'm so grateful for her belief in my story—and to everyone else at Crown who helped me realize my dream—including the thorough and thoughtful Fariza Hawke. Thank you all for the role you played in helping to make dreams come true.

There are so many others who have played a pivotal role in making this book a reality, including Ellie Reichlin and her husband, Dr. Seymour Reichlin. I must acknowledge and thank them both for the sacrifices made on behalf of my enslaved ancestors. It was Ellie who first realized the incalculable historical value of the daguerreotypes and invested countless hours in piecing together their checkered history. I firmly believe that were it not for Ellie, the daguerreotypes might have been discarded or overlooked and thus leaving a dreadful part of Harvard's dark past undiscovered. And to Dr. Reichlin, Ellie's adoring husband, thank you for running the last leg of Ellie's race. After her passing, you picked up the torch and carried it home. You continued her research and ultimately found Renty's descendants. I can only imagine how incredibly proud Ellie is of you right now. There are simply no words to express my gratitude.

And to the man who changed the course of my family's history, Rich Morrison, the ice cream shop owner from the small rural community of Franklin, Connecticut, I commend you and thank God for you. Although you were not commissioned by Harvard to research the history of those captured in the slave daguerreotypes, you, in your spare time, succeeded where Ivy League scholars failed.

You are an internet supersleuth, responsible for finding my Papa Renty, and with all the gratitude that I can muster, I thank you.

To Rose Shiver, a woman I call sister and soulmate, I believe that the stars had to align perfectly to bring us together as friends. I searched the South, calling and connecting with educational and academic institutions throughout the greater Columbia area. I found no one more informed or resourceful than you. I must publicly acknowledge that were it not for you, I could not have placed my ancestors on land owned by the slaveholder Benjamin Franklin Taylor. You are also responsible for my meeting with Dr. Edmund Taylor, the linear descendant of the man who enslaved our ancestors. It was a transformative moment that I will never forget. To Dr. Edmund Taylor, the great-grandson of Benjamin Franklin Taylor, thank you for welcoming me into your home and your heart. You didn't know me, but you extended an invitation to me, and you provided me with invaluable information. For that I thank you.

To Marian Moore, Susanna Moore, and the Agassiz descendants, we are truly two families forged together by history. Thank you for your unwavering support and commitment. Without reservation or hesitation, you stepped outside your comfort zone and into the fight. You stood side by side with me and lent your voice in the call for reparations. For that, I am grateful.

To Meredith McKinney, Jarrett M. Drake, and the entire Harvard student body, you are amazing, and I extend my deepest gratitude to you for your courageous support and unrelenting pursuit of institutional accountability. You stood in solidarity with me; you voted to condemn the university because of its unethical stewardship. Above and beyond this, you used your extraordinary talents to pen an amicus brief that was cited by the Massachusetts Supreme Judicial Court. Your commitment to justice and unwavering dedication to hold your academic institution accountable embodies the true spirit of *Veritas*. Thank you for your invaluable support.

To my dream team and the brilliant attorneys of Ben Crump Law LLC, and Koskoff, Koskoff & Bieder, there are simply no words to express my most deepest and sincere gratitude for your steadfast and unwavering support. You are to be commended for your fearless and relentless pursuit of justice for my enslaved ancestors. To Attorney Crump, for as long as I live, I will remember fondly that moment when I mustered the courage to press my way through an eager crowd, praying for just a few moments of your time. And when we first met to discuss my case, I was sick with anxious anxiety, but you gathered the hands at the table and said, "Let's pray." I knew in that moment that our faith would carry us through to a favorable conclusion. I cannot thank you enough. To the late Michael Koskoff and the entire Koskoff family, I want to thank you for the love and support you have shown me throughout the years. The fine counsel I received from Mike enriched my life in countless ways and I will always cherish my fond memories of him. His kindness and generosity will forever inspire and guide me. Words cannot express the depth of my gratitude.

And finally, I am grateful beyond measure to all the scores of people worldwide who are inspired by my Papa Renty and who want to see a fair and just conclusion for him and his daughter Delia. I'm claiming this victory in advance! The cultural property of my enslaved ancestors will ultimately find a fitting final resting place. A place that celebrates their legacy and restores their humanity.

Tamara K. Lanier
April 2024

Bibliography

Associated Press. "'Mr. Fortune' Honored More Than 200 Years After His Death." September 12, 2013.

Azoulay, Ariella Aïsha. *Potential History: Unlearning Imperialism.* Brooklyn, NY: Verso, 2019.

Barbash, Ilisa, Molly Rogers, and Deborah Willis, eds. *To Make Their Own Way in the World: The Enduring Legacy of the Zealy Daguerreotypes.* Boston: Aperture and Peabody Museum Press, 2020.

Barry, Amy. "Norwich Woman Thinks Famous Photo Is Her Ancestor." *The Day,* February 21, 2011.

Carmichael, Mary. "Louis Agassiz Exhibit Divides Harvard, Swiss Group." *Boston Globe,* June 27, 2012.

Coates, Ta-Nehisi. "The Case for Reparations." *Atlantic,* June 2014.

Crump, Benjamin. *Open Season: The Legalized Genocide of Colored People.* New York: Amistad, 2019.

Farrow, Anne, Joel Lang, and Jenifer Frank. *Complicity: How the North Promoted, Prolonged, and Profited from Slavery.* New York: Ballantine, 2006.

Fässler, Hans. *Reise in Schwarz-Weiss: Schweizer Ortstermine in Sachen Sklaverei.* Zurich: Rotpunktverlag, 2005.

Huber, Sasha. *Rentyhorn.* Helsinki: Museum of Contemporary Art Kiasma, Publication 126, 2010.

King, Martin Luther, Jr. *Where Do We Go from Here: Chaos or Community?* Boston: Beacon Press, 1967.

Lechtreck, Elaine Allen. "Racial Science and Early American Photography." *Journal of African American History* 98, no. 1, Special Issue: "Women, Slavery, and the Atlantic World" (Winter 2013).

McLoughlin, Pamela. "Family Tree: African Slave's Remarkable Life Traced to Connecticut." *New Haven Register*, January 30, 2011.

Murray, Yxta Maya. "From Here I Saw What Happened and I Cried: Carrie Mae Weems' Challenge to the Harvard Archive." *8 Unbound: Harvard Journal of the Legal Left 1*, September 11, 2013. Loyola-LA Legal Studies Paper No. 2013-31.

Paz, Franco. "Who Should Own Historical Images of Enslaved People?" *Washington Post*, October 25, 2022.

Reichlin, Elinor. "Faces of Slavery: A Historical Find." *American Heritage*, June 1977.

Rensberger, Boyce. "Earliest Pictures of Slaves Found in Harvard Attic." *New York Times*, May 31, 1977.

Rose, Julia Anne. "Rethinking Representations of Slave Life at Historical Plantation Museums: Towards a Commemorative Museum Pedagogy." PhD diss., Louisiana State University, 2006. https://repository.lsu.edu/gradschool_dissertations/1040.

Rogers, Molly. *Delia's Tears: Race, Science, and Photography in Nineteenth-Century America*. New Haven, CT: Yale University Press, 2010.

Schoeffler, Nancy, and Rick Hartford. "In Search of a Truer Picture of Papa Renty." *Hartford Courant*, February 17, 2014.

Sehgal, Parul. "The First Photos of Enslaved People Raise Many Questions About the Ethics of Viewing." Book review. *New York Times*, September 29, 2020.

Sinha, Manisha. *The Slave's Cause: A History of Abolition*. New Haven, CT: Yale University Press, 2016.

Thornton, Cedric. "Attorney Ben Crump Wins Historic Ruling: Black Woman Can Sue Harvard University for Displaying Photos of Enslaved Ancestors." *Black Enterprise*, June 27, 2022.

Wallis, Brian. "Black Bodies, White Science: Louis Agassiz's Slave Daguerreotypes." *American Art* 9, no. 2 (Summer 1995): 38–61.

Washington, Harriet A. *Medical Apartheid*. New York: Doubleday, 2006.

Webster, Noah. *A Grammatical Institute of the English Language* [the Blue Back Speller]. Hartford, CT: Hudson & Goodwin, 1783.

Williams, Heather Andrea. *Self-Taught: African American Education in Slavery and Freedom*. Chapel Hill: University of North Carolina Press, 2009.

Wood, Peter H. *Black Majority: Negroes in Colonial South Carolina from 1670 Through the Stono Rebellion*. New York: Knopf, 1974.

ABOUT THE AUTHOR

Tamara K. Lanier is a tireless champion for truth and justice—and a plaintiff in the *Lanier v. Harvard* reparations lawsuit. She is a descendant of Papa Renty. She is also a twenty-seven-year veteran of the State of Connecticut Judicial Branch, from which she retired in 2017 as a chief probation officer.

Lanier has a long and distinguished record of public service and social advocacy.

She is a board member of the Connecticut Racial Profiling Prohibition Project, the past vice president of the New London NAACP, and an active member of Saint John's Christian Church of Groton, Connecticut.

Lanier has several passions, one of which is to eradicate racial and ethnic disparities in Connecticut's criminal justice system and to put an end to the ugly practice of racial profiling. She has been a constant voice for change and has traveled the country promoting the need for a national dialogue relative to slavery and its impact on society. She lives in Norwich, Connecticut.